THE
COMFORT FOOD
DIARIES

THE
COMFORT FOOD
DIARIES

My Quest for the Perfect Dish
to Mend a Broken Heart

EMILY NUNN

ATRIA BOOKS

NEW YORK   LONDON   TORONTO   SYDNEY   NEW DELHI

ATRIA
BOOKS

An Imprint of Simon & Schuster, Inc.
1230 Avenue of the Americas
New York, NY 10020

First Atria Books hardcover edition September 2017

ATRIA BOOKS and colophon are trademarks of Simon & Schuster, Inc.

For information about special discounts for bulk purchases, please contact Simon & Schuster Special Sales at 1-866-506-1949 or business@simonandschuster.com.

The Simon & Schuster Speakers Bureau can bring authors to your live event. For more information or to book an event, contact the Simon & Schuster Speakers Bureau at 1-866-248-3049 or visit our website at www.simonspeakers.com.

Interior design by Kyoko Watanabe

Manufactured in the United States of America

10 9 8 7 6 5 4 3 2 1

Library of Congress Cataloging-in-Publication Data

Names: Nunn, Emily, author.
Title: The comfort food diaries : my quest for the perfect dish to mend a broken heart / Emily Nunn.
Description: First Atria Books hardcover edition. | New York : Atria Books, [2017]
Identifiers: LCCN 2016055910
Subjects: LCSH: Nunn, Emily. | Comfort food. | Cooking, American. | Food Writers—United States—Biography. | LCGFT: Cookbooks.
Classification: LCC TX649.N86 A3 2017 | DDC 641.5973—dc23 LC record available at https://lccn.loc.gov/2016055910

ISBN 978-1-4516-7420-0
ISBN 978-1-4516-7427-9 (ebook)

For John (April 8, 1934–April 4, 2017) and Mariah Nunn,
who taught me to rethink my definition of family.

"No one who cooks, cooks alone."

—Laurie Colwin

Contents

THE
COMFORT FOOD
DIARIES

One

CHERRIES JUBILEE AND
OTHER DANGEROUS DISHES

"No one knows how Ezra Pound came to be born in Idaho." That's something an English professor at the giant magnolia-shaded southern university I attended announced one day during my freshman year. *What a ridiculous statement*, I thought. *Ezra's parents probably had sex in or around Idaho*. The joke about this school, back then at least, was that someone would throw a diploma in your car window if you drove through town. So I thought, *Perhaps this man is not a top quality academic*.

Decades later, I believe I understand what he was trying to get at: there's no real logic to where we start out and what we end up with. It's like cooking. Once you get your ingredients, how you put them together at any given time is up to you. Maybe you have a book of recipes that has been passed down to you, maybe you're winging it. Either way, it's your responsibility to create something good, which you must then attempt to parlay into something better, never knowing exactly how things will turn out. It helps to have a high tolerance for disasters, in the kitchen or otherwise.

The place where I came to be born, and the place where I learned to cook, is Galax, Virginia, population seven thousand, nestled in the Blue Ridge Mountains. It's hard to imagine my parents doing what Ezra's did (in Galax, in Idaho, or anywhere), but it happened, and something about my upbringing flung me far away rather than keeping me in the fold.

I ended up in New York City, heaven to me after small-town life, where my first job was at a magazine called *Wigwag* (the word means "to signal someone home"). A group of upstarts had left the *New Yorker* magazine to start *Wigwag*, which ran out of money during an economic downturn and stopped publication a year after I arrived in the city. When a few of them returned to their old jobs, I tagged along and landed at the *New Yorker*, too, and for almost a decade ended up covering theater plus editing and writing the original Tables for Two column.

My assignment, basically, was to go to the theater (sometimes five times a week), eat in restaurants, and have engrossing conversations with interesting people. I often felt like the luckiest person in the world. Why would I ever leave? I wondered this immediately after I took a job at the *Chicago Tribune*, despite the fact that they almost doubled my salary, gave me my own restaurant column, and promised I could write on any other topic I wished: the world would be my oyster.

If I was lonely at first, a few years after arriving in Chicago my life had fallen beautifully into place. I loved my job, and I'd met a local engineer who was tall, handsome, funny, wore Brooks Brothers suits, had pale blue eyes, and shaved his face exactly the same way every day. I adored him; I didn't doubt for a second that he adored me back. Less than a year and a half later, we moved in together to a building a few blocks away from the *Tribune*'s hulking gothic headquarters and even closer to his firm.

And as great as this man was, he came with an added benefit: a seven-year-old daughter who also had blue eyes. She was as enchanting and lighthearted as a fairy princess, even when she was covered with mud from sliding down a clay embankment in the rain, even with her arms tightly crossed and shoulders up in fury, or when she had rats' nests from days of not brushing her long, shiny chestnut-brown hair, just because she was not in the mood. She had an affinity for the natural world that was reciprocated: I once watched her tiptoe extremely close to a deer as if she were indeed a woodland fairy princess; she and the animal stood staring at each other for a long while, as if they were trying to remember where they had met before, until the deer bounded away.

A few months after we met, the Engineer told me I came first in his life. *First.* Since I had grown up in a family of seven—an *exquisitely* dysfunctional southern family, in which various members had stopped speaking for years in various convoluted and confusing configurations—you can imagine how alluring that was, in spite of how rushed it seemed. A few months after we'd moved in together, he took me to Tiffany and bought me the prettiest platinum three-diamond Etoile engagement ring. It didn't seem to matter much when the *Tribune* laid me off during the recession, along with a lot of other people who had high salaries and a Pulitzer or two. I threw myself into a life of heretofore unthinkable, at least for me, domesticity.

Back when we told the Fairy Princess's mother, the Co-parent, that we were setting up household together, she had immediately announced plans to take the Fairy Princess away with her to Paris, where she had gotten a job. When she did finally leave for Paris, though, she left her wonderful nine-year-old child in our care. The day the Engineer and I moved in together was the exact day I became an almost full-time stepparent. Previously, when I had thought of the word *family*, I'd imagine cavemen sitting around a fire chewing on a bone—a human bone. I was afraid of what a family could do. So I had naturally avoided creating one as an act of lonely self-preservation, as well as a service to all humanity.

But I found I absolutely loved it, loved the natural flow of rituals that took over my life: at night, sitting down to a dinner I'd cooked for my little family, bedtime reading (*Little House on the Prairie*), walking the dog, cleaning up the kitchen, an hour of television with the Engineer on the couch, turning off the glowing living-room lamps, seeing the moon on Lake Michigan, the stars outside before sleep, feeling the dog jump onto the foot of the bed, then hearing the Engineer's snoring, taking his reading glasses off and putting them on the nightstand with the folded *New Yorker* he'd started reading regularly and I'd begun to ignore.

I began to believe in the idea of family and thanking God for mine almost every single day.

●

Two and a half years later, I lived through the darkest winter of my life, after the sudden death of Oliver, one of my two brothers. The new family and the life I had loved collapsed into a flat mess like a soufflé after some unthinking person slams the oven door.

I got the news that Oliver had killed himself—a late-night text from my other brother, Michael, who lived in Santa Barbara—while on a culinary and architectural tour of Barcelona, a birthday present from the Engineer. But rather than telling the Engineer right away that my brother was dead, I waited until we'd finished our nightcap at a dark grotto bar, after our local friends had said good night and walked away. Because I didn't want to spoil the evening.

In Barcelona, I felt curious and connected to something good. I fell in love with the medieval claustrophobic streets, modernist architecture, and murky Catalan mood right away, and I've missed what I felt there ever since. The wonder you feel in great foreign cities is easy to confuse with the wonder you feel when you first fall in love with a person you imagine to be great, who seems at the same time to be so strange and novel. I was hoping to feel that way about the Engineer again.

"Don't come home early. You should finish your trip," my sister Elaine said, when I finally reached her by phone the next day. "There's nothing you can do."

Well, there isn't now, I recall thinking.

And so it came to pass that we were still in Barcelona two days after I'd heard the awful news. Glass of wine in hand, I was standing in line to eat at Cal Pep, the fabled tapas bar in the hipster Born district, right around the corner from the contrastingly steadfast twelfth-century church Santa María del Mar, as if nothing had happened at all. *La-di-da.*

When the Engineer came striding across the cobblestone plaza to meet me, he was wearing the blue-and-white striped scarf I'd tied around his neck that morning along with the rumpled mackintosh I'd given him for his last birthday. He looked so handsome that I kicked up a leg to show off a new pair of shoes he'd bought for me earlier that day.

"New boots!" I said, and then backward I fell, landing flat on my back, like a floor lamp that had been pushed over. Lying there, wondering what had happened and if I'd cracked my head open, I saw the face of my dead brother Oliver: super-pale green eyes the color of beach glass, heavy-lidded and half-closed, blond hair that he cut very short, ham-steak cheeks, and a semipermanent scowl, which would become a radiant smile, but only if you could make him laugh.

A couple from New York finally had to pull me to my feet; they seemed disappointed when I thanked them in English rather than Catalan.

When I stood up, I felt significantly altered, which I attributed to the wine.

Soon, the two of us were installed at the long granite counter at Cal Pep; some tremendous white beans with sausages arrived, then calamari, beautifully flash-fried, followed by a lovely piece of grilled turbot.

When I tried to lift my glass of wine, though, my wrist went limp with pain. I looked down at the pretty food. "I think we should see a doctor," I said to the Engineer, who'd barely gotten to touch the *pa amb tomàque* (bread smeared with tomato), a customary snack set down the minute you arrive in Barcelona restaurants.

As the cab banged and bounced its way over cobblestones to the closest Barcelona hospital, the Engineer said, "Why are you crying? Does it hurt, or are you just upset?"

I couldn't see that it mattered exactly *why* I was crying. My arm hurt really badly and my brother was dead, and either reason seemed acceptable.

"I don't know," I answered.

But I knew. And the truth would begin to buzz around my brain like an insect I could never swat away: while Oliver was completely alone in a hotel room, preparing to say goodbye to the world and everyone and everything in it, I was on British Airways drinking champagne in first class, a fact that would strike me later as a betrayal so incomprehensible that it made me quite sick.

When we got to the hospital, the Engineer was silent as a female doctor who looked like a movie star gave me a shot for the pain and took X-rays. She showed me a ghostly outline of my hand and arm on a computer screen, pointed to a blur, and said in a heavy accent, "It is broken." I just nodded and let her splint my limp arm and wrap it in a soft, temporary contraption, which she said would not "esplode" if my arm swelled up in the pressurized cabin during our flight home to Chicago the next day.

After we left the hospital, we went into a bar across the street to watch some of the World Cup, but it was too crowded to see the television, and neither of us wanted to find another place. So we went back to the Hotel Neri, and sat in the empty bar for one more glass of Cava before going home and to Oliver's funeral.

"I know you're not equipped to help me with what I'm going through—or what I'm going to go through," I told him, hoping he would say, *"Of course I am. I have your back. We'll get through this together."*

"Well, maybe the Fairy Princess can bring you some joy," he said instead.

"That's very sweet," I replied, trying to smile. But I was confused. He seemed to be offering up his child as some kind of compensation for his own emotional deficits. How in the world was that supposed to work? I suddenly felt afraid.

•

Nothing prepares you for the death of a sibling, even if it's not a surprise. Oliver had almost killed himself, whether intentionally or not, just a few weeks earlier by downing Trazodone and vodka. When I had last spoken to him, the conversation had become tangled. We left it unfinished. But he was reaching out to me. He needed me. "I just want it to end," he'd said a couple of weeks before we'd left for Barcelona.

I wouldn't say that Oliver and I were extremely close, although I did follow him to college, where we'd speak by phone every other week or so, just to tell jokes. But we barely saw each other at all by the time he killed himself. And that is part of what was hard to accept. Had I ever been there for him? We were never good at taking care of each other; my brothers and sisters and I had all apparently internalized the message that that was not what we were meant to do. Our job was to focus on our mother. We didn't really know how to pull together; we always ended up pulling apart. Oliver and I were somehow just the same: our lives were parallel in their unnecessary loneliness. Oliver had attempted suicide when we were just out of college many years ago. When my mother read me his suicide note over the phone, she began to weep. I didn't know why; the note was pretty tame and Oliver was alive. He'd lived. "Oh, Mom, I'm sorry. Why are you crying?" I asked her. Her response: "Do you realize there was not a word to me in that suicide note?"

He was my doppelgänger. I was born on his first birthday; he thought I was his present. Twelve years later, I cut my very long hair very short, a pixie cut, and his friends began to call me Oliver, sometimes to be mean, sometimes by accident, because we were both blond, scrawny, tall, awkward, and talked too much, snorting over our own dumb jokes. In my favorite picture of the two of us, when we were six and seven, his fly is half-unzipped and my white knee socks have slipped down to my ankles in a pile, making me look like a Clydesdale in a skirt; his arm is slung across my shoulder, his head thrown back in laughter, full of joy in that long-lost minute, two happy nerds. The same year I cut my hair, I went to a Halloween party at my friend Amy's house dressed as Oliver, in a pair of his old wire-frame glasses, corduroy pants, and a crew neck sweater with a pointy shirt collar folded over the outside. Which made him really angry. He was funny, loved a great joke, and was an amazing storyteller: he could be charming. And he was off-puttingly smart, but also infuriating. In fact, he became so intolerable one year in junior high that my mother sent him to live at my grandmother's house in Galax for several months. He had a photographic memory and could recall pages and pages of books he'd read and presidential speeches and monologues from plays. As a kid he did spot-on impersonations of John F. Kennedy and Sean Connery and, when he grew up, Bill Clinton. He had a giant coin collection and his own stockbroker who showed up at our house one day looking for "Mr. Nunn" and was surprised to meet a fourteen-year-old boy in corduroy pants and a T-shirt rather than a grown man. I once sneaked into his room when I was twelve and found a pipe with a half-smoked bowl of cherry tobacco.

I won the role of Springtime in our kindergarten play and Oliver was Mr. Winter, so I got to melt him.

He was neither saintly nor angelic, nor was he the quietest person in the world. In fact, it seemed he yelled half of what he said. He was scarily impatient and a scary driver. On a trip home from college together, he got two speeding tickets in three hours. He told me to drive after the second one. I ran over a curb pulling out of a filling station and he immediately made me turn the wheel back over to him.

Growing up, he regularly called me dumbbell, as if it were my name. But as we got older I suspected that, underneath his showy, outward dislike, he adored me. I began to think he avoided me because he knew I truly recognized him and understood that his anger came from not being able to be himself.

Although neither of our parents were big drinkers, we'd both gotten the alcohol gene, handed down from both the maternal and paternal sides of our family, the latter of which included our great-uncle Kenneth Messer, a brilliant and handsome air force man and inventor who drank himself to death after my great-grandfather made him come home following the war to help run the family's furniture factories. When I was in grade school, my best friend Melissa's uncle lived in the house where Uncle Kenneth bled to death on a stairway landing. She took me there once and pulled back the rug to show me the giant bloodstain on the wooden floor. They talked about him as if his ghost was still living there.

Oliver had always transformed himself: from a skinny kid with glasses who read all the time but made lousy grades to a dean's list student who won an ROTC scholarship to pay for school, a field organizer for the Republican Party in California at age twenty-one, and then a muscled marine who blazed through Officer Candidate School, and later a business executive who eventually managed his own company.

But when we were well into adulthood, he told me that when our mother came into our rooms to tell us good night and that she loved us, so many years ago, he would think to himself, *Not if you knew.*

Because he was gay (or bisexual). And he seemed to think that fact disqualified him from being loved. As a conservative Republican born in the sixties in the South, it had tortured him all his life—so much so that after he had come out in his twenties—and fallen in love with a man, at some point he had gone back to pretending it wasn't true. After he'd been sober for more than a decade, he'd gotten married to a woman he loved and had a child he loved, too. "This was my second chance," he once said to me, about his family whom I never knew him to betray. Living the life of a faithful, happy father and husband seemed to give him joy for so many years. But he was not faithful to his sobriety. He'd tried to hide the fact that he was drinking, and drinking a lot, but with every year that passed, he'd begun disappearing more and more. I'm pretty sure he'd been drinking heavily again for the last four years of his life.

Oliver had gotten tired of trying and had given up a long time ago, I think. For him, making an effort in life had always had mixed results, with wonderful highs and puzzling lows that seemed unworthy of a guy as brilliant and charming as he could be.

●

When we arrived back home from our ill-fated trip to Barcelona, I saw that Oliver had called and left messages on my phone. I imagined him alone, waiting for me to pick up. I deleted them without listening to them. I couldn't bear it, knew I never would be able to. That same day the Princess arrived at the apartment, too.

I was happy to see her bright face, and she said the most perfect thing once we sat her down to tell her about my brother: "I hope Oliver got to have a good Thanksgiving dinner before he died."

On Saturday we were scheduled to be greeters at the holiday fair at the Princess's alternative school. As we drove up Lake Shore Drive toward the school, Lake Michigan looked like some kind of steel-blue heaven, so gorgeous in the winter sunlight that it made me tear up. "I might have to sit in the car for a while," I said.

The Princess fluttered away into the gymnasium, excited for her big event, but I couldn't get out of the car to face the happy crowd. I pictured myself standing in the entry hall at this relentlessly quaint event full of handmade holiday crafts, folksy musical performances, and happy intact families.

I couldn't imagine what I would say to them.

"Hello! Welcome to the holiday fair! Come right in! My brother is dead! We were like twins, but not really. I hope your families turn out well! Good luck getting your kids into Harvard! Hello! Welcome! Hello!"

The Engineer didn't seem to understand my pain, but he sat with me outside the school before going in. "Exactly how long do you think a person should grieve?" I asked him, after we'd acknowledged my inability to focus on my responsibilities to our family. "What if your brother had died?" He stared back at me as if I were speaking an ancient, very boring language he had no desire to learn. "I don't know," he said impatiently, his face turning red. "Five days?" Which was exactly how long we'd been home. I was thinking that he was certainly the biggest fucking asshole in the universe, but also that he was *my* tall, handsome, engineer asshole whose frayed filament of affection was still attached to mine.

After he'd gone into the school that day he sent me this text: "It's ok if you don't feel like coming in. Plenty of help here. *I love you.*"

I got out of the car and went inside, into the gym, hypnotized by the idea that love was in there.

From that day forward, we never talked about Oliver or how I was feeling about any of it. We were supposed to go on like none of it had ever happened, even though the funeral had still not been planned.

I continued to cook delicious meals for him and the Princess during the next few weeks, despite my clumsy broken arm. I filled my cast-iron Le Creuset pot with white bean and sausage stew and fried up cornmeal arepas topped with black beans and avocado; I made the Princess's favorite spicy sweet potato and kale stew with coconut; we had vegetable soup, lentil salad. Also, caramelized pear tart, fish fillets smeared with mustard, Indian dishes that made the Princess wipe her tongue with a napkin (which made me laugh; thank God for her), and sometimes fudge sauce for vanilla ice cream that made her stand very close to me, waiting for it to be ready.

The Engineer seemed unable to understand that I was in the kind of pain that takes you by surprise, the kind that feels less like pain than like an inability to see any of the brightness in your life.

"What did you do all day?" he asked one night as I served them Chef Thomas Keller's amazing curry chicken breasts and my special butternut squash roasted with just a sprinkling of cayenne and a lot of lime, along with onion focaccia I had baked.

"I cried," I replied, somewhat operatically. I'd gone to the grocery store and I'd cooked, and I had started walking the dog more than once a day, but I wasn't really sure if I'd cried. I couldn't remember what I'd done, actually. I was trying to get some solace. The dog seemed to understand and was sitting at my feet now, slumped against my calves.

"That's sad," he replied, then continued quizzing the Princess about her day at school, whispering and laughing, as if I were no longer there.

I understood that he was concerned how the Co-parent would react to my sadness playing out in front of the Princess. It also occurred to me that he just couldn't understand or tolerate my tears.

Once he even told me that my tears were "diabolical"—as if I were the Riddler or the Penguin rather than the person who had taken the Princess to get her first bra at Marshall Field's and made vegetable soup with *pistou* to go in her lunch box. Rather than the only person who'd shown up at her Christmas concert after we'd all moved in together, because both the Engineer and the Co-parent had been out of the country for work.

Whatever the reasons, I'd considered myself under a strict crying ban ever since the time Oliver had ended up in the hospital in early November (after his run-in with Trazodone and vodka). I had openly cried in front of the Princess. It had gotten back to the Co-parent, and the Engineer made it clear to me that concerns had been raised. So a few days later, on my birthday, which was also Oliver's birthday, I spent all day by myself. The Engineer was unhappy with me (for many reasons, I have no doubt) and had canceled our birthday dinner reservations. It seemed impossible that we'd gone to Barcelona three weeks later, but we had.

And after we returned, I began to feel like a ghost in my own home—insubstantial but still hanging around for some reason, haunting everyone or, at the very least, annoying them.

"Don't you have some friends you could talk to about this until then?" the Engineer asked me one night, when I mentioned I was worried that weeks after Oliver's death no date had yet been set for the funeral and that I felt like I was in limbo.

"I have you. You're my friend!" I said. But I was coming to see that while the Engineer could do friendship, I was depressed and he couldn't do depressed.

No one seemed recognizable to me. At the same time, I couldn't say anyone had changed very much. What scared me most was that I was beginning not to recognize myself, either.

A few nights later, the Engineer and the Princess came storming into the house. "Dinner is ready in ten minutes," I said.

"We're not ready for dinner," the Engineer replied, as he followed her into her bedroom, where they had a heated conversation about her clarinet tutor, a lovely man with messy hair I'd hired myself. When the Engineer came out, he was furious. I stirred a pot as he told me about the clarinet-tutor situation; as he was talking I had the overpowering sensation that I was seeing him from miles away, through a tunnel much too small for me to fit through. No matter how much I yearned to be over there with him—in a place where you could be mad about something like a clarinet tutor—I could not go into the tunnel.

A month before we had left for Barcelona, the Engineer had asked for my social security number to make me the executor of the Princess's trust.

Three weeks after my brother's funeral, which he didn't attend (neither did my mother or my younger sister), the Engineer and I broke up.

We'd argued briefly, and after a familiar wall of silence rose up between us, I felt like I needed to be alone to cry. I bought a bottle of wine and took it to a hotel room across the street, hoping to grieve. Instead, in one of those grand moments of sweeping clarity that usually come only with alcohol, the universal truth serum, I sent a text to the Engineer saying that I thought we should break up. I remember feeling triumphant, light, released.

And he must have felt the same way because when I tried to take it back the next day, it was too late. "No, we're done," he said, and I could see in his eyes that this was true.

At first it was all relatively friendly. "You can stay as long as you want/need to," he texted me after we broke up. But the following week, after he'd stayed a few days at the Co-parent's apartment, the Engineer told me I had to leave our beautiful, sunny, high-rise, industrial-concrete-and-glass apartment with sweeping views of Lake Michigan (which I had found for us). He wanted me out in two weeks but I was pretty sure it would be impossible to find a new place to live in Chicago in two weeks.

I had just buried my brother, was crushed by shame and guilt, and suddenly it became blindingly obvious that I had absolutely nothing to show for my life. I was an unemployed former stepparent with $240 in the bank and a seriously drained IRA. I had lost, quite literally, almost everything I had in the world.

But I couldn't help noticing that I *did* have a half-full bottle of gin in the freezer, left over from a dinner party we'd had that fall on our building's rooftop terrace (I made fish tacos on the grill, with lime and cilantro). The blue Bombay bottle held an almost soulful, spiritual allure. I closed the freezer. No way. Not going there.

I had always credited my move to Chicago with changing my life after more than a decade of genetic, creeping, high-functioning alcoholism (*Why am I this way? Should I stop drinking? How can I keep doing this? Open a bottle of wine.*) Less than a year after I'd started working at the *Tribune*, I'd gone to rehab, on my own, without telling anyone in my family. The slower midwestern pace had allowed me to face the truth about my life and do the things I needed to fix it. Alcoholism is like charisma: you either have it or you don't, but how you choose to deal with it decides your fate. Like a lot of addicts, the allure for me was that it made my dark side seem brighter—until it didn't.

By the time the Engineer and I had met (*"You have such beautiful eyes!"* I'd said; *"So do you!"* he'd replied), I'd been a faithful nondrinker for more than four years. I'd told the Engineer right away that I didn't drink, and explained why. People tend to want to hear exactly why you quit, in great detail, a lot more than they want to know why you ever drank so much.

"I don't care about that. I care about who you are now," he told me, pulling my head to his warm shoulder. It was so comfortable there.

I began dabbling in white wine a little over a year into our relationship. "I can never do that again," I said, the first time I had a glass with him, horrified with myself.

"Well, I'm not going to police you," he replied; we'd had fun.

I felt safe. So rather than viewing myself as a relapsed alcoholic, once we'd moved in together I chose to see myself as a prissy sailor: taking my shore leaves, drinking with delicate purpose, then heading back to the ship of sobriety before things got too out of hand. And the Engineer had been fine with that, until I did something stupid—like smoke a cigarette with his business partner's wonderful wife after too much wine at his company Christmas party, creating a brain buzz that hit me like general anesthesia. I ended up having to leave the party early, walking like Frankenstein's monster, which made him furious. I thought he was worried about *me*, and maybe he was. But what he'd said the next day was, "I can't stand people thinking I've made the same mistake again." Meaning picked the wrong partner. Meaning me. It never seemed to occur to him that he was part of the equation.

Nonetheless, he asked me to marry him the very next week. And I accepted. A few weeks later, he bought a case of his favorite red wine and put it in the Princess's closet, since our kitchen was so small.

The possibility that my occasional social drinking could swerve, without much warning, into full-blown alcoholic behavior did not dissuade him from openly wanting me to be able to have cocktails with him.

But it was my responsibility. I knew that some kind of jerky behavior would always be the reward for the stupid, unforgivable risk I took having those few glasses of wine with him. No matter how good you seem to be at drinking, when you have the gene it always leads to the same place, eventually.

After the breakup, as my life started to spark and smell like smoke, I poured alcohol on it and watched it burst into blazes, as if I were preparing cherries jubilee for a crowd.

Sometimes only a flaming dish can serve as the proper ending to a dramatic meal.

One night I drank several glasses of sauvignon blanc and, in a fit of uncensored self-pity, broadcast the details of my wrecked life on Facebook for the unsolicited elucidation of around 350 so-called friends.

Pouring out my heart, I wept a bit while I typed, pausing to gaze out my floor-to-ceiling windows at Lake Michigan, a landscape where clouds and moonlight cast strange shadows across giant chunks of ice that rubbed together and made mournful creaking sounds that seemed to come from deep inside the earth. It was the modern-day version of going down to the river, rending my garments, beating my breast. Except stupider.

It went something like this: "My brother's funeral was three weeks ago, and my fiancé just broke up with me. I have almost no money, no job, no home, no car, no child to pick up after school, no dog to feed, no one to care for. I am cold and alone." (It was actually a lot more detailed than that, and a lot more embarrassingly melodramatic, but I deleted it and I don't remember all of it nor do I ever wish to.)

By the time I'd finished typing, I was comfortably numb, unmoved except by a flicker of the sensation that comes from watching a spectacular explosion in a movie. Even if it destroys something you'd never want to hurt, like the White House or Disneyland. *Kablooey!* It's satisfying.

I went to bed, unconcerned about webcasting my plight. It had seemed like the only thing to do.

The morning after my pathetic post, I swallowed my slightly hungover dread and logged on to receive a remarkable surprise: instead of punishment for my honesty, I had been rewarded with kindness.

The little Facebook comment button displayed a big number, but it was not the sign of a virtual scolding. It turned out to be a bright flag signaling that people from all around the country were willing to come down the river with me, so I wouldn't be alone.

A community had gathered around me that included not just my accustomed associates, but people I'd forgotten I'd once loved so much, people whom I'd never known cared about me, people I'd always admired but had never made the brave effort to get truly close to, and people who were almost strangers. Some I hadn't actually spoken to in years—since leaving my hometown, since leaving college, since leaving New York City, since throwing myself into what I'd believed was my real family in Chicago. Since leaving all the places I'd left without saying much of a goodbye to anyone, convinced it made no difference. It had never occurred to me that people wanted to stay in touch with me.

"You'd better cheer up or I'm coming back to give you a tune-up," wrote a high school classmate who was in our small-town production of *South Pacific* (starring my mother) when we were fifteen (probably the last time he and I spoke). We had spent lots of evenings together, waiting for hours in the hallway or the band room, doing our homework, until the extras were required to stand on the high school stage, sing and dance in the chorus, say a line or two, then go sit in the hall again. Since then, skinny, boyish John had grown big muscles and acquired a weathered face after years stationed in Iraq. He was writing from a war zone, and in his Facebook photos he was dirty and sweating, with dusty trucks and sand in the background. I was on the thirty-fifth floor of a Helmut Jahn high-rise in Chicago, overlooking gorgeous Lake Michigan. In my pictures I was clean and smiling, wearing red lipstick and standing on a street in Barcelona, or posing with our sweet Labrador retriever as she stretched out on our large comfortable bed.

Beyond the kind, cordial notes—sweet pats on my back—personal stories arrived detailing sorrows that were not my own.

There was a message from an old college roommate, the kind of blond southern belle who knew which boys would not break your heart, what to wear to a mixer, why it was okay to have sex but not talk about it, and other things I couldn't figure out. She had a constant hum of happiness that was leavened with a sharp sarcastic edge that made her seem ideal to me. But she was writing to tell me how her longtime husband left her for another woman. How she became so depressed after their children left for college that she couldn't get out of bed. And how much it hurt to take him back, despite her love and sense of relief.

A very funny woman I'd never met in person, whom I'd gotten to know through the growing internet food community (created by Twitter and Food52) before officially friending her, told me that when she was in her twenties, her brother and sister died within a few years of each other. "I was an only child," she wrote. I remembered how lucky I was to have my remaining siblings.

I read things I never would have guessed from all the happy family pictures that I'd scrolled through, thinking everyone else in the world had gotten an instruction booklet for life that I'd been denied.

Former *New Yorker* coworkers encouraged me to move back to New York City and offered to help me find a new job. One high school classmate even offered me money (he was my ninth-grade date for the homecoming dance; his gesture was pretty embarrassing, but so disarmingly sweet).

And so many people wrote simply to say they were thinking of me. Whether I received this unexpectedly soothing balm because these friends didn't know the kind of person I'd turned into or because people like slowing down when happening upon a disaster, I wasn't sure. I honestly could not discern straightforward human kindness any longer. But one thing was certain: it was a second chance to reconnect with people from my past and make new friends in a way that others seemed to do with grace. I grabbed on to this opportunity as if it were a giant piece of driftwood in the ocean, bobbing toward me as I flailed miles from shore.

A lot of these people were terrific home cooks or food writers or chefs or cooking instructors or plain old food lovers, so their suggestions leaned heavily in a culinary direction. It was as if they'd arrived at my frozen Chicago home, where the snow had been falling for days and the gray sky never cleared, bearing covered dishes for an impromptu winter potluck.

"Hey! You should visit us, and we can cook for you," wrote Eileen, a former sorority sister from Savannah who makes great peach and strawberry jams from local fruit.

"Or you could cook for us," wrote a wry illustrator from the *New Yorker*, who wore a short bob haircut and played in the magazine's summer softball team in Central Park, facing off against teams from *Vanity Fair* and *Time* with life-or-death seriousness.

Eileen then suggested I embark on a culinary tour to see them all. "It should be your comfort food tour," posted one of my oldest friends, Kevin, who'd sat at the desk next to mine the entire time I was an editor at the *New Yorker.*

And we all "Liked" that idea—very much.

It was the moment of crisis in a Mickey Rooney–Judy Garland movie. Except rather than gathering around the barn to put on a show, my friends and I were in separate homes, miles apart, staring at glowing computer screens, alone but together.

Their offers seemed to me extraordinarily generous. We often hear about the isolating, numbing qualities of the internet, but in my case it had an inverse effect, perhaps because I was already feeling both numb and isolated. Either way, Facebook saved me. It really did. I'll always be grateful to my virtual guardian angels. Thanks to them, the kernel of an idea began to form right then—a Comfort Food Tour that would allow me to reconnect with people I'd dearly loved, and get to know new ones I'd admired from afar. I wondered what secrets they would reveal to me about how to become a happy, healthy person, with a happy, healthy family, in a world that seemed awfully forbidding from where I was sitting.

In honor of all those guardian angels, here is the recipe for my cousin Martha's Angel Biscuits, passed along to me one spring afternoon in my aunt Mariah's apple-green kitchen in Galax during a lovely weekend with a group of some of my favorite female relatives. These are perfect for country ham biscuits, the sandwich of the South. They are what I imagined having in my knapsack as I ventured out into a different world, hopefully one in which connection and solace and renewed love were possible.

Angel Biscuits

Makes approximately 48 biscuits, to be served with country ham

5 cups all-purpose flour

¼ cup plus 2 tablespoons sugar

1 tablespoon baking powder

1 teaspoon baking soda

1 teaspoon salt

2½ teaspoons dry yeast

2 tablespoons warm water

1 cup shortening

2 cups buttermilk

1. In a large bowl, sift together the flour, the ¼ cup sugar, the baking powder, baking soda, and salt; set aside.

2. In a small bowl, combine the yeast, water, and the 2 tablespoons sugar; it will begin to foam. If it doesn't you need to start again with new yeast.

3. Incorporate the shortening into the flour mixture until the texture resembles gravel. You can use a pastry cutter. I use my hands.

4. Pour the yeast mixture and the buttermilk into your flour bowl and mix gently until a ball forms. Fold the dough over on itself a half dozen times or so, until a uniform texture is achieved, being careful not to overwork it (you can do this in the large bowl). Cover the bowl with a damp cloth and place it in a warm area of your kitchen to let it rise for 90 minutes. At this point, you can refrigerate half the dough for later use, which is kind of amazing. It will keep for 4 to 5 days.

5. Meanwhile, preheat the oven to 400°F. Lightly grease a cookie sheet, or, if using a cast-iron skillet, place it in the oven about 10 minutes before baking.

6. On a floured board, roll the dough to ¾-inch thickness; fold the dough over on itself and press down evenly to make it ¾ inch thick; repeat once, pressing the folded dough out into an even ½-inch slab. Cut with a biscuit cutter. (I use one the size of a half dollar for small ham biscuits, but you can make larger biscuits according to your whims.)

7. Place on a lightly greased cookie sheet or in a preheated cast-iron pan and bake for 20 minutes, until lightly browned. You may brush the tops with melted butter halfway through baking for a prettier brown.

Two

EZRA POUND CAKE

Unfortunately, before I could begin to receive all that love and light—before I could start planning my Comfort Food Tour and take the first steps away from the isolation I'd been cultivating over the last couple of months—I momentarily fell back into the deep darkness.

I stayed in the apartment longer than two weeks, withdrew, and started caring less about my life than I ever had before. Eventually, even though I was a wine drinker and generally a lightweight, I opened that pretty blue bottle of gin that was still in my freezer. And when it was gone, I hardly thought of Oliver at all.

The Engineer was staying elsewhere most of the time, but when he came over, he played the guitar and sang Wilco songs in a loud, off-key voice that I'd once found endearing. He blasted the television and banged on our locked bedroom door, asking me why I was still there.

Not that I was pleasant to be around. It's hard to say, in retrospect, who was the bigger, scarier jerk—whose personality changed most dramatically under pressure. At the time I felt like I at least had an excuse, but all active alcoholics think that they have a great excuse for their bad behavior.

In a way, drinking is not so different from being in love with a narcissistic charmer. It makes you feel so good at first. You keep going, even though you know it will separate you from friends, family, and the rest of the world. And you keep relying on it, even when it starts to make you feel bad.

So I went out and bought more gin. It kept me company as I started filling boxes with the few things I cared about—my cookbooks, Le Creuset pots and pans, KitchenAid mixer, a few pieces of art, and my clothes. I figured I could store stuff in the garage of my sister Elaine's vacation house near Palm Springs until I determined my next move. And the rest I would put in storage. It was hard work, stacking the boxes onto a cart from the UPS Store on our block and rolling it down the street all by myself in the ice, wind, and snow, but the medicinal, evergreen-scented gin made it much more pleasant.

On the third night of my gin binge, after a month of this ridiculous semi-cohabitation, I was awakened long after midnight by plain terror.

I realized that I was drowning in guilt and shame and slowly killing myself with alcohol. But when I asked myself who might be able to help me without compounding the shame or guilt or anger or denial I was feeling, I drew a complete blank.

Then it hit me: it was me. Only me.

I got out of bed and found the number of a local crisis hotline on the internet. The person who answered the phone told me what to do. I knocked on the door of the Princess's pink room where the Engineer had been sleeping part of the time.

"I'm taking myself to the hospital," I told him, my legs shaking.

"Why are you taking yourself to the hospital?" he asked. He always had a way of making my own statements seem absurd by turning them into questions.

It was clear to me then that there was no understanding left to be had in this relationship. And I had no right to drag him into the ocean with me.

"I just have to," I said.

The Engineer walked next to me on the icy sidewalk to Northwestern Memorial Hospital's emergency room just three blocks from our apartment. I sobbed the whole way.

The minute an emergency room attendant took me by the arm, the Engineer left without saying a word, and that was the last time I saw him.

A nurse led me to an empty room for emergency admissions and asked me some questions.

"Are you afraid that you will harm others?"

I shook my head no, though I knew I had. And I didn't want to anymore.

"Are you afraid that you will hurt yourself?"

"I already have," I told her.

After talking to the nurse, I signed myself into the hospital's Stone Institute of Psychiatry, where I stayed for the next nine days on lock-down.

•

Each morning at the center, we received a three-part paper menu card with choices for our next day's meals, the only respite from our long days of classes, private sessions, and group therapies. It was a thrilling document that you could tear into sections for breakfast, lunch, and dinner. It was decorated with a drawing of funeral gladiolas, "Your Menu Selection" written in swirly letters on the front, and the latest food pyramid printed on the back. "Circle one for lunch," it read: Meatloaf or Seasonal Fruit Plate (with Homemade Zucchini Bread), Rice Pudding or Lemon Meringue Pie. Whatever you chose would then appear on your tray the next day, along with a little bowl of something delicious, like Italian Wedding Soup, to start. Miraculous!

After I made my choices in the early morning, while waiting for the rest of the patients to arrive for breakfast in the multipurpose cafeteria/art room, I could stand on a bench and get a look through the floor's only unfrosted windows onto the snow-covered cityscape with pink skies above Lake Michigan, the same view as the one from my former home.

The main lesson I learned at the hospital, the one I chose to cling to, came from a young psychiatrist there who explained to me that my recent crisis was just one event and that it didn't have to dictate the rest of my life. "You are on a forward path, which you can control to a certain extent," she said. "But you have to put your head down, keep moving forward, up and down the hills, no matter what."

Over the next few years, there would be so many times when I wanted to just quit and go home before remembering, once again, that I didn't have one anymore. That I might never have had one.

Keep moving forward. I wrote it down in my notebook.

•

By the time I was sprung from the center, the remaining immediate family members who gave a damn about me, meaning Elaine and Michael, had come up with a plan. In a few days, my brother Michael was to arrive at O'Hare Airport to escort me to Elaine and her husband Kevin's home in Santa Barbara, after which I was to live in their vacation house in the desert near Palm Springs for the time being.

Until Michael arrived, I would be at my friend Jessica's. I'd called her from inside the hospital to ask if I could stay at her place while I tied up all my loose ends, and without any hesitation she'd said, "Just tell me when and where to pick you up." She treated me as if I had done something splendid, something deserving of congratulations. She made cups of mint tea for us while we watched *Modern Family*, had cupcakes and licorice (which we both love) on hand, and later let her wry, scruffy dog, Clyde, sleep in my bed in the guest room, where there was a little basket of gifts for me. She seemed so surprised by my relief and gratitude that I realized something I'd never before considered: the things people truly need from us at the very worst times in their lives are often much smaller than what we try to give them.

So that I wouldn't be alone, she came with me to my former apartment the next day to finish the packing job I'd started before my late-night trip to the hospital. No one was there. The little origami fashion kit I'd bought for the Princess in Barcelona across the street from the Picasso Museum was left out on the table. A little pink paper bra and a little pair of yellow paper high heels that she had folded lay next to the open box of chocolates I'd also brought her.

As the Russians from Moishe's Moving carried my cinnamon-colored velvet sofa and kitchen appliances out to their truck to place in my storage space along with all the things I'd packed away when the Engineer and I moved in together, my phone rang. It was my first cousin and oldest friend in life, Toni. Oliver and I had seen her almost every day when we were very small; we were all close to the same age and lived right across the street from each other—our fathers were brothers and their wives and their eight kids ran back and forth all day long.

Her voice was like a healing tonic. "Everything is going to be fine, Emily. Just keep forging ahead, and don't stop respecting your own life." She told me that no, I was not crazy; that she was in fact *proud* of me for taking myself to the hospital. That gave me courage.

On my last night in Chicago, Jessica and I bundled up and walked from her apartment to a tiny pizzeria called Great Lake, one of my favorite restaurants back then, owned by our friend Lydia and her husband, Nick, the brilliant pie maker. Lydia brought us one of her simple salads made from local herbs, baby greens, organic purple and yellow carrots, lemon juice, olive oil, and lots of sea salt. It was like getting a bouquet, followed by an equally simple Neapolitan pie with a crust from heaven, light and airy but sturdy and crisp in places, with subtle hints of that good burnt flavor that comes when great dough meets a well-tended pizza oven.

Oh, this pizza: it was extraordinarily important to me. I wasn't ready to process other people enjoying their happy lives on the streets or in the small dining room at Great Lake. The hello hugs and welcoming handshakes, the intimate conversation and laughter, the cute woolen caps and cool new boots all belonged in the world I'd been ejected from, a world I both resented and yearned for. I needed to focus on the habits of happy people, to study them, but it was too hard at the time.

Instead I focused on our enormous, freshly made pizza—with its sweet, barely melted homemade mozzarella, that fragrant crust, the sparky tomato smeared between the two. The first bite transformed me temporarily, filled a place where sadness was trying to wedge its way in for good. I ate three giant slices and felt sleepy. This pizza was better than any hospital-prescribed drug in my purse. It connected me to the world in a way I could not on my own. Without trying too hard, I had accepted another gift from Jessica.

By giving me my first unofficial stop on the Comfort Food Tour, she had shown me how easy it could be; that in real life, it could all just unfold naturally if only I'd let it.

Great Lake is closed now, but a really good homemade pizza can have a similar effect on anyone. And I happen to make an excellent pie. You will need a pizza stone for your oven to get a proper crust, but making the dough is the easiest thing in the world. I like the recipe in Jason Denton and Kathryn Kellinger's *Simple Italian Snacks*. Underneath the cheese (and basil, thinly sliced red onions, and bits of high-quality, oil-cured olives), I use this luxurious, potent sauce that Toni taught me long ago, adapted from her mother's much less spicy version. Because of the large amount of butter, when you refrigerate the sauce it turns into a rich paste that you can spread like icing over the dough, but you can also use it as a base for pasta sauce. I make a giant batch and freeze half for pizza emergencies.

Toni's Tomato Sauce

Makes about 1 quart

8 ounces (2 sticks) butter (don't try to make this healthier)

5 tablespoons minced fresh garlic (feel free to add more)

2 teaspoons red pepper flakes, or to taste

2 (28-ounce) cans whole peeled Italian plum tomatoes, preferably San Marzano, with their juice

1 (14.5 ounce) can petite cut diced tomatoes

1 tablespoon sugar (optional; I leave this out)

Handful of chopped fresh basil and/or oregano

1. Melt ½ stick of the butter in a heavy pan, add the garlic, and cook over medium-low heat until fragrant; don't let it brown. Add the remaining 1½ sticks butter and let it melt.
2. Add the red pepper flakes, whole tomatoes, and diced tomatoes,

crushing them with your hands over the pot. Don't forget to include the juice. (In the summer Toni grows a variety of terrific tomatoes, so she skins, seeds, and dices her own.)

3. Simmer uncovered over low heat for what will feel like forever—2½ to 3 hours—stirring occasionally, until it is pudding-thick and potent, before adding the sugar (if using) and herbs. Then cook for another 30 minutes over very low heat.

•

When my brother Michael, a decorated cold-case detective for the Santa Barbara Police Department, arrived in Chicago the next night, we stayed in a cheap airport hotel room together before our flight the next day. Elaine paid for all of it. She is a former PR executive and always in charge.

"Elaine wanted me to check your luggage for alcohol," he said with a straight face, in his just-the-facts-ma'am voice. Michael thought this was hilarious. But it made me feel lonelier than ever: all alcoholics were the same desperate cartoon. I briefly wondered if I could go back to the hospital. But he talked me into watching one of his favorite shows on the History Channel, *Ice Road Truckers*, and we ate junk food from the hotel gift shop. This calmed me. When he got up to shower, he put a chair under the door—so I couldn't get out?

"Very funny," I said.

"You may as well laugh about it," he replied, adding: "You don't exactly have a choice."

He was right.

As we hurtled toward California the next day, I said goodbye to Chicago, which looked like a chunk of black ice from the airplane window. Michael was sitting next to me, not talking, just being tall, strong, kind, and alive. I dozed, relieved I'd escaped all the ghosts down there, but with absolutely no idea where I was going to end up.

It turned out to be the Betty Ford Center.

When I got to Santa Barbara, Elaine told me that the offer to live in the desert house near Palm Springs now had a condition: I would have to go to the Betty Ford Center, a twenty-minute drive away. She and

Kevin would gladly pay for my time there. "Think about it," she said.

I said yes, of course, and thanked them. I had no money and no place else to go. If she'd told me I could stay at the desert house but that I had to wear a dunce cap the whole time, I would have jumped at the chance.

Which was kind of what was happening.

I'd already caused so much turmoil and misery that I didn't remind Elaine I'd just gotten out of an expensive, very intensive program three days earlier. That rather than crazy and unspeakable, going there was probably the smartest thing I'd ever done in my life. Or that I had felt safe there and had had no desire to drink since. But no one wanted to talk about the hospital, as if it was somehow shameful, the same way no one wanted to talk about Oliver. So I just kept quiet and went along with Elaine's plan, even though it seemed tailored not for me but for another person altogether.

When I called the Betty Ford Center, I was told that attending the program as an outpatient would shave about $25,000 off the bill—eight weeks cost $5,000—which made me feel a little better about the expense.

Before I enrolled, though, I had to undergo a complete ten-day makeover under the guidance of Elaine, who is a perfectionist and seems to believe that perfection is a real possibility. Back in high school, she started cutting everyone's hair. Quite a few of the cheerleaders and majorettes, and some of the marching band, began showing up at school with the same floppy bowl cut. She likes to fix things. And she didn't want me falling apart again. Presumably, the more fetching I looked, the lower the probability of this happening.

"You don't even look like yourself," she said. ("*But I'm not myself*," I wanted to reply.)

She told me I was fat. (I had gained ten pounds, a side effect of the antidepressants I'd begun taking a year before the breakup.) "Please don't say that," I replied. "You sound like the Engineer."

"Well, do you want me to lie to you or do you want me to tell you the truth?" she asked.

It seemed like a trick question. Those two choices had always gotten confused in my family: the truth or fiction? They were interchangeable.

But I was so grateful to have Elaine, who took me to her hairdresser to have my shoulder-length curly hair straightened and lightened, because I "looked like Rapunzel." (Anjelica Huston was there with her dog, which should give you an idea of how much the whole thing cost.) She bought me Vera Wang dresses with matching shoes and threw in expensive hand-me-down purses to go with it all. ("Dresses! You need to lose weight before you wear pants!") We went together to her George Clooney–lookalike trainer, who hounded me through a series of squats, crunches, and barbell exercises. I took long walks every day in the beautiful sunshine to a local café to get the *New York Times,* drink coffee, and get in a bit of secret crying.

Sometimes, if necessary, I took several walks a day.

We also made a searching and fearless inventory of my closet.

"What is *this*?" Elaine asked, holding up an article of my clothing with pincer fingers.

"That's my favorite coat," I replied, even though I think she knew this. It was brown corduroy, and when I wore it, I imagined it made me look casually elegant, almost raffish.

"It makes you look like a hobo," she said, stuffing it into a giant black garbage bag to give to her maids, before I could snatch it away. Apparently, most of my favorite clothes made me look fat or as if I should be roasting a sausage over a burning trash barrel near the railroad, because we gave away the majority of my remaining wardrobe.

"Throw it away," she said to me, again and again. This had always been her mantra. "You can get new stuff later."

I can? I could not imagine how that was possible.

I love my sister Elaine madly—she had always been my best friend and confidante, and I her adoring, loyal ally. We talked on the phone twice a week. She was taking care of me, which I desperately needed. So while some of this makeover hurt my feelings, I went along with it gratefully. Whenever I tried to discuss the fact that I had just over $10,000 in resources, which I needed to conserve, she'd dismiss me. And I thanked her so often she got annoyed: "Will you *stop*?" she said. "You can pay us later if you want to, when you're back on your feet."

Back on my feet. How in the world did I get there from here, from this posh limbo, so far removed from all the things I had to face?

I decided the first step was admitting that I'd had the kind of old-fashioned nervous breakdown my southern forebears used to have. But since we would never talk about it—at least not directly, to one another; that's not how my family has ever worked—I would just have to admit it to myself and be done with it.

Neither Michael nor Elaine had really had the time to absorb Oliver's death, and now they were worried about me. Like many of my southern-family interactions, this was comforting, humiliating, and guilt-inducing at the same time.

So the second step, to my mind, was to start cooking: I would repay them in the only way I was capable.

For Elaine I made my healthy and low-calorie pounded chicken cutlets with a Parmesan and black-pepper crust, served with a dressed arugula salad on top, a dish that speaks for itself, as well as my excellent lentil soup that Elaine renamed Beauty Soup, because we added extra carrots, spinach, garlic, and onions, all of which are supposed to be fantastic for the complexion.

This is more of a vegetarian stew than a soup, really. If you are watching your weight (even though you might have only gained ten pounds!), this is a good dish to live on because it has no butter. However, you can start the dish by browning a few strips of chopped bacon, then adding the vegetables. Elaine likes to sprinkle hers with grated Parmigiano-Reggiano; I like to drizzle mine with a little good olive oil.

Beauty Soup

Serves 10

1 tablespoon olive oil

1 large onion, chopped

6 garlic cloves, minced

2 large carrots, chopped

2 bay leaves

1 cup black lentils, picked over and washed

1 cup French green lentils, picked over and washed

1 (28-ounce) can whole peeled Italian plum tomatoes, preferably
    San Marzano
10 cups water
Salt, to taste
Freshly ground black pepper, to taste
A couple of pinches of cayenne pepper
Splash of cider vinegar
1 large bag baby spinach (or 1 head of escarole, cut into thin strips)

1. In a large pot, heat the oil over medium-low heat, then sauté the onion and garlic until the onion is translucent, 4 to 5 minutes. Add the carrots to the pot along with the bay leaves, and sauté until tender and fragrant, 3 to 5 minutes.
2. Add the lentils to the pot, stir to coat, and cook for 5 minutes.
3. Crush the tomatoes with your hands before adding them and their juice to the pot. Let simmer for 5 minutes.
4. Add the water, salt, black pepper, and cayenne.
5. Bring the soup to a boil, then lower the heat and simmer at a lively pace for 30 minutes or so, until the lentils are tender.
6. Add a big splash of vinegar and the spinach, and cover the pot, continuing to simmer for about 10 minutes more. You have to try really hard to overcook this soup, but you can undercook it. It is generally better the next day.

Note: You can substitute lemon juice for the cider vinegar if you'd like. Escarole cut into strips is a great substitute for spinach, and gives the soup added texture. If the soup gets too thick (since it is rather like a stew), add a cup of water or more and let cook a bit.

•

For Kevin and Michael, both of whom love cake, I decided to make Elvis's Pound Cake, a variation on a popular recipe I inherited from my mother.

Growing up in the South, I had often thought that everyone was on a permanent quest for the perfect recipe—for pound cake, spoon bread, deviled eggs, shrimp and grits, pimento cheese, bread-and-butter pickles. And this sought-after recipe, once secured, could somehow serve as a solution, an explanation, an antidote, a balm for whatever damage had been done to the recipe seeker, which he or she desperately wanted to forgive. For me, however, this is the pound cake that simply landed in my life by default, which I consider a lucky break.

The name, like so many other things about my childhood, confused me as a kid. (Mother surely never met Elvis; I doubted he was ever a baker.) But as a grown-up, I have the power to change not just the recipe but also the name of the cake if I want to. And as an overdue nod to my long-suffering English Lit professor in college, I have done so.

It's a cold oven cake, dense and buttery yet somehow not too heavy, so it results in very little remorse once you've had a slice. You must sift the flour twice as instructed.

Ezra Pound Cake

Makes one 10-inch cake

8 ounces (2 sticks) unsalted butter, at room temperature, plus
   more for the pan
3 cups cake flour, sifted twice, plus more for the pan
3 cups granulated sugar
7 large eggs, at room temperature
1 cup heavy cream
2 teaspoons pure vanilla extract

1. Butter and flour a 10-inch tube pan.
2. Thoroughly cream the sugar and butter in a large bowl.
3. Add the eggs to the mixture one at a time, beating well after each addition. Mix in 1½ cups of the flour, then the heavy cream, then the remaining 1½ cups flour. Mix in the vanilla.
4. Pour the batter into the pan. Set in a *cold* oven and turn the heat to 350°F. Bake for 60 to 70 minutes, or until a knife inserted into the center of the cake comes out clean. Remove from the pan and cool.

Three

THE GRAPEFRUIT DIET
FOR NON-DIETERS

After dark and icy Chicago, the Betty Ford Center was like Oz, but in the desert—surreal silver-green mountains and exotic plants surrounding sand-colored buildings whose expanses of glass reflected a white sun and slumping palm trees.

Camp Betty, as it is called by alumni and locals, is in the town of Rancho Mirage, which reminded me of those old *New Yorker* cartoons of the single lost traveler crawling on his hands and knees over endless sandy dunes, dying of thirst, his pants torn in zigzags, inching toward an oasis that would turn out to be a dry mirage. As if that were funny.

The day Elaine took me to register, an inpatient in trunks was playing guitar by the outdoor swimming pool, while a stray brown duck floated in the chlorinated water a few feet away. Volleyball nets were set up on the forced-green side lawn. Lizards skittered across white gravel gardens. A cute campus dog trotted around. ("He's sniffing for drugs," my intake manager said, when I asked if the dog was the Betty Ford mascot.) Inside the wood and terrazzo offices, portraits of Betty herself hung everywhere. She looked pretty and poised, the wife of an American president, clearly unashamed to be the most famous lush in the entire free world.

Elaine went back to Santa Barbara after a few days, and I had a couple of weeks to get settled into the desert house before starting the two-month program. I was alone and free, for what felt like the first time ever, to do or say or feel anything I wanted. I was pleased to discover that did not include drinking or even craving a drink. I barely thought about alcohol at all until I actually started classes at Camp Betty, where it was the main topic. So I had a lot of time alone to think about what I'd done wrong, and how I was going to make it better. But it felt like I'd been exiled.

Granted, my banishment to the desert was in an airy modern house at the world's most heavenly country club, where Dwight Eisenhower and Gerald Ford and the Bushes had been members. But during the long, contemplative hours I spent stretched out under palm trees reading, riding my bike at the base of the rocky Santa Rosa Mountains, or watching hummingbirds drink from the yellow acacia blossoms, I could not feel the truth of my good fortune, despite how grateful I was to be there. I was dumbfounded by my own life.

Once I finally started making the twenty-minute drive out to Rancho Mirage each afternoon, to join all the other alcoholics in their various stages of surrender, I started feeling connected to something outside myself; I was sick to death of my inner dialogue, and it thrilled me to notice other people's pain.

Some of us were sad and racked with guilt, some glowing and refreshed, some very young, some very old. Why stop drinking at eighty? A few of us were defiant and snarly. One of us (a business executive who spoke to no one and spent all his spare time on the terrace smoking expensive cigars) seemed to be in complete denial. But everyone, however damaged, listened when you talked, no matter how unpleasant you were. It was okay to cry, but not many people did. No one removed their pants during group, the way someone had at the hospital in Chicago, and the stories were fascinating and often much more shocking than anything I'd ever done or considered doing, even at my most sozzled. *Why would you, a successful banking executive, smoke crack, ever?* I'd wonder. *How could you lose your car? Your ex-boyfriend sold you to his drug dealer for a night? But you're so pretty and smart and well-adjusted. And you're wearing Chanel flats.*

Before leaving me at her desert house, Elaine had given me a cover story (I was working on a book) to tell all the neighbors, in case they asked why I was there. (No one ever did; from what I could see they were too busy having lots of cocktails of their own to worry about why I wasn't.)

I was supposed to be ashamed, but among my recovering friends it was okay *not* to feel that way every minute of the day. In fact, being able to tell the truth made us less so.

The Betty Ford Center is a bit of a magical kingdom, but it's also a high-class reform school for adults, meant to break you down and build you back up with a permanent fear of your old way of life. In addition to yoga in the Elizabeth Taylor Gymnasium, guided meditation to find our "spirit animals" (mine is a wolf), and seeing movie stars in workout clothes picking through the salad bar—*Was that a cherry tomato or a carrot? Is he really going to eat that much Thousand Island dressing?*—we worked the famous Twelve Steps, had meetings with a spiritual adviser, heard scary lectures on codependency, and endured grueling four-hour-long group therapy sessions that included reading aloud entries from our so-called private diaries that explored the personal consequences of yielding to addiction—as if recalling them in the first place weren't hellish enough.

Every once in a while, during our group therapy gatherings in our counselor's glass-walled office, we outpatients would hear whooping and laughing from a distance. Then we'd see the inpatients, a raggedy band of kids, old people, and midlife professionals running through the manicured grass together on their way to whatever nonaddictive evening meds (Trazodone, Seroquel) were allowed in a rehab joint. (We got tested for palliatives like tranquilizers and Ambien and for alcohol on a regular basis.)

After a couple of weeks of driving back and forth every day to Camp Betty, I noticed the bare trees in the neighborhood had puffed up into pink and white pom-poms and the air smelled like citrus blossoms. When had that happened?

When I wasn't at Camp Betty, I spent less time inside watching the Food Channel and more time on my bike. I found a ratty yet regal standard poodle on a local rescue website and when I pointed her out to Elaine, she adopted the dog during one of her two brief visits, named her Maggie, and left her with me for acclimation before her transfer to Santa Barbara. Maggie and I slept together in the prettily made-up queen-size bed, with her scratchy black paws at my face, her head at my feet—two damaged rejects who were strangers but needed each other terribly. She followed me from room to room, even when I showered, and would stare deeply into my eyes the second I glanced in her direction, which was something no one had done for a long time.

Maggie and I took long walks during the too-bright mornings when the air was still cool; the citrus blossoms fell to the ground like summer snow. By the time the trees produced tiny green balls that turned out to be baby grapefruit, I had started going to the Palm Desert library to check out stacks of vintage cookbooks by local characters like Dinah Shore. I read these cookbooks in bed, and began to dream about the dinner parties I'd have someday for my own sparkling friends, when I would use food to lead me back to love, to some kind of family.

But I was still thinking about the Engineer way too often. My Camp Betty counselor pointed out that giving the Engineer "so much room in my brain" was a big mistake that could slow me down from being able to process Oliver's death or begin to make plans for my future.

How could she know that that had been the way I'd grown up, putting my own life aside to focus on the off-kilter emotions of people I adored, even if they were incapable of loving me back? I was loyal long past the point when it was clear that no one there had my back. It was my comfort zone.

When I'd strayed off my path—lost touch with the sober, competent, independent person I'd been so proud of becoming when I first moved to Chicago—I'd stepped back into a very old role. I'd re-created a home where unconditional love flowed in one direction only, a home with close to no boundaries and a screw loose somewhere I could never quite locate, no matter how hard I tried.

When I'd desperately needed someone to care for or comfort me at the worst time in my life, my new family had disappeared: poof.

The truth is that I picked the Engineer; I helped create our patterns. And more than half the time, my life with him had been wonderful. We drank coffee together in bed. I knew the whorl of his ears. I knew the size of his feet and bought him handsome shoes to go on them.

We got so close at the beginning, so fast, and I cooked more and more. I wanted to comfort him. My own apartment, the home I'd built, was beautiful and pacific; I had a great kitchen stocked with everything I needed to make him love me forever.

I began to keep a diary of the meals I made for him and, later, the Princess, when they came to my place together on weekends. I'd make them toasted cheese with both cheddar and blue, super-thin slices of red onion that charred under the broiler, and some chopped walnuts on top, a little celery salad, some iced tea, and then they would both fall asleep—one in the living room on my velvet sofa, the other on my bed. I don't think I'd ever been happier. We had baked bananas with brown sugar for breakfast, potato soup for lunch, Marcella Hazan's veal stew with buttered noodles for dinner. I made banana bread, popovers, chocolate mousse; shrimp and feta, scallops on spinach with lemon orzo, steak salad; pan bagnat, green-hatch-chili chicken on creamy grits, butternut squash risotto; ham biscuits, pork tenderloin with maple and sage, cucumber and avocado salad with red onion. I needed to take care of someone, and now I had two people to look after. In the years that followed, I cooked dinners and made lunches and breakfasts at what you might call an advanced level.

When we moved in together, to the gorgeous high-rise apartment I found near the *Trib*, I'd made sure we had an extra bedroom for the Princess and a good kitchen for all of us to use together (she loved to make chocolate mousse). I embraced the caretaker role with the gusto of someone who never thought she'd have a child to love in her life.

But things change. When they disappear suddenly, you wonder

if they were good or bad, true or false—if they were ever real at all. In the end, it's the path that needs inspection. Now I knew what I wanted to get out of my time at Betty Ford, what I wanted to learn. How does a person make choices about relationships, ones that might lead to a stable happy family, when she's never been given a recipe that makes any kind of sense at all? And how does she learn to let go of the bad recipe, even though it's a family heirloom?

●

The trees all around Elaine's desert house had begun to produce lemons and oranges and tangerines and tangelos and fat pink and yellow grapefruit, which eventually got so heavy they spilled all over the grass and onto the black street like oversize confetti. Occasionally, I'd hear a pleasant thump as they hit the ground.

I started picking grapefruit in my pajamas, for breakfast and lunch, from trees off the patio. I brought shirt-loads of lemons inside, and placed them all over the house in bowls like flowers. I squeezed the multicolored fruit into a big pitcher and drank the mixed juices with seltzer every day.

Grapefruit has always been my favorite fruit, and these were extraordinary, with so much sweetness leavening the satisfying bitterness. The world still seemed alarmingly painful to me; it was also more beautiful than I'd noticed in quite a while.

It was a very good thing all this fruit was available, because I had barely turned on the stove, even though the house had the kind of warm sunlit kitchen I'd always dreamed of: room enough to cook with friends without also wanting to kill them, and a really long counter with stools for everyone who was staying out of the way and just eating.

But unlike Santa Barbara, where I had Elaine and Kevin and Michael to cook for, I was completely alone in the desert, except for Maggie, who had been so damaged by her previous life that she only liked kibble. (I'd waved a piece of really good salami under her nose, and she'd recoiled as if I was trying to poison her.) It had never been so clear to me that the reason I cook is to show people how much I love them. Or to make them love me. Since I was not exactly crazy about myself at this point in my life, though, I didn't get the pleasure of a home-cooked meal very often. I didn't think I deserved it.

I am such a loser, I thought one morning, during a bit of dark backsliding, before slumping to the floor, feeling like Scarlett O'Hara when she realized she had nothing but curtains left to wear. After about a half hour down there on the gorgeous terrazzo tile, being ludicrously self-pitying, I recalled that a lot of other people thought I *did* deserve comfort. "Let us cook for you!" my friends had written back when I was still in Chicago.

I got up off the floor and dug through my Betty Ford tote bag ("Who the *hell* is going to carry that?" Ann, the director of the out-patient program, said to me when she handed it over as a welcome present, along with my official Betty Ford water bottle). In it I found my old recipe/idea notebook, which was the closest thing I had to a thoughtful journal. I hadn't opened it since leaving Chicago. I'd scrawled, "Do baked eggs in custard cups; lemon cake w/strawberries; warm bacon vinaigrette—cook pecans in fat before deglazing; potato watercress soup/buy nutmeg grater."

I started a new list in my notebook: the names of friends who'd invited me into their homes, people I wanted to cook for, people I felt like I could learn something from, both culinarily and otherwise. I wrote down the names of friends who'd been there for me all along, when I was wearing my blinders and couldn't see them.

I would use this list as my guide for the Comfort Food Tour, the idea of which came back and seemed more important, more neces-sary, than ever before. I'd been knocked off my path, ejected from the kind of world where happy people and families gathered around the table, but I could try to turn that around. Why had I not reached out to these friends? Now I had the chance.

But before I could begin again, my counselors and friends at Camp Betty helped me to see that I needed to mourn. Whatever I'd been doing, I sure as hell had not been mourning. All my presumed objects of grief—Oliver, the Engineer, the Princess, the dog, my home, my idea of family, my career, every last cent I'd made or saved and most of what I'd invested, my independence, my old way of life—had become a mystery to me once they'd suddenly disappeared, just a few months earlier. I juggled them all constantly, not daring to let a single one come to rest, not ever focusing on any one of them.

The idea of trying instantly to accept Oliver's death seemed selfish and inappropriate: Why the hell should I accept it? How could anyone? Despite what it said in his obituary, Oliver had not died peacefully at all. In a family of seven, he'd ended up alone in a hotel room; a stranger found his body.

Grief was a luxury I did not deserve.

It was only after he'd died that I thought about why crushing lows followed his numerous self-transformations: maybe because none of them changed the truth of who he truly was, and he could not accept himself. I didn't know all his secrets, and no one should, but I knew enough. Including the fact that every time he fell, he probably took people down with him, too. Collateral damage: maybe he didn't want to do that anymore.

All of which is why it was so very contemptible of me, after my tortured alcoholic brother had killed himself with alcohol, to get drunk and give up, too. Because that's what drinking is when you're an alcoholic. According to one of my oldest friends, who quit alcohol when he was twenty-five, "Drinking is no longer trying."

At Betty Ford, they told us that you're only as sick as your secrets. But I always wanted to point out that the secrets you keep, in order to protect other people at your own expense (especially if those other people don't give a damn about you, especially if you're hiding things that no one should be ashamed of to begin with), can do more than make you sick. They can be fatal.

If I entered that grieving room, I was sure the door would lock behind me for good. And I believed that whatever was in there was worse than what happens to a person who never accepts death and loss, a person who never mourns.

Which, it turns out, is bitterness.

So I became bitter about Oliver's death. It just happened. A minuscule black dot grew into a creosote lining; an emotion turned into a trait. There was nothing I could do about it for a very long time, other than try to hide it as much as I could.

Take some advice: never be bitter. People will treat you as if you have willingly welcomed bitterness into your life like a vampire you've allowed through your front door. They take it to mean you've given in, given up. And because of that they will give up on you, too. You get nothing back from bitterness. It goes in one direction only.

But I have discovered much later that sweetness comes, in one form or another, to anyone who reaches out for it and opens up to receive it.

Here is a salad of bitter herbs, which you can make as large or as small as you'd like—for yourself alone, a family, friends, or complete strangers. Not a single person I've made it for has failed to adore it. Some people won't eat grapefruit because of the bitterness, but I encourage you to give it a chance, and you'll find it tastes as sweet as a ripe peach in contrast to the salad's sharpness. All proportions are adjustable to individual fancy, of course, but I like a lot of grapefruit. Do not omit the avocado, which is an essential middle ground for your palate to turn to.

A Bitter Salad with Grapefruit and Avocado

Serves 2 to 4, depending on how much you like salad

1 cup or so torn herbs (a combination of mint and basil is my
    favorite)
1 or 2 pink grapefruit, depending on size, peeled with a very
    sharp knife
⅓ small red onion, cut into very thin slivers, or finely chopped
    (reserve 1 tablespoon)
4 handfuls of assorted greens—mostly bitter (choose from
    watercress, arugula, radicchio, endive, escarole, mizuna,
    even slivers of kale) but also gentle (Boston, Bibb, or butter
    lettuce, soft red leaf lettuce, baby spinach)
1 or 2 avocados (alligator, not the giant shiny ones), peeled and
    cubed (do this last)

1. Wash the herbs, remove any tough stems, spread the herbs out on a cheesecloth towel to dry, then roll up the towel gently and refrigerate while you prepare other salad items and the dressing.

2. Section the grapefruit by slipping the knife along each membrane until the fruit slips out. Do this over a bowl to catch the juice, which is good mixed with seltzer.

3. Place the grapefruit sections and onion in a small bowl, and pour some of the dressing over it; toss gently and let it sit at room temperature while you tear the greens into bite-size pieces if they need it and make a chiffonade of the herbs; reserve a few shreds for garnish.

4. Once you're ready to serve, place the greens and herbs in a large serving bowl, arrange the fruit mixture attractively in the middle, sprinkle on the freshly cut avocado, and decorate it all with the reserved herbs and a little of the red onion. When you get it to the table, and everyone has seen how pretty it looks, fold it all together gently. The dressing on the grapefruit and onions should be enough, but you can always bring extra dressing to the table in a little crystal cruet. Or the jar. I especially like to serve this salad with freshly roasted chicken (with slices of lemon, rosemary, and garlic cloves slipped under the skin before cooking) and new potatoes cut in half, sprinkled with olive oil and sea salt, and roasted until their skin is as crispy as the bird's.

My Usual Mustard Vinaigrette

Makes ¾ cup

I triple or quadruple this recipe to leave in the refrigerator whenever I visit my aunt Mariah and uncle John, because Mariah claims it never turns out right when she does it, which is what I say when I try to bake her rolls.

8 tablespoons good-quality extra-virgin olive oil
1 tablespoon Dijon mustard
3 tablespoons red wine vinegar

½ **teaspoon sea salt**
Freshly ground black pepper, to taste

In an appropriate size jar for which you still have the lid, stir together the oil, mustard, vinegar, salt, and pepper. Place the lid on the jar and shake vigorously, until emulsified. Check for balance. If it tastes like straight olive oil, sprinkle in some more vinegar, shake, and taste again. You may want a bit more mustard, but be careful; it's supposed to be in the background. If you like garlic on all your salads, start this recipe by mashing a clove of garlic together with a teaspoon of sea salt using a mortar and pestle, until it is reduced to a paste; from there, you can proceed with the directions above, leaving out the ½ teaspoon of salt.

●

After sixty days, when it was time for me to leave the Betty Ford Center, I was proudly carrying my tote bag, but I did not feel brave in the way people always seem to at the end of rehab movies—raw but raring to take on the world. In fact, the next steps on the journey I'd planned—going out in search of comfort from my friends and recipes for their most soothing foods—made me feel remarkably uncomfortable. When it comes to love and support, or, for that matter, standard hospitality and offhand gestures toward normal friendship, I have a blank spot in whatever area of the brain helps distinguish the difference between what's acceptable from immediate family and what's acceptable from friends or mere acquaintances or strangers.

Somehow, it goes back to food. The Grapette Incident of 1968 comes to mind.

"Would you like a Grapette?" my great-aunt Flo asked my three older siblings and me. We were visiting her and Uncle Kyle's mod white and turquoise ranch house in Johnson City, Tennessee, where my mother had grown up. Grapette soda was insanely delicious and so dark grapey purple it looked black through its squat glass bottle. We couldn't get Grapette in Galax. The intense flavor and lovely perfume were ten times better than an actual grape to me, and its particular flavor has never been measured up to or replaced in my Grape Department.

"No, thank you," I said to Flo. On my mother's side of the family, politeness meant not openly wanting or asking for anything from anyone and feeling guilty if you allowed nonessentials to be pressed upon you—gestures of kindness or gifts that you did not absolutely require, say, a tourniquet when your leg has been severed, or an oxygen mask on a crashing plane. I have no idea why I, unlike the rest of my siblings, adopted this psycho-torture form of etiquette as my own. It was stiflingly hot in Flo's house and I was extremely thirsty, and I grew despondent as everyone else enjoyed the Grapettes they'd gratefully accepted. Just take the gift and say thank you—what could be so bad about that? Nothing at all, if you didn't mind guilt and shame.

●

One day soon after the Engineer and I had started dating, I said, out of nowhere, "Don't worry, you can't break my heart—it's pre-broken." I thought I was being hilarious.

He never asked what I meant, but I was talking about my family. If I figured out anything during my time at Betty Ford, examining the path that had brought me there, it was that my upbringing, and possibly generations of off-kilter rearing before mine, had led me to the Engineer like an arrow through William Tell's apple: *zing*!

I come from a long line of divorces and broken relationships, people who gave up on their lives and a lot of the people in them. It was a tradition it would have been wise not to carry on. And in my family, both before and after it fell apart, accepting kindness and comfort was tantamount to taking it away from someone else who deserved it a lot more than you did. So in a way, even mentioning that you were scared or sad equaled stealing. Once you committed this crime, you'd never hear the end of it. Or you'd be drowned in silence. So it was best to keep it to yourself. One of my earliest memories was being sent to my room for screaming when a daddy longlegs climbed across my shoulder as I played near a hibiscus bush in the yard. "I thought you'd been hit by a car!" my mother yelled before sending me to my room, where I felt guilty. A year or so later, when I actually did get hit by a car—driven quite slowly by a local high school student, who was turning a corner as I was crossing our very unbusy street to see a dog—I felt guilty about that, too, even though I was not yet six years old.

Simply existing was very close to more than you deserved, a fact that the five of us were frequently reminded of with the Lipizzaner story. My beautiful and fascinating mother had given up a life of fame as an actress and an abstract painter to give life to me and my siblings and move to boring Galax. This had been a giant risk to her own personal welfare, because as we children were told, she and my father had "incompatible blood types," and she should have died in childbirth. But knowing this she gave us life *anyway*. She reminded us that she'd had two miscarriages, one of which was brought on while she was at a circus; the Lipizzaners escaped and came charging toward her, frightening her so badly that she lost a baby, who probably would have been more helpful around the house than I or any of my living siblings were.

As a grown-up, on a day-to-day basis my inability to accept loving support has generally escaped the notice of those around me. (With the exception of my college friend Tripp: "Why won't you let anybody help you or be nice to you? It's offensive," he said, not realizing what a favor I was doing him by not letting him help set up my bookshelves.) Eventually I learned to fake it—or I became extremely good at accepting drinks, at least.

But over the long haul, it's the kind of thing that can build up so much that people begin to think you don't need or want them, when you do, quite desperately. For a very long time, I might as well have become a giant conch, washing up on the beach now and then, just often enough to let people know I was still around, doing just fine—*hey, check out my ever-growing, ornately twisted shell*. But they can't understand me. They do not speak conch.

Before arriving at Betty Ford, I had finally allowed myself to be vulnerable in my search for love, and I had gotten pounded. But at Betty Ford, they had insisted on ripping off the rest of my shell, anyway. It had never worked that well, but I felt naked without it. It was excruciating.

I had a choice: reach out to other people, preferably not jerks, let them help me find the sweetness in life, and learn to give and receive love.

Or end up like Oliver.

Four

FINDING THE COMFORT
IN COMFORT FOOD

Continuing on down the path that had been set so far, I packed two bags and went to Elaine and Kevin's place in Santa Barbara for a short visit. From there I planned a trip to see my cousin Toni in Atlanta that was to culminate with all of us meeting up at the Old Fiddlers' Convention in our hometown of Galax, after which I was to return to the desert house to live while I sorted out what to do next.

Before heading to Toni's, I took my time in Santa Barbara to seriously consider my project: simply looking for comfort food per se would get me nowhere, I realized. First I needed to get a feel for the comfort landscape—find out what comfort food was to other people, what it was to me.

The blithe definitions slung about—by the Oxford English Dictionary, for example: "food that provides consolation or a feeling of well-being, typically any with a high sugar or other carbohydrate content and associated with childhood or home cooking"—seemed to insist that everyone enjoyed gross food and had grown up in a happy home.

In every city or town or village in the United States, down sterile fluorescent grocery store lanes, the standard dishes await you—so-called comfort foods frozen behind glass, calling out to the wounded like easily available online drugs: meatloaf and mashed, potpies, tuna-noodle casseroles, giant lasagnas to serve a crowd, single man-size bowls of chili. Iconic dishes fueled by the idea that your mother used to make them for you at home. Or, at the very least, that someone's mother, somewhere, made them for her family, and it soothed them.

Purchase this processed food memory, thaw it out, heat it up, stuff it down your pie hole, and you'll feel better. And if you don't feel better, well, you can just buy some more. But true comfort food is a much more complicated concept.

Take the country ham biscuit—funky, potent, leathery, salty ham that has been placed on a biscuit whose edges crumble from crisped fat and whose center is sweet in comparison. It's one of my very favorite foods, something I will almost never turn down, and that's probably true for most of the people I grew up around in the Blue Ridge Mountains, just north of the North Carolina line.

I might have become deaf to the magical chime that triggers the opening of your heart or stimulates a key area in your brain in order to deliver a sense of peace and calm. Because when I asked myself if a ham biscuit was my "comfort food," I didn't know.

My grandmother, who had little interest in housekeeping but plenty of interest in food, always had a ham on her kitchen counter, with a wrinkled piece of foil floating over it as a stab at food safety. But my mother never made country ham for me and my two brothers and two sisters; she was a master of casseroles and stews and cakes. I have cooked a country ham for a party, which was an enormous pain in the ass. But I have never made ham biscuits for myself as a balm, never eaten seven in a row as a distraction from sadness or worry. And I would never make them to soothe a heartbroken friend any more than I would want that friend to show up at my house with a box of revolting black-walnut penuche fudge. Because the wrong food just might make things much worse. My point is, you can't really know what comforts a person until you ask. And then you have to listen.

●

And yet, as we all know, when somebody dies the predictable comfort canon appears at the after-party—kept warm in silver chafing dishes until it is lifeless, too, then placed in empty Tupperware the bereaved must wash and return.

I like macaroni and cheese just fine, but it certainly doesn't *comfort* me, whether in its purest state or after a modern upscale reinvention loaded with four kinds of artisanal cheese and chunks of lobster; it's a waste of good cheese and a criminal act toward a lobster.

Apparently, the very idea of comfort food is often a scattershot longing, an elastic and suggestible concept. "I used to like potato chips. After I stopped drinking, I couldn't get enough ice cream," a close friend from college told me, while holding an enormous bowl of peanut butter ripple topped with hot fudge sauce and an extra-large double-thick Reese's Peanut Butter Cup, broken into pieces.

I have certain other friends and relatives who look down on sugar freaks with a telling sense of superiority. When you meet one of these types, who may tell you they never eat sweets—*ever!*—I can tell you that person probably drinks an enormous amount of alcohol, hence the total lack of desire for the drug in its edible form.

Like the Food and Drug Administration's food pyramid, your "gaydar," or your decision about, say, whether or not you are a "hat person," your choice of comfort food may be subject to change according to outside influence, your current state of mind, or simple whims. However, it does not require signing a lifetime contract, nor is its source subject to regulation of any kind.

And one person's comfort food can easily be another's nightmare. Which is why, when you are trying to comfort someone else, you have to stretch a little in terms of what's appropriate and what's not.

"We're going to have the *green salad*," a handsome college boyfriend joyfully informed me before I arrived to share the Thanksgiving holiday with his family.

A special Thanksgiving salad? Charming. I imagined an enormous wooden bowl darkened from use, rubbed with garlic and filled with many kinds of greens, pale and dark, bitter and soft, with crunchy slivers and slices of many-hued vegetables, maybe an avocado for buttery contrast, a little thinly sliced red onion for bite, even nuts or dried fruit. It would have a lemony vinaigrette that was also slightly creamy, made so with the addition of egg yolks or heavy cream. I imagined sprinkling a little sea salt on it and digging in. There is nothing quite like a nice big salad. A salad can be the whole world.

But this salad was in a mold, a lime-gelatin compound turned celery green by the incorporation of a block of cream cheese, in which were suspended shreds of raw cabbage and pecan pieces. I focused on maintaining a neutral facial expression as we all watched his mother turn the asterisk-shaped mold over a plate to release the jiggling thing and bring it to the table. This was my boyfriend's culinary signifier of home. Like the heart, the stomach wants what it wants.

Seeing someone reunited with his special food, gelatin salad or not, is like watching him realize that a person who'd stopped loving him had returned: the nostalgia, the hope, then sweet relief. And sometimes, a hint of worry that it might not be the same this time around.

If you can't be happy for his reunion, despite natural reservations about how healthy it might be, you have to ask yourself if your heart is working properly.

And yet, this can be difficult. I was in love with a short, dark-haired man whose Ecuadorean parents never spoke English at home when he was growing up. He was fluent but confused me with a hybrid language that sounded like not-quite-right translations of English. I often could not figure out what he was saying. But we loved eating out together; he was unpretentiously adventurous and came along when I was reviewing restaurants for the *New Yorker*. At one of them, he stood up from our table, grabbed a handful of raggedy popcorn from a community bowl at the bar, and sprinkled it onto his beautiful parfait glass filled with ceviche, a dish the restaurant was known for. I wondered aloud why anyone would mess up something so pretty and perfect: pieces of white and pale pink fish, shrimp and scallops, "cooked" with lime juice, stirred together with minced onion, a few jalapeño-type peppers, and a dash of chili sauce. It was tonic and tangy, sweet and refreshing. But Ecuadoreans created ceviche, and he had been eating it long before it became fashionable in New York City. "Try it!" he said, dropping three kernels on top of my parfait before I could stop him. I did, and then had kernels in my teeth, which distracted me from all the beauty going on in the mouthful.

"I don't get it," I said. "It just gets in my way."

"That's right," he replied. "You do not want to get it."

The ceviche chasm might have been a sign of what ended us: I could not recognize this intimate longing for food eaten in a way that, in truth, rightfully belonged to him. In his eyes, I now suppose, I was ignoring an invitation to come home. Home—mine or anyone else's—did not appeal to me.

Here in the United States, we have a giant array of regional foods that people adore and often seem to remain loyal to on principle alone. Perhaps it's a way of standing up for their small patch of land, asserting their individuality in a nation that has homogenized so many of our melting-pot markers out of existence.

Take, for instance, scrapple, which a 1969 book I own, *A Dictionary of Cooking* compiled by Ralph and Dorothy DeSola, defines this way: "Bricklike food combination composed of bits of pork cooked up with cornmeal and herbs; scrapple, supposedly a Philadelphia specialty, is usually sliced and baked or fried for breakfast." My mother, who was born in Philadelphia, loves it.

Before my parents got divorced, my mother took a trip to Pennsylvania Dutch Country with her friend Patsy, who lived across the street. She returned from this vacation with wonderful stories and a green spiral-bound cookbook whose cover was decorated with a drawing of what I assumed was a Pennsylvania Dutch woman, dressed in a giant bonnet that hid her face and a long apron over a puffy ankle-length dress. She was holding up a pie, to no one in particular, probably shoofly pie. My mother used this book to make me and my siblings scrapple. She sliced and fried it. I imagine it gave her back some of the happiness that was permanently taken from her by her mother's early death when she was only nine years old and her father's subsequent and immediate disappearance, and it might have even delayed the inevitable disintegration of my parents' marriage.

In 1997, after her cooking had faded somewhat from my memory, and before everyone in my family had gone to separate corners to sulk permanently, she sent each of us an "Illustrated Cook's Notes," in which she had inserted notes written in her loopy, elegant script, "Recipes from your life . . ." as well as a quote from the musical *Mame*, a Robert Louis Stevenson poem, and a food-related limerick: "A wonderful bird is the pelican/His bill will hold more than his belican/He can take in his beak/Food enough for a week/But I'm damned if I see how the helican."

I loved getting it. It was a sweet gift that reminded me of how funny she was. I cherished many of the recipes; others—Dot Foster's Mother's Chicken Salad or Liz Vaughn's Egg Mold with Caviar— made me wonder where the hell I'd been when everyone else was enjoying them, or how in the world the broccoli cheese soup had been attributed to me. I've never made it in my life.

Opening this book again recently, the recipe that came closest to ringing my lost chime was Flo's Barbecue "Oliver's favorite!," meaning my great-aunt Flo and my late brother, Oliver. It was the one I wanted to make as soon as possible.

Here it is, verbatim:

1. Boil a large chuck roast or large fresh ham until tender (when it shreds.) Cool. Shred. Save the broth.

   In a large pot mix together:

   1 tablespoon allspice
   1 tablespoon chili powder
   1 teaspoon celery salt
   1 large bottle Heinz Ketchup
   Dash of cayenne pepper
   Broth from the meat
   Salt, to taste

2. Add the shredded meat. Cook down very slowly to desired thickness. Must serve on large buns that have been toasted, with slaw
(below).

SLAW

  2 cups cider vinegar

  Salt and sugar, to taste

  1 cup sweet pickles, chopped (or use jarred sweet relish or sweet
    pickle cubes)

  1 cup finely chopped green bell pepper

  1 small green cabbage, chopped

Mix together the vinegar, salt, and sugar. Heat to boiling and pour
over chopped vegetables. Refrigerate.

(Wonderful with Mom's potato salad, beer, and dessert. Great
picnic fare.)

●

This dish isn't true barbecue, of course, and it's not really trying to be.
Yet I'd pick it over some of the best I've had. You should go heavier
on the cayenne if you like a bigger kick, but taste it first, and do not
deviate from the other instructions. The slaw's texture and tang are essential to the sandwich's overall embrace, as is toasting the bun—not
just to hold it together longer, but for the toast flavor.

However much I loved this sentimental handmade book, it still
made me recall a very telling thing about Oliver's eating habits. No
matter how much he loved or craved a favorite meal or pushed everyone away to get an extra serving of some precious dish we were rarely
served, like steak, he never finished it. He always left a substantial
portion on his plate. I once asked him why there were always three
or five bites left, and he replied, "I don't know. I'm always afraid I'll
get sick if I eat everything." The food that was supposed to make him
feel good might make him feel bad.

I sometimes think he went a lifetime without comfort.

Back to the scrapple: I disliked it intensely, but the mere memory of the brick substance and the barbecue recipe made me lonesome for something, without making me homesick at all.

I hadn't fully realized that trying to understand the fondness a person feels for a certain food—or her inherited ideas about food in general—can give you insight into why she is the way she is, and even help you love her in a better way.

"You could be eating out of a Dumpster," my mother would occasionally say when I was very young, if my siblings and I complained about the idea of eating the chicken liver badly disguised in a shawl of bacon she was trying to feed us or if we didn't finish our food, which was not very often for most of us. We tended to race to the finish. "There are children in this world who have only garbage to eat," she would continue, once she'd gotten our startled attention. "Children who have to dig through other people's *trash*. And they don't complain."

Really? I wondered, through the muddled curtain of empathy young children are capable of. How did she know they didn't complain? And why would I ever end up eating out of a Dumpster when we had a packed refrigerator, a pantry in the basement full of canned and dry goods including asparagus, *petits pois,* tamales wrapped in paper, Space Food Sticks, bags of rice and various dried legumes, giant jars of Tang, not to mention a freezer on the back porch containing half a cow we'd had butchered, flounder fillets stuffed with crabmeat, honey buns from the day-old bread store, and boxes of Eskimo Pies and frozen strawberries. The fruit bowl on the breakfast room table was full of bananas and apples and picked-at grapes. The kitchen cabinets held five or six boxes of breakfast cereal at any given time and jar after jar of dried herbs and spices. If it came to it, we could live off cinnamon. And barring that, in the summer there was a man in an old pickup truck who showed up selling corn from his farm, and sometimes there was a strawberry man, too.

But I think we all began to get her point as the years wore on: there were many people in the world much less fortunate than we were. Even if we were in a full-body cast, as she had been as a child, having contracted polio, we were a lot luckier than all the children we didn't know who ate out of Dumpsters.

Eccentric families—especially in the South—hand down their craziness through the generations the way other families pass along silverware and secret recipes. I got a bit of crazy from my mother's side of the family, along with some jewelry, some gigantic studio cameras, and my grandmother's dresser for storing lingerie.

My inherited neuroticism manifested itself in immobilizing stomachaches that seized me late at night, after school, and on Sunday afternoons, after the sun had gone down and I knew my father would be leaving the next morning for Tennessee, where he traveled each week to sell furniture for the family factory. I'd double over when my parents went away, even if it was just to a country club dance across town, which became so annoying for both of my parents that in the fourth grade I was sent to the hospital overnight for ulcer tests. Absolutely dreadful. I didn't have an ulcer, I had a "nervous stomach," according to a doctor who gave me a brown glass bottle of green liquid called Cantil; I don't remember its exact effect but I do remember that my mother remained convinced that my pain was related to what I was eating, as if I were an old Italian man consuming peppers and sausages on a daily basis rather than a willowy fourth grader who took everything way too personally. Her solution was to make my favorite sandwich to put in my lunch box almost daily because it was considered bland. It's not. It's delicious.

Cream Cheese and Olive Sandwiches

Makes 1½ cups filling

1 (8-ounce) package cream cheese, at room temperature

⅔ cup coarsely chopped stuffed green olives (don't buy the presliced or pre-chopped ones, just the ordinary whole grocery-store kind; you can cut the olives back to ½ cup but I love olives)

1 tablespoon mayonnaise

2 to 3 tablespoons of juice from the olive jar, to thin the mixture

Place the cream cheese, olives, and mayonnaise in a bowl and blend together by hand. Thin it a bit with the olive juice. Refrigerate until it is time to make your sandwich. You may add more olive juice to taste, but go easy on the mayonnaise—it's just used to smooth out the cream cheese. And you can always put mayonnaise on your sandwich, which ideally should be made on white bread or white toast, with the crusts cut off. Cut on the diagonal, otherwise the entire sandwich is ruined.

•

Even when I was in my stomachache phase, I could always eat a little something. So my cream cheese and olive sandwich, rather than bringing back memories of whatever caused my pain, reminds me that people tend to do the best they can in loving you—even if they're the reason you feel bad.

Back when I was still in the peaceful desert, I went back on Facebook and crowd-sourced my comfort food question. I asked everyone to answer the question: What is your comfort food? In return, I was generously rewarded with a lot of gems, some forgotten but familiar, some I would never have dreamed of, others that were insane, and a few so precise that my memory of these friends became much more vivid than it had been in a long time. This is exactly how they arrived:

"Pineapple upside down cake in the cast iron skillet"

"Spaghetti with garlic, red pepper flakes, pecorino and black pepper."

"Corn bread (the good stuff with creamed corn and sour cream) with lotsa buttah. When I need it, I'm hard-pressed not to eat the whole thing."

"Paella with lots of seafood, chicken and chorizo"

"Great Mac and Cheese and Pot Roast"

"Your artichoke risotto!"

"Naaahhhchos with lots of sour cream and cheese, just a little salsa, peppered with black beans and little bits of jalapeño sunken in, I feel better already"

"Homemade beef/vegetable soup with cheese toast. My daddy would add Tabasco."

"Toast"

"Breakfast would be Charleston style grits (made with milk, not water—duh) and eggs. Dinner would be mashed potatoes, squash and onions, and fried chicken the way only Alma knew how to fry it. And now that I'm all grown up I find comfort in my own version of fish tacos (homemade corn tortillas only) and my own version of baked French toast. Wow! That's a lot of comfort food!"

"Ground rice pasta with olive oil, anchovies, and cracked black pepper OMG!!"

"My mother's scalloped potatoes and cheese and ham. My own pasta with Bolognese sauce or pomodoro sauce or pasta carbonara."

"This is hard, maybe pot roast, with onions, potatoes and carrots OR pork roast and gravy, sweet potatoes, cooked apples and green beans and any dessert!"

"Chewy Blueberry brownies with a cigarette for after."

"Chicken pot pie on a bed of white rice or shrimp creole also on a bed of white rice or fried shrimp, hush puppies and baked potato"

•

There were lots of other great suggestions, but my favorite was from my old friend Bruce, who is gay and has always seemed to possess inherent kindness but also immense insecurities and longing, which may be a burden but is part of what makes him so lovable and insightful. He once said to me, many years ago when we worked together at the *New Yorker,* "We're alike, Emily. We know what we *don't* want but have no idea what we do." At the time, I had no idea what he meant. His response to my call for comfort food, though, was revelatory.

"Mash 6 or 7 Oreos in a glass of cold milk. Eat with a spoon, but not in front of anybody."

It said so much in so few words. Even if the underlying shame was just a joke, it broke my heart . . . in a good way.

Should comfort food make you nostalgic for the past? I had no idea, but I felt pretty sure that neither comfort food nor your home should ever make you feel worse, much less ashamed. Everyone in the world must yearn for the solace associated with home and comfort food, even if they've never experienced it.

I had just lost the last place I had called home, which had offered little comfort for a long time. Even so, I still believed in the idea of homemade comforts. There's great truth in the saying that "the best damn sandwich is the one someone else makes for you."

So setting out in search of a good sandwich (made by someone else) began to make perfect sense.

The pan bagnat is great to make for someone else; this classic French sandwich has a little bit of something for everyone to love. I created this smaller version when I lived in Chicago. It's also a very portable sandwich, good for long journeys.

Mini Pan Bagnat Sandwiches

Makes 4

4 round French rolls

3 (6-ounce) cans good-quality solid light tuna in water

⅓ cup plus 1 tablespoon olive oil, plus more for drizzling

1 very small red onion, quartered then thinly sliced

1 pint grape tomatoes, coarsely chopped

1 (14-ounce) can artichoke hearts, thoroughly drained and
   coarsely chopped

1 (7-ounce) jar roasted red peppers, drained and coarsely
   chopped

1 cup chickpeas, drained, rinsed, and coarsely chopped

20 pitted black olives, chopped

1 garlic clove, crushed

¼ cup red wine vinegar

1 teaspoon salt

Freshly ground black pepper, to taste

4 to 8 lettuce leaves

1 cucumber, unpeeled, thinly sliced

8 oil-packed anchovies, drained

1. Split the rolls, remove some bread from each side to make room
   for the filling; feed excess to the birds and set aside the rolls. Drain
   the tuna and break it apart in a bowl. Drizzle with the 1 tablespoon
   oil; set aside.
2. Combine the onion, tomatoes, artichoke hearts, red peppers,
   chickpeas, olives, and garlic in another bowl; set aside. Whisk
   together ⅓ cup of the oil, the vinegar, salt, and black pepper in a
   small bowl; pour over the vegetable mixture, stirring to combine.
   Let stand for 10 minutes.
3. Place 1 or 2 lettuce leaves on the bottom half of each roll; top with
   a quarter of the tuna mixture. Add a layer of the cucumber slices,
   a quarter of the vegetable mixture, and 2 of the anchovies. (It will

appear overloaded.) Drizzle the filling with additional oil, if desired. Place the top of the roll on the sandwich; carefully wrap tightly in foil or plastic wrap. Wrap each sandwich again in more plastic wrap or a plastic bag. Press firmly under a plate; let the sandwiches sit, weighed down with cans or books or a cast-iron skillet, for at least 10 minutes. It's traditional to sit on this sandwich (while it's wrapped, of course) rather than weighting it.

Five

THE PEANUT, PICKLE,
COUNTRY HAM CURE

Despite my dive into the mysteries of comfort food, my plans were not suddenly tied up in a neat bow. And unlike what you might expect from a story like this, I didn't have a road map for the next year of my life, a rock-solid time line, or an uncharacteristically smart but rustic man hovering in the wings to make my life happy and perfect again. The truth was that I had absolutely no idea what I was going to do with the rest of my life, except in the short term. And even the short term was sketchy.

The night before I was scheduled to fly, Elaine said offhandedly, "Maybe you should stay *there* for a while."

What? What did that mean? I didn't ask her which of the many possible "theres" on the planet she was referring to—which "there" I might make my next headquarters, without the clothes, cookbooks, notes, computer, and all the other belongings I'd left in the desert, thinking I'd be back in a few weeks. She was in the living room and I was in the kitchen making a salad, so she couldn't see the expression on my face. "Oh. Okay!" I yelled. And when I left for the airport the next morning, I told myself that I hadn't just been given the heave-ho.

In the back of my mind was the certainty that I'd end up like Maggie the dog, with her hobo sensibility. A few weeks after Elaine and I rescued her, my brother Michael and my nephew had come out to visit me, and together they'd taken Maggie for a ride in the golf cart, which she usually loved. Ten minutes later my cell phone rang. "She's going about a hundred miles an hour!" Michael said breathlessly. "We lost her." Maggie had leapt out at the dog run two miles away, but rather than running off on a freewheeling canine adventure she'd headed straight back at full speed to Elaine's house, which was now the only home she knew, even though she still didn't seem comfortable there. I went out and stood at the end of the driveway, and in a few minutes saw her tiny black figure zooming toward me, past palm trees and pristine cacti gardens, then right past me and into the house, trailing dark footprints on the white terrazzo floor, which turned out to be blood. She had been so terrified that she was being taken away from yet another home that she'd torn the pads on her feet getting back to it. Before she even knew if the home made her happy or not.

Naturally, when I was finally on my way to take Toni up on her bighearted invitation to visit her in Atlanta, I worried I might end up staying longer than was okay under any circumstance. And yet being with her and her family turned out to be extremely comforting, even though none of my relatives were on the original list of hosts I'd made back in the desert. The longer I stayed with her, the more I felt content to let my Comfort Food Tour unfold more naturally, using my list as a guide rather than a binding holy grail.

"Stay as long as you want! You can even live here," she had said.

Toni's home in Atlanta included not just her comically grouchy husband, Richard, and their two preteen daughters, Mariah and Addie, but two outdoor cats, a caged bird, an elderly white standard poodle who sprang and spun around like Twyla Tharp when he wasn't asleep, and a hamster that everyone thought had run away, until Mariah found it in a lidless plastic toy bin in the basement playroom, where it must have accidentally walked the plank off the arm of the couch.

"Emily, did you even *know* we *had* a hamster?" Mariah shrieked at me as she ran up the basement steps grinning wildly, squeezing the rodent in her hands with rough affection. Her giant blue eyes reflected absolutely no knowledge or concern that this hamster had just returned from hell and was starving—just happiness to have it in her hands again.

The morning after I had arrived in Atlanta, I woke up in the guest room in one of the flowered twin beds I'd slept in as a kid at my grandmother's house, and Mariah and Addie were standing over me. They had made me breakfast in bed: a Yoplait yogurt with a spoon poked through the closed foil top; some tiny purple figs they'd picked from the neighbor's yard; a few large strawberries; a cup of black coffee; and a small bowl of Raisin Bran, along with a folded paper napkin on which they'd written, in pale pencil: "Emily, we ♥ you."

"Thank you, girls," I said, tasting the mangled purple fruit they'd gathered. "Figs are one of my *favorite* fruits." Addie made a face that asked: How could that be? They shrieked, "You're welcome!" jumped in the air, and ran away, slamming the door behind them. I took a picture of the note.

I wasn't sure if anyone else had ever made me breakfast in bed before.

Toni is a blond bombshell who genuinely gets a kick out of life. She had worked in finance since college and, in order to spend more time with her girls, had recently left a high-profile job as a member of one of the first all-female private wealth management teams ever hired at Goldman Sachs. She'd started a business with her next-door neighbor, installing and maintaining raised-bed vegetable gardens for suburbanites, for which Toni bought an old red pickup truck. She became a tomato expert. Toni will do anything, ask for anything, and always counts on things going her way. Her name is short for Antoinette, which seems slightly ridiculous when you meet her, except that she does sort of consider herself a queen. She once told me she doesn't read the newspaper because she doesn't "*know* any of those *people*."

"Jesus Christ, Toni, would you like a newspaper called *Toni's Universe?*" Richard asked her, frowning.

"Yes," she said, grinning and frowning back at him, as if it were a stupid question. *Off with their heads!*

Last Christmas, Aunt Mariah had party crackers at the dinner table, containing gold paper crowns, which we all put on. "That looks so very natural on you, Toni," I'd said. Her eyebrows went up in that expression that means, "I *know*! Right?" as if she were glad that someone else had finally noticed.

Toni loves an adventure, large or small.

"We can go to Courtland!" she said. Courtland was the eastern Virginia hometown of her mother (my aunt Mariah; she'd married my father's brother John). There, on a plantation built in 1805, in the low, hot, and humid Tidewater region, Mariah grew up among rows of tobacco, peanuts, and cotton worked by black families, the descendants of slaves, which no one ever talks about much.

In my fantasies, Courtland was the cradle of American comfort food, so I was thrilled to go. Wherever I am with Toni feels like home—something better than home, actually. A place where people don't look for reasons to get hurt or worry about everyone else's flaws. A place where it's okay just to have a life, or have a conversation, be the way you are.

Before we left for Courtland, Toni made perfect, giant, thinly sliced fried onion rings right in the middle of the afternoon, salted them, and passed them over, crisp and hot, without even asking me if I wanted them. (Which would be the right way to give someone a Grapette, too, come to think of it. Just hand it over.) I'd had no idea Toni knew how to make onion rings or knew I loved them, or that they were exactly what I needed at that very moment. We had them with Richard's Special Cajun Spice, since he is from Louisiana Cajun country (he threw an authentic crawfish boil for Toni's fortieth), and I had some ketchup on mine, too. They hit the spot, as the Princess used to say: *pow*!

Toni's Onion Rings

Makes 4 servings

2 large sweet onions, such as Vidalia

1 cup all-purpose flour

1 tablespoon granulated sugar

1 teaspoon baking powder

Richard's Special Cajun Spice, to taste (recipe below; you can use
    cayenne pepper, to taste, if you choose not to make the giant
    vat of spice mix Toni keeps on hand)

2 cups buttermilk

Vegetable oil, for frying

Salt, to taste

1. Slice the onions as thick as you like, then separate them into rings.
2. Whisk together the flour, sugar, baking powder, and about 10 shakes
   of Richard's Special Cajun Spice, then whisk in the buttermilk.
3. Pour 2 inches of vegetable oil into an iron pot and heat to 375°F, or
   until water droplets pop and sizzle.
4. Meanwhile, dredge the onion rings in batter, coating them well. Fry
   a few at a time until golden; drain on paper towels.
5. Sprinkle the onion rings with salt, and more of Richard's Special
   Cajun Spice, if desired.

Richard's Special Cajun Spice

Makes about 5 cups

1 (26-ounce) box salt

4 ounces black pepper

4 ounces cayenne pepper

2 ounces garlic powder

2 ounces chili powder

1 ounce Accent (Toni's note: or less; it is full of MSG)

Combine the salt, black pepper, cayenne, garlic powder, chili powder, and Accent in a large container with a tight-fitting lid. Toni transfers the mix to a large metal shaker as needed.

•

All my life, I'd heard tales of the Kello cousins who lived in Court-land, Virginia (where Toni's mother, my aunt Mariah, had grown up): the big Easter celebration at the plantation house, afternoons spent paddling down the Nottoway River, the homemade butter, the butter beans, the pickles, the biscuits, the peanut products. My sister Elaine got to visit once, and she ate so much peanut brittle she threw up, but that never made me want to go any less. Especially after I tasted the real butter that Aunt Mariah brought back one summer, and the salty, pungent country ham that we rarely got in Galax.

Later, when I was working at the *New Yorker*, John and Mariah sent me an assortment of the family-produced peanuts at Christmas, and the editor in chief, David Remnick, would come to my desk and snack on them without waiting to be asked.

A few days after I arrived in Atlanta in mid-July, we packed up Toni's SUV and zoomed off to Galax and then to Courtland with Mariah and Addie. Until then, I'd never been invited to Courtland, even though Toni and I had been inseparable as kids (until we ap-proached puberty, at which time Toni began brushing her hair and wearing a clean shirt, eventually joining the cheerleading squad). She took our friend Joan Milgrim, who later became head majorette, instead. This still absolutely burns me up.

"Are you *sure*?" Toni said when I reminded her, as we drove with the girls in the back, wearing headphones, ignoring the fascinating scenery, sitting in their giant nests of kid junk.

"I'm *sure* I invited you," she said again, over the country music station, as we drove through Hillsville.

"No." I shook my head. "You didn't."

"Huh," she replied, frowning. We drove over the Dan River bridge and onto what Toni's husband, Richard, calls our "country-ass roads," curving and hilly and lined with diners advertising plate lunches, antiques stores, Pentecostal churches, unpainted houses with tractors and other farm machinery in the yard, places with both corn dogs *and* live bait for sale, Porky's Barbecue, Lover's Leap, a banner announcing a cantaloupe festival. We drove through Brunswick County, the alleged home of Brunswick stew (traditionally a squirrel, chicken, corn, and tomato stew, now made without squirrel), and also home to a lot of Confederate flags hanging right out in the open on houses and stuck to car bumpers, which a large billboard tried to explain away: DON'T BE OFFENDED. UNDERSTAND THE FLAG'S HISTORY.

Beautiful, mesmerizing, wrongheaded, amusing, and repulsive, it was my neck of the woods. A place I loved and loathed in equal measure.

Toni pulled over on a peaceful stretch of highway to get the girls snacks at what looked like a regular gas station but was actually a filling station with a full-service, sit-down pine-paneled diner. Howell's Grocery, as it was called, was packed with locals sitting in baby-blue booths, chatting and eating, in the middle of the morning. Homemade fried apple hand pies sat by the cash register next to trays stacked with ham biscuits in plastic wrap and homemade cake with thick icing cut into fat slices on paper plates. On a regular kitchen stove and a large flat grill, short-order breakfasts were being slung.

"Bye, y'all," said the winsome lady who sold us our food. I wanted her to hug me, let me rest my head on her shoulder. When we drove away, I wondered where the people inside came from, as there were no houses or a town in sight. I imagined that the same people were in there all the time, never leaving, just eating this wonderful food given to them by this sweet woman, and filling up their cars with gas outside for no reason, since they had no jobs or homes to go to. I could be happy in a place like that.

I unwrapped a ham biscuit in the car, and opened it up to inspect the properly pan-fried, leathery slices of ham and the biscuit with slightly crisped exterior and dense buttery interior, stained by the fried meat. I took a bite: it was delicious. The ham in a restaurant ham biscuit should always fight you just a bit, and it did. (At home, we never fry it.)I took a picture of my receipt for the biscuit, coffee, and small orange juice, which came to $4.79. It made me feel like a cartoon character who, having fallen off a cliff and been crushed flat by the impact, springs back to life, albeit still folded up like an accordion.

As a kid, I was jealous of Toni's Courtland family, the Kellos, these impostor cousins, the family of Toni's mother, my aunt Mariah; they cut into my Toni time. Since settling there before the Civil War, they'd all been named James or Jim or Richard or Antoinette. I'd never been able to tell them apart.

Now, as we headed their way, I became jealous again as Toni filled me in on what had been going on with the Kellos over the last thirty years. And not all of their history was the sunny storybook I'd imagined, but they had stuck together through very tough times, living on their ancestors' land, just blocks away from one another, tightly knit and as loving as possible.

From the age of nine through her teen years, Martha Kello, Aunt Mariah's niece, visited John and Mariah's home in Galax each summer for several weeks, although I only remember her as a teenager. She eventually moved to town, after getting her advanced education degree and a local teaching job.

Everybody adored Martha, with her super-low, slow voice, glossy jet-black hair, and aquamarine eyes; with her millions of stories and true interest in all the kids. Now, many years later, she had moved back to her deceased parents' crumbling but still regal farmhouse in Courtland, on land that had once been part of the thousand-acre plantation.

"Martha is going to show you her famous pickle-making art and also take us to the peanut-brittle dude and the country-ham dude," Toni told me.

I focused on this promise in a way that I could not focus on other things. Oh, these chunky, murky pickles: not quite bread-and-butter pickles, not quite flat-out sweet pickles, neither salty nor sour, green nor gray, sliced nor speared, but something in their own Platonic category of crunchy-spicy tartness. The thing to do is just put a few on the side of your plate, to accompany absolutely anything you are eating, but especially some chicken salad.

My relatives hide jars of these cucumber chunks from one another, wrapping them in brown paper bags and shoving them under car seats. Others measure the contents of jars in the refrigerator once they've been opened (*Who's been eating so many pickles?*), even though a half dozen *unopened* jars are stocked in the pantry, and even though each year, if her neighbor's cucumbers grow in excess (they always do), Martha makes another giant batch, along with wild plum jelly. These are not finite pickles, and yet the Nunns and the Kellos always worry about the false inevitability of consuming the last jar.

As we sped down the road, way too fast, Toni produced and began eating a MoonPie, a hockey-puck-size sandwich cookie made of two soft graham wafers filled with stiff marshmallow, covered in chocolate. Where had she gotten it? I hadn't seen one in twenty years, since leaving the South, and I took a picture of her biting into it. Not much later, I took a picture of her giving herself a manicure; she had wedged an emery board into the space between the horn and the steering wheel, rubbing each fingertip up and down along the nail file, driving and talking on the phone at the same time. I could feel my heart starting to open up. This was the way life could be! By this I suppose I mean: you could be yourself, without worrying about being judged for having a MoonPie. I started taking pictures obsessively, to make sure I didn't lose anything else.

"What?" she asked as the camera clicked. The girls laughed like crazy at this. They were intermittently loud then stone silent in the back seat, reading, watching a video, or hooting at something only they understood.

The first thing we did after we hit Courtland's flat, lush fields was swing by to pick up Martha. When we got to her old slumping house at the end of her long gravel drive, surrounded by more tall fields, it was hot as an oven outside. Inside, it was cool and dark and her kitchen floor was half-covered with large white plastic buckets containing cucumbers in various stages of pickling and bags of cucumbers all over in various stages of cleanliness (some were in the sink, some were on the floor covered in dirt). "Toni, you and Emily are going to wash all those cucumbers," she said. There were a billion of them.

But she wanted to go to the peanut-brittle maker first. "They tore down the drugstore," Martha pointed out as we drove on bumpy dirt and gravel roads that gave one the odd sensation of being *in* a farm field rather than driving past them. I didn't see much of a town to speak of, except for the Southampton County courthouse on Main Street, where a Kello was the first clerk of court, and Mahone's Tavern, now a museum, which was once named Kello's Tavern.

"Emily, those are soybeans in that field over there; corn over there, as you can tell. That was cotton in my front yard." Educator, historian, crocheting expert, tour guide, hostess—Martha was exactly the same as I'd remembered her.

Bobby, the seventy-three-year-old peanut-brittle man, whose house was also surrounded by tall fields of plants I didn't recognize, was standing in front of a detached hut behind his old white house, wearing a Hawaiian shirt. A mutt named Sadie was sleeping in a shallow hole she'd dug in a pile of hot sand.

"She sleeps with me inside at night, but during the day, no matter how hot it is, she sleeps out here," he said to me after we were introduced. "If it storms out, she gets under my bed, but she doesn't do too much panting."

I pointed my camera at the dog.

"She does *not* like to have her pit-cha taken," Bobby commanded, in that outlandish Tidewater accent.

I pressed the button on my camera anyway, and the dog ignored me. The girls looked at me with open mouths, scandalized that I'd gone against Bobby's ridiculous counsel.

This is the way southerners are. No one simply tells you something directly and then leaves it at that. Each conversation is loaded down with other conversations and extraneous information and inconsequential observations and non sequiturs. While discussing a neighbor who has rudely nailed ugly PRIVATE PROPERTY signs on the trees near your house, suddenly someone else will start telling a story about how her husband killed a giant snake in the driveway in the *dead of winter*, "just chopped its ugly head off with the snow shovel."

It's not entirely meaningless; it's circular, a secret code you either learn to decipher or just not worry about too much.

Inside, the hut smelled like smoked caramel. I liked the scent, and even felt a little hungry, though I imagined smothering, hot sugar floating through the warm air and attaching itself to my lungs, drowning me in sweetness.

"I don't even smell it anymore," Bobby said, as the five of us crowded into the ten-by-ten-foot kitchen house with him and his longtime friend, Ed, with whom he'd worked at the now-defunct local paper mill and had hired when it closed. They and a woman named Debbie continued to make the brittle over a couple of electric stoves.

Bobby had never intended to make brittle at all, yet he produces the lion's share sold by peanut and souvenir shops in the area, like the Peanut Patch, usually under each store's own label. Fame didn't matter to him.

"The women from Peanut Patch were at the academy where my daughter was at school. They were married to a set of *twins*. When they said they wanted someone to make peanut brittle, I tried to get my mother to do it. She was raised in this house, and I grew up here. I used to catch the school bus down at that mailbox. I would almost freeze to death.

"She said no, she wasn't going to do it. Then I went to a Christmas party and the Peanut Patch women told me the woman they'd gotten to make the brittle's mother was dying of *cancer*. I told them I wanted to give them some brittle my mother had made. They took it to the Peanut Patch, where everybody liked it. 'I told you I was *not* going to do it,' Mother said. I said, 'That's fine, but you have to tell me why.' She said, 'I only have a ninth-grade education and don't know how much to charge, and things like that.' I said, 'I have a bit more education and will help you.' She had never worked. They wanted a hundred pounds. She got her check for thirty dollars and was thrilled."

I was sort of falling in love with this Bobby, but I also wanted to knock his block off. I'd forgotten how long it took for anyone to get to the point down here.

I had tried to read his messy recipe notebook lying on the counter while he talked and cooked. "So here's how you make peanut brittle, right?" I asked him. "You melt the sugar with the syrup, boil it, throw in the peanuts, and spread it all out on a buttered pan to cool. Right?"

"No," he replied, looking out the window, as if in some reverie.

"My mother taught me to make it," he continued, wandering off in his own mental direction. "I changed it a little. She made it right in the kitchen in the house, but when I took over in 1984, I moved it back here," he said, mixing the peanuts into the caramelizing, liquid sugar, then spreading it out on a large tray to harden, exactly as I'd just described to him.

"You melt the sugar, just warm it. Add the syrup. I don't use any thermometers. I do measure, though, yes I do. We have a timer that gives us a general i-dear.

"These are Number One Virginia Redskins. I use some blanched, too, to sell to the guy in Enfield, North Carolina."

Martha started talking about how she was just driving through Enfield the other day. Debbie asked me what I was writing about, and then started listing her favorite foods before I could finish answering her question. Toni was trying to get the girls interested in what was going on in this kitchen because it was educational.

We ate some samples, and it really was perfect. Not thin, lacy-candy brittle; this is a thick brown slab you have to break apart with a mallet. The candy part is not tooth-crackingly hard, but it is certainly not soft—it submits as gently as the toffee in a Heath bar, which gives it perfect textural contrast to the nuts. Also, it leaves a lovely stickiness on your lips, which lasts so long you start to think your lips are melting.

"It's how long you cook it. That's your secret, right?" I asked.

"No," he replied.

Goddamn it.

"This is Mother's recipe, I changed it a little bit," he said. "Peanut Patch started doing mail order. Mother said, 'I can't keep up.' Her niece came to help for a while. But then I took over.

"She was sharp as a tack. She thought she had Alzheimer's. I said,

'Mom, if you had it you wouldn't know.' I tried to joke about it, but it made her *mad*.

"I asked her what she wanted to eat one night. I cooked for her. 'What you got in the refrigerator?' She said, 'I'm going to sit down and rest.' The doctor had told her that swollen feet were just because of old age. I had set up a fifty-five-gallon aquarium, and she was talking about how peaceful it was to look at. And then *whoosh*—she was gone. That was eleven years ago. And that's exactly the way she wanted to go: just like that."

It was time for us to go as well, but first we bought some bags of brittle. "I was going to go dancing this evening, but I'm going to pick those butter beans instead," Bobby said, even though I hadn't asked him about his plans. "It's seven dollars a pound. You gowin-ah share it with anybody? Get two pounds."

That sounded like a lot. I remembered Elaine throwing up all those years ago. But I bought it because I felt an odd sense of gratitude toward his mournful brand of happiness blended with industry. I felt like he had something I needed. I still felt like chatting with him. I wanted to know what he liked to eat.

"I don't eat much peanut brittle. I just do that for the money," he said. "But I like country food. Pork chops, ham, collards, potatoes with smoked meat, butter beans. And we used to have fish fries at the paper factory—coleslaw, potatoes with smoked meat. We need to do one of those again."

"I like the sound of that potato thing," I said.

In response, he ambled into his house and returned with a photocopied recipe, which I glanced at and put in my bag.

"I'll tell you what," he said. He was standing close to me, with the heat coming off the earth, but he stared past my shoulder, at the fields or the dusty road beyond. "I didn't want to eat much of anything after Mother died. I like peanut butter fudge. You call me and I'll give you that recipe."

I told him I surely would.

When I got into the car, I read the potato recipe, which uses frozen hash browns. "Just because you make great peanut brittle doesn't mean you can make an acceptable potato casserole with frozen hash browns and call it country food," I said to Toni and Martha, who pointedly didn't respond. "But it was very sweet," I added.

"Bless his heart," said Martha, in her deep drawl, as we pulled away.

Martha pointed out bits of information about the places we passed along the road, including who lived in that house I'd been admiring and exactly what it looked like inside, down to the color of the wicker furniture in the back sunroom; where the last slave in the Nat Turner rebellion had been hanged; when the courthouse was built; what that giant vat in the side yard of that enormous plantation house was for (making lye soap from lard); how peanuts are cultivated and harvested; the various tribes of Indians who once lived in the area; child-rearing methodologies; the stages of cotton (it grows a purple flower, which turns white, and then a boll forms); what that small stone house close to the road was (a farm poorhouse, from the Depression, where women and men lived and worked off their debts, women on one side, men on the other); what muscadine grapes are good for (jelly); why the owner of that beautiful mansion with the crape myrtle trees was selling it so cheaply (he was old, his wife was much younger and wanted to live at the beach, and his kids didn't want to move back).

Our next stop: Grayson and Emma's Garden Spot, a farm stand with a café that was wonderfully familiar even though I'd never been there. Yellow squash was $1 a pound if you bought ten pounds or more; okra $2.95 a pound; eight cucumbers $4.50. They also sold jars of watermelon rind pickles, birch beer, side meat and ham pieces, souvenirs, and cookbooks. In a sunny little area decorated with a giant gray hornet's nest, mounted deer heads, and red-checked curtains, we sat near a man in a cowboy hat who nodded at us. While in Courtland, we ate here more than once: chicken and dumplings, pimento-cheese sandwiches on white toast, chicken salad on whole wheat with fat slices of good tomato, plastic cups of cubed sweet watermelon, and hand pies—or jacks as they're called here—with a crisp fried crust, filled with sweet potato or fried apples. Hand pies are a reason to live in the South, where you can find them at filling stations, hand wrapped in plastic, next to such treats as a snack-size chunk of cheddar (also wrapped in plastic) or a baggie full of pork rinds. And perfect country ham biscuits, of course.

I drank a birch beer. Martha pulled out her crocheting and worked with the girls until the food came. When the girls got restless they inspected the various vegetable bins and played with the pigs' feet, wrapped in plastic and as *en pointe* as a ballerina's.

After lunch we paid a call at Rose Hill, the Kello family plantation house, just up the dirt road from Martha's. Aunt Mariah and her sister Glynn had lived in the house from the time they were born until they got married and moved away. Even after Rose Hill fell into neglect, the family still gathered here for reunions and the big Easter celebration, until Glynn and her late husband, Freddie, came back to town, restored it, and moved in after Freddie had retired from the military in the early eighties.

The long dirt drive was lined with soy and peanut crops, but there was also a graveyard (where slaves and, later, free workers who had lived in houses still standing on the land were buried). But the house itself, which was notable as one of the earliest and best preserved houses in Southampton County, was set back, close to the river, with an enormous rolling green yard, giant magnolia trees, and rows of boxwoods that led from nowhere up to the front door, as if there was a walkway (there is not). Just to the west were a kitchen house, boathouse, and dock for embarking on the Nottoway River, named for the Indian tribe that sold the thousand-acre plot in 1792.

Since their mother, Glynn, wasn't around, Toni's cousins Bob and Jim, whom I remembered well as my Toni competition in the summers, took us on a tour of the house.

The enormous windows downstairs still contained the original glass panes, wavy and full of bubbles. Over the course of two hundred years, the glass had survived—even through the War Between the States, as people down here refer to the Civil War. The house had its original paint and heart pine floors, with no finish on them, just wax, and four fireplaces with the original mantels. The original doors on the house have no locks; they're barred.

Down a shallow hill alongside the house was a waist-high miniature steam engine train on a circular track laid down on a piece of land the size of a soccer field. Jim had built it years ago, complete with a covered bridge and railroad signs, to entertain the kids. It really worked and even had a whistle, so of course we all took a ride in the miniature passenger cars with Addie and Mariah.

The day was beautiful and clear, and fat magnolia blossoms still hung in one of the enormous trees. We went around and around in circles with the kids, just as the Kellos and my Nunn cousins had in the past.

I liked the idea of holding on to your history the way Courtlanders do. I liked the loyalty and the faith and the clarity; the love. But maybe I needed to let go of some of my own recent history. How long did I want to remember Oliver's funeral, and afterward, when we all sat in the lobby at the hotel getting drunk? At one point, Elaine and my brother Michael and I were sitting around a little table alone. Elaine looked at us and said, "It's so weird, isn't it? It's almost like we're the last ones left." It seemed hopeful, as if she thought it might not be true that Oliver was dead. And it was crushing, too, because she'd left out the fact that our sister and mother were both still alive. We were just the last ones Elaine wasn't mad at, the ones who'd come to the funeral.

"That's because we are," said Michael, who never minces words.

On this little train with all these cousins, moving forward seemed way too precarious. But it wasn't safe to go backward, either. So I imagined my own history draining away, seeping into the soil here for me to leave behind as we went round and round in circles.

Late that afternoon, Martha got out two cast-iron pans and fried an enormous batch of hoecakes—cornmeal, water, and a little egg, molded into patties. We took them down the road to Martha's brother (and Aunt Mariah's nephew), James, and his wife, Betsey, where they lived on a piece of land that was once part of Rose Hill, with a forest of tall pines out back. A cute teenage football star in his youth, James came out the side door of his house as we pulled up and poked an oven thermometer into two great-looking pork butts that he was cooking on low heat with the grill top down. He didn't say hello or anything else as he did this. Then he looked up, smiled, and taunted, "Too bad this isn't for you." Although it was.

I remembered James and Betsey from their voices. Betsey has a sweet girl's voice that she'd apparently kept ever since she'd married James very young, back in the early seventies, in a wedding that might not have happened if she hadn't set him straight on how to court. This was Betsey's story, and it made my heart open up a tiny sliver more to hear her tell it that night.

James was dating another girl when he and Betsey met in high school (in separate towns). "I'm going to keep dating Kay, but I'd like to *write* to *you*," he'd told her, according to Betsey herself.

"'Noooooooooo,' I said." Betsey's voice got higher, mad all over again, even after all this time, while James laughed through his big silver mustache, as if he'd never heard the story.

I loved the way Betsey said James's name, it seemed to take her about twenty minutes to get it out (it still had music in it after their long marriage), and the fact that even though they were both in their early sixties, he called her Girl.

"Girl, you better stop telling that story."

But nobody ever stops telling stories.

In addition to shreds and chunks of James's incredibly tender pork, for which he gave us several different barbecue sauces in squirt bottles, we had smothered cabbage with hot smoked sausage, fried squash and onions, corn on the cob with butter, boiled potatoes, the hoecakes with butter, and Martha's homemade plum jelly, which was the color of a camellia blossom. For dessert, Betsey had made soft, custard-style ice cream.

It felt natural to be there with them, even though I barely knew them, eating this forthright, glorious food. They hadn't seen me in years, but the fact that they'd cooked with me in mind—the generosity of heart—made me feel like I'd been in their house a hundred times. Everybody at the table knew that Oliver was dead, but aside from Toni, no one else was aware that I'd crashed and burned and was now a pile of ashes sitting at their table. Or I assumed as much, although the truth is, usually everybody knows everything.

"What do you eat when you're blue?" I asked, as we all ate, though I didn't need to look much further: I was having the best meal in the world at this very table.

"I want mashed potatoes," said Betsey, right off the bat. "Boiled in salt water, drained with a little water left, salt, pepper, butter, and milk.

"But my favorite *meal* is Dan Doodles," she added. "And collard greens, boiled potatoes, boiled eggs, corn bread, and spring onions, chopped up with vinegar."

I love anything that combines eggs and potatoes. Anything called Dan Doodle sounded wonderful, too, but it turned out to be the southern version of my culinary nemesis, haggis: smoked pork sausage made of small intestines, chopped, mixed with cubes of fat, and stuffed back into sections of large intestine.

Martha said, "My favorite meal is slick collards with ham, smoked sausages, peach pickles, deviled eggs, and corn bread. I always got to have that on my birthday, because I never had a party."

That had to be an incredibly comforting meal, and I was going to try it. Her comfort foods also included sweet potatoes "any way that is not sweet, and watermelon. We'd put the melons in the watering trough to cool, under the sycamore tree. Then we'd put a piece on the picket fence, like a holder, to eat it."

Of course, Toni's answer was a dose of pure, happy Toni: "Maybe comfort food is not always something you eat when you feel bad, or when something bad has happened," she said.

Great point—who says you can't have comfort food to make you feel even better than you already do? Her choice was green beans and cucumber sauce: very thinly sliced cukes in vinegar with onion and a tiny bit of sugar. "But I don't ever make it because it's so much better when Mom makes it." Aunt Mariah makes cucumber sauce to eat with a pot of green beans, cooked to death with some country ham.

The opposite of comfort food, for me, is canned tomato soup. In the early nineties, when my younger sister, Lisa, was living in New York, too, I went over to her apartment to drop off a dress she wanted to borrow. She'd heated up a can of soup and made herself a grilled cheese sandwich, because she wasn't feeling well. I didn't know why it made me sad, as I left her, watching her eat this food alone, waving at me before I shut the door. This image has stuck with me through the years. She moved to Italy, where I've not heard from her since 2004, hurt and silent and, like Oliver, never coming back. Sometimes, all my family's collective interactions seemed to be based on a single misunderstanding that no one could remember if pressed.

While eating all this food, the cousins told more stories. Betsey's flying squirrel: it got into the house late one Christmas night, zooming and rattling around their peaked rustic living room. But James wouldn't believe her, until it flew into their bedroom.

Kello family pranking: they take newcomers off in James's truck somewhere "interesting"; when the prankee begins to politely examine a log or gravestone or an unusual pumpkin of note, someone, usually James, says, "Let's leave him," and everyone jumps back in the truck and does that. Which explained why Toni objected when she heard James wanted to take us for a ride in his pickup.

James is obsessed with stealing watermelons as a prank, too. "You stand right here and if anybody comes, you gotta warn us," James told Tom, my cousin Susan's husband, after they got married. Tom had obediently stood for some time, guarding the entrance to the watermelon field, when James came speeding back as if being hotly pursued, with melons in the back of his truck, yelling, "Get in! Why didn't you warn us?" (In truth, James is friends with the watermelon farmer.)

His pranking aside, James is a naturalist, intimately familiar with the local geography and its history, and knows the name of every species of tree, plant, and animal in the area. He rides his horse, Tinny, rather than driving (which is what his father did, too) and has a room full of shadow boxes containing the ancient arrowheads he's collected over the years while exploring with Tinny along the river, or while hunting or fishing. His great-grandfather was one of seventeen survivors of Pickett's Charge; among his Civil War relics is a fierce-looking bayonet from the era.

The next day Martha and Betsey took us to nearby Smithfield, in Isle of Wight County, which I knew only as the town where the most famous country ham in the world originated.

The streets in Smithfield are lined with landmarked gorgeously preserved colonial, federal, and Victorian buildings.

From the 1978 edition of *The Smithfield Cookbook*—really a history book with great recipes—I learned that the county had been settled by Englishmen around 1619. The local Warrascoyack American Indians gave Captain John Smith thirty bushels of corn to take back to famine-struck Jamestown around 1607. If they hadn't been so generous, Warrascoyacks might still be living here today.

Because back in England, Smith talked up the area, describing its attractive plains and marshes; the fertile valley lush with trees; the fish, oysters, deer, fowl, and grain; and its many creeks and brooks. By 1634 an influx of new European settlers had learned from the American Indians how to live off the land by farming, fishing, hunting, and preserving food (including salting and smoking meat). These native methods, along with the African slave influence, helped create the distinctly local cuisine.

The unusually wonderful hams and peanuts made the port town of Smithfield rich and famous by the 1750s. As Captain Smith had pointed out, geography "entrenched the inhabitants," most of whom were bound by water and living on plantations large and small that were pretty much inaccessible to the outside world. This sort of archetypal self-sustaining community lasted well into the twentieth century, a way of life, with its peculiarly deep connection to the land, which is still starkly evident in the local manners, customs, and cuisine. Despite the decaying plantations, the disappearance of much of the early mainstay farming, and all the refinements associated with them, the locals treasure the remaining heirlooms. They continue to find a way to dine on food that has not changed at all, like Betsey's Dan Doodle, a relic of hog killing dinners that were once common.

Factory farming transformed the agrarian customs and almost killed off the old-style country ham that was cured and aged in small batches. It was reassuring to visit the Darden Country Store, where country hams were still being prepared in the old style. There's not much on the shelves, but they'll cut off some ham, make a sandwich, or sell you some rat cheese (an old name for cheap cheddar) from the giant orange wheel, or side meat (pork belly), which truly is the one indispensable thing. It goes in everything.

The store's smokehouse was across the street, a dark, smelly, high-ceilinged two-room building where dismembered pig parts covered in mold hung three layers deep from the ceiling. A hock and the saw that had just removed it were lying on a table like an old Flemish still life (I took a photo of that, of course). The place horrified Addie and Mariah.

Tommy Darden, whose father started the business back in 1952, and his wife, DeeDee, showed us how they layer green hams in salt in late January or early February, let them sit for about forty days, then take them out and wash them thoroughly.

"Then we cover them in three parts black pepper to one part borax. We're not sure why. That's the way we've always done it. It works, so we don't change," he said.

The hams are then hung by ropes from the ceiling; a barrel of apple wood is brought in to smoke them during the rainy spring days of April and May. They continue curing until the Fourth of July, by which time they've lost about 20 percent of their weight but gained giant flavor and texture, and grown a layer of that scary mold, which actually protects the meat. "You can eat this raw, like prosciutto," said DeeDee.

It's hard to find anyone else who makes country ham on such a small scale, over a comparable time span. "Factory hams have a turnaround of six months," DeeDee said. "You can't get ours by mail, like Edwards, only in the store." And people buy it from the store, since pig farming is pretty much gone for good around here, along with the days-long family hog-killing rituals described in *The Smithfield Cook-book*. A hog-killing menu included fried tenderloin and pork chops, fried pork liver, fresh sausage, chitterlings, snap beans, collards, baked sweet potatoes, corn, applesauce, fried apples, corn bread, biscuits, and crackling bread. Which was not that different from how I'd been eating since I'd arrived. But now people rarely buy or cook an entire country ham (partly because factory farm pigs are so gigantic). So the Dardens began cooking the hams, too (first you wash off the mold and then boil, never bake, them), to sell by the pound. They started out in their kitchen at home, "two hams at a time, while Dad was working at the Navy Yard," said Tommy. "Then we got a pot so we could do four, then we got one that we could cook seven or eight of them in, outside."

Toni and I later dropped by to see her cousins Bob and Jim at Parker's Peanuts, which produces a peanut I have often felt like writing a musical about: a simple blanched and fried version with a few tiny bubbles puffed along each legume, and the perfect amount of salt. I've probably eaten two hundred pounds of these peanuts in my lifetime and wanted to see how they'd updated their father, Freddie's, methods.

I suddenly remembered that Freddie had been a suicide, a fact that everyone who knew their family knew very well. The Kello-Parkers hadn't tried to hide it. It was just a sad part of their history about which no one seemed to be particularly ashamed. It was tragic for Freddie, not some kind of reflection on who they were as a family. So they continued being a family.

Freddie had started the peanut business in their home kitchen after retiring from the military, until the kitchen got so oil-slicked that Glynn kicked him out and made him move down to the river house. Jim and Bob have since computerized and updated the final building their late father left to them—the mechanization of frying, salting, and packaging. But it's still a boutique, small-batch, family enterprise, dedicated to earlier ways. "Dad's mother taught him how to do the peanuts this way," said Bob. "She told him, 'Cook them till they rattle.'"

The peanut-brittle man, the Kellos, the Dardens, and the Parkers were all essentially engaging in family home cooking that got out of hand. This food connects people to their history, to a sense of place. They know who they are and they have a place in the world. And when that world changes, they try to adapt, however much resistance they might instinctively feel.

On our last night in Courtland, we all crammed into Toni's SUV—Mariah and Addie, Martha and James, and Betsey and me—to drive the narrow roads to the Virginia Diner, famous for its country food: pulled pork, collards, spoon bread, country ham, fried apples, black-eyed peas with stewed tomato, peach cobbler, and peanut pie, which was hot and prepared chess style, meaning like traditional southern pecan pie, made with a lot of sugar, eggs, and butter, a bit of cornmeal, and with a texture neither custardy nor pudding-y but pleasantly gelatinous and sugary. And, of course, a giant basket of biscuits and large tumblers of sweet tea.

After we finished, it was pitch-black out. Toni pulled over on a curve in the road when James commanded her to stop. With the headlights shining, we could see fat striped watermelons out in the fields, waiting to be stolen. Toni drove into the field, the doors opened, and James and the girls went running into the darkness, looking for the perfect melon. The rest of us got out, too, so we could take pictures of the girls' first watermelon-related crime, and then we all crowded back in, like clowns into a circus car.

We never ate the watermelon, though it was a real beauty, because Toni and the girls and I were driving back to Atlanta the next day. And we were so busy we never made the pickles. I spent our last afternoon at Martha's house talking with her, while Toni took the girls rafting down the Nottoway River with Bob and Jim.

Martha's old house was filled with antiques and family pictures. The dining room was piled with gorgeous jars of jam and preserves. We installed ourselves in her TV room amid crocheting magazines and piles of yarn, and talked about food and family for a couple of hours; I told her how lucky she was to have her brother James so close by, part of her day-to-day life, picking the plums and grapes for her preserves each year, and bringing over all the buckets of cucumbers (which I was immediately sorry I had mentioned, since they were still there in the kitchen, unwashed).

When the conversation turned to my search for comfort foods and I naturally praised her famous pickles, I was surprised to hear her say, in her slow, unmistakable voice, which sounds amused no matter how happy or sad a thing she might be saying is: "Emily, pickles are not my comfort food."

I don't know why I'd assumed they would be. But I was dumbfounded she could even bring herself to make them at all after she told me that her enviable domestic skills—including making jams and jellies and putting up food, like the pickles and wild plum jam—were forced on her from a very early age.

"I was my family's maid," she told me.

Her mother was cruel to Martha all her life, especially during the years before she left home for college: she told Martha she was unattractive and overweight, and forced her to stay home and work while her friends and her brother, James, were allowed to just be kids. "She only wanted me around so I could cook and clean," Martha said. Unimaginable.

I was well aware that one person's comfort food could be another person's poison, but this was certainly not the wonderful story I'd imagined for Martha, who seemed to have surprised herself by telling me the truth. Her revelation made me so angry that I felt sick to my stomach. It also made me love Martha even more. She seemed brave to me, a wonder. And I was glad that just down the gravel road, her brother was there for her, and a little farther away, all those cousins pulling together, as best as they could, at any given time.

Martha's Virginia Sweet Chunk Pickles

Makes about 6 quart jars or 12 pint jars (this may vary)

You will need a 5-gallon (or larger), heavy-duty plastic bucket for one batch of pickles. Martha's mother used an earthenware crock.

6 cups pickling salt (Martha has also used rock salt; never iodized
   salt)
Water (enough to almost fill your 5-gallon bucket)
6 to 7 pounds fresh small cucumbers, as uniform in size
   as possible (Martha tries to use ones that have the
   circumference of a quarter), thoroughly washed in clean
   water
3 tablespoons powdered alum
1 gallon cider vinegar
4 to 5 pounds granulated sugar
⅓ cup pickling spices
1 tablespoon celery seed

1. Working in 1-gallon batches for ease and safety, use a very large pot
   to make a brine with a proportion of 2 cups salt to 1 gallon water.
   Boil until the salt has dissolved and pour boiling hot over the whole
   cucumbers in your 5-gallon bucket. Repeat this step until all the
   cucumbers are covered with brine. You will have extra brine. If any
   of the cucumbers float to the top, weigh them down by placing a
   plate or two in the bucket. Let stand for 1 week. In hot weather, if
   mold develops just skim as needed. Do not be disturbed by mold;
   this is normal. Martha's mother used to start a batch before the
   family went to the beach for a week, then skimmed the mold upon
   returning.
2. At the end of the first week, drain and rinse the cucumbers and cut
   them into ¾-inch chunks. Wash out the 5-gallon bucket and return
   the cucumber chunks to the bucket. Make a boiling hot solution
   of 1 gallon water and 1 tablespoon of the alum and pour over the
   cucumbers. You may have to repeat this step to cover the chunks
   in the alum bath. Repeat this process for a total of three mornings,
   after draining the cucumber chunks and rewashing the bucket.
   Make this fresh hot alum bath each morning.
3. On the fourth morning, drain the alum water and rinse the cucumber chunks well. Rinse the bucket well and return the cucumber
   chunks to the bucket. In a large pot, mix together 6 cups of the

vinegar and 5 cups of the sugar, and bring to a boil. Add the pickling spices and celery seed tied up in cheesecloth and pour the vinegar mixture over the pickles. (You can use the pickling spices and celery seed without cheesecloth; just scrape them out of the strainer when it's time to return them to the liquid.) You may have to repeat this step to make sure all the chunks are covered with the vinegar mixture.

4. On the fifth morning, drain the sweet liquid into a large pot, and add 2 cups of the sugar. Include the spices. Heat to boiling until the sugar is dissolved and pour this syrup over the pickles.

5. On the sixth morning, strain the liquid into a large pot, add the remaining 1 cup sugar, and heat until the sugar is dissolved and the liquid comes to a soft boil.

6. On the seventh morning, pack the pickles in the jars. Heat the vinegar mixture to a soft boil and remove the spices. Using a ladle, carefully pour the hot syrup, spices now removed, over the pickles, to about ⅛ inch from the top of the jars. Wipe the top of the jars with a clean, damp cloth and cover with a ring and lid. Seal the jars. You can eat them at this stage, but they're better after a month or so. Keep them on your shelves for years.

●

Obviously this pickle recipe is a lot of work, but Martha herself says they are worth the effort in spite of the fact that she has no fond childhood memories attached to them at all. Martha keeps making these fantastic pickles and probably a lot of other foods the family clamors for because we love them, and she loves us.

Six

GREAT-GRANDMOTHER'S
MEAN LEMON CAKE

The simple act of cooking for another person, while beautiful, is not a substitute for real love nor can it induce it. I'd learned that back in Chicago. Now that I'd visited the Kellos of Courtland and eaten their wonderful homemade food, though, it occurred to me that cooking might be one of the things that keeps many families together. Or helps families continue to understand how to love one another and feel loved. It had worked for Martha, who had so much deep affection in her life, including for her late mother, in spite of everything. "When my mother was dying of ALS, at age fifty-six, I told her: 'You always viewed me as your scapegoat,'" Martha said. "And she replied, 'No, it was just that you were my best friend.'" Martha sighed. "I really have many wonderful memories of her, especially as a cook; I learned to cook with her."

At the very least, home cooking can certainly soften certain realities and create fond memories of an imperfect home. So that's something.

On my side of the Nunn family, neither my mother nor my father had had a very good example of what a family was supposed to be like, and not just because both of them had been abandoned at an early age by fathers who seemed to feel no responsibility for their own children once things had fallen apart.

But the food was often excellent. Without her amazing lemon cake, for example, I'd have almost no fond memories of my paternal great-grandmother, Augusta—a bitter Frenchwoman who seemed to have very little cause to feel that way. I try to withhold judgment, because I only knew her when she was very old, although I did hear appalling stories from her daughter, my grandmother Bea. Because of this cake—moist but not-too-sweet layers, filled with lemon curd, dusted with confectioners' sugar—she persists in my memory with a sliver of love, even though she scared me.

When I say this cake is mean, I use that word as a compliment. Some relatives on my father's side of the family recall this cake fondly but incorrectly: topped with whipped cream, or with a glaze that melted if you didn't eat it in the morning, before the day got too hot. And some of them also remember my great-grandmother with surprising tenderness. When I asked my aunt Mariah about this cake, she didn't remember it at all, and she pointed out that Great-grandmother had a cook, which I'd never known. I never saw a cook in her kitchen, but I also never saw Augusta make the lemon cake. Aunt Mariah also remembers my great-grandmother as a joyful woman who loved children. It's really hard to determine the absolute truth about cakes or people from the past.

●

Here is what I have been told. Augusta's husband, my father's grandfather, John Alvin Messer, born Jtzig Mesoritzky, was a Russian Jew who arrived in the United States from Kiev with his parents when he was nine years old. His parents lived the rest of their lives in New York and were buried in Brooklyn. But my great-grandfather claimed that he grew up in a newsboys' home on the Lower East Side, which turned out not to be true, a story he made up once he moved south to High Point, North Carolina, presumably to hide his true origins. That's where he met Augusta while working for her father in the mirror business. They married and moved to Bassett, Virginia, where he was hired to run a mirror factory before moving to then-nascent Galax, which existed because of the furniture business and was originally named Bonaparte, later renamed after a plant with waxy, deep-green, heart-shaped leaves native to the region and found on the forest floor throughout the Blue Ridge Mountains. Florists are crazy about it.

My great-grandfather became a business leader and eventually owned his own furniture and mirror companies in Galax. He was so industrious that he became a millionaire during the Depression, according to my uncle John.

John Messer loved Augusta deeply, by all accounts, even though according to the family lore, she was raised a Catholic and was the one who persuaded him to hide the fact that he was Jewish. Together they raised a family in a stunning mansion called Cherry Hill, outside the city proper where he lived out his days as a wealthy town leader and philanthropist and secret Jew. My younger sister refers to our family as "Jewbillies" because of this. Galax grew quickly but then leveled off forever, never getting much bigger or smaller regardless of the closing of the factories or the creation of the Twin County Regional Hospital, which added a *Peyton Place* dimension to the social mix as egomaniacal doctors and their adoring nurses settled in, or the influx of tourism for the bluegrass music and crafts scene that has blossomed there, or the blue-collar Yankees and trust-fund hippies who bought cheap land off the Blue Ridge Parkway in the seventies. Today, my great-grandparents' mansion is long gone. Uncle John has photos of it being burned to the ground to clear the land, now the site of the Cherry Hill Walmart at the Cherry Hill Plaza.

Again, Augusta Messer was pretty old by the time I was born, and as I recall from our Sunday after-church visits, she always seemed peeved. One year she sent all of the presents my mother had wrapped for Christmas back to our house, unopened. At the end of her life, she lived in a smaller, pink house built after my great-grandfather died. The lawn was dotted with lush lilac bushes, and she had greenhouses and raised beds built to a height perfect for kneeling comfortably while gardening. The house was modern but filled with pretty and dainty things. One room held a collection of creepy dolls in fancy dresses that none of us was allowed to play with. Great-grandmother wore the most beautiful clothes—accessorized with handmade hats with netting and flowers and tiny fruit; millions of pairs of kid gloves of various colors and lengths; and tiny ornate purses. She had a surprisingly modern kitchen, where I naturally gravitated during visits.

Plenty of my family members would be surprised by my memories of her. But here is the way I have learned to see it: you have your version of the past, I have mine. And, at least, we have the cake. This is my own adaptation, which I cobbled together from various family recipes and my own trial and error. I was able to admit that the cake needed the whipped cream that I accused my relatives of fabricating. In fact, the whipped cream, in lieu of my remembered dusting of confectioners' sugar, is essential: it balances the tartness of the lemon curd and turns the whole enterprise into something altogether voluptuous. It's a nice cake to serve on the Fourth of July, decorated with a few strawberries and blueberries, especially if you've always pretended the Fourth of July is your birthday, the way Great-grandmother Augusta did for some reason.

Great-grandmother's Mean Lemon Cake

Makes 1 two-layer cake

FOR THE LEMON CURD

3 lemons, zested and juiced (about ¾ cup juice)

½ cup granulated sugar

½ cup brown sugar

4 tablespoons (½ stick) unsalted butter

3 large eggs, at room temperature, well beaten

FOR THE CAKE

1 cup granulated sugar

6 ounces (1½ sticks) unsalted butter, plus more for the pan

5 large eggs, at room temperature, separated

2 cups all-purpose flour, plus more for the pan

1 teaspoon baking soda

1½ teaspoons cream of tartar

1 cup milk

2 teaspoons pure vanilla extract

1 pint heavy cream, very cold

Strawberries and blueberries (optional)

1. To make the lemon curd, combine the lemon zest and juice, granu-lated and brown sugars (you can use all granulated sugar, which is prettier, but the brown sugar tames the sharpness and gives it depth), and butter in a saucepan over medium-low heat until the sugar is completely dissolved. Let the mixture cool slightly. Mix the eggs into the liquid, continuing to cook over very low heat until the mixture is thick and one or two bubbles surface, about 10 minutes. Once the mixture has cooled, strain it by pushing it through a large wire mesh strainer with a spatula or wooden spoon. This takes a while but is worth it. Refrigerate the curd for several hours before filling the cake.

2. Preheat the oven to 350°F. Grease and flour two 8-inch round cake pans.

3. Using an electric mixer, cream the granulated sugar and butter until light and fluffy. Beat the egg yolks well, add to the sugar-butter mixture, and beat until light.

4. In a bowl, sift together the flour, baking soda, and cream of tartar; slowly incorporate into the sugar-butter mixture, alternating with the milk. Add the vanilla and mix well.

5. Beat 3 of the egg whites until stiff (reserve the remaining egg whites for another purpose) then gently fold into the batter. Divide the batter evenly between the pans, and bake until golden on top and a toothpick inserted into the center of the cake comes out clean, 25 to 30 minutes. Let them cool completely.

6. To assemble the cake, use a long-bladed knife to carefully remove the domed top crust of one of the cooled cakes, creating an even surface. This will be the bottom layer. Remove the bottom crust

from the other cake, which will be the top. (If you don't do this, the two layers will slide around; the curd soaks into the cake.) Place the bottom layer on a cake stand and spread it with a thick layer of the lemon curd. You may have extra curd (it is delicious on scones). Carefully place the second layer on top. It's okay if the curd oozes out, but do not press down; you can also place some sliced strawberries or whole blueberries on this layer. Whip the heavy cream in a chilled bowl to stiff peaks immediately before serving, then pile it messily and bountifully on the top layer of the cake. Really pile it on there. Again, you may drop some berries here, for decoration.

●

To give her the benefit of the doubt, it's possible that my great-grandmother was unpleasant not because she was an anti-Semite married to a Jew, as I'd assumed, but because she was bored. Galax was not New York. It was not Chicago. However, I imagine my dysfunctional upbringing would have been a lot worse if not for the fact that Galax allowed us to grow up in fresh air, around green fields, with horses and cows (not ours) visible from my bedroom window. We built a big house, a modern glass and stone thing with five bedrooms; I had cute clothes and plenty to eat, lots of friends, a dog, a pretty bedroom with violet floral wallpaper, and lots of books to read. Unlike kids in the surrounding rural areas, we were town kids who had easy access to a movie theater, a pool hall (not to play pool but for the chili-slaw dogs), a drugstore with a lunch counter, and a bowling alley.

I suppose it was a good place to raise children, because my very immature parents miraculously produced five kids who were popular, smart, and attractive, and who excelled at sports and social activities, like *The Brady Bunch*—if you didn't look too closely. Eventually they got divorced and moved on to lives that had little to do with us.

People cooked every day in my hometown, mainly because they had no other choice. When I was very young the only restaurants were at the two local hotels as well as a place called the Red Barn.

We had not one but three drive-ins, where a woman in stretch pants would come out to your car to take your order after she'd finished smoking a cigarette—if she didn't just bring the cigarette with her. Two of the drive-ins are still there; you can order corn dogs, cheeseburgers that have been flattened in a press and wrapped in wax paper, and Boston shakes (a giant milk shake with a sundae on top) or lime flips (a lime sherbet shake). The Red Barn and one of the hotel restaurants had Sunday buffets with all the Thousand Island dressing you could pile on your iceberg salad, fried chicken, pork chops, mashed potatoes, collard greens, green beans, and biscuits, and any number of pies for dessert.

I loved my mother's cooking. But like a lot of mothers of her era, mine reminded her children, more often than was probably necessary, about her hardships growing up. Whatever emotional deprivations marred your childhood, none was nearly as tragic as those my mother had endured during her childhood in Johnson City, Tennessee, during the Great Depression.

Her mother, Mid (short for Mildred), a Zelda Fitzgerald flapper figure judging from an old photo I have, died of cancer when Mother was nine years old, but she was not given that news until long after her alcoholic newspaperman father, Joseph McKendree Ramsey Rees, aka Ramsey Rees at the *Philadelphia Inquirer,* dropped her and her sister, Patricia, in Johnson City, Tennessee, to live with his dead wife's two spinster sisters. He never saw either of his daughters again. I have heard from other relatives that he started a new family not far from Johnson City, but remained uninterested in their welfare.

Because of this, it is very easy to understand why my mother was not the best parent in the world. She was very good at other things, primarily at being fabulous for everyone to admire. (If you didn't admire her, though, watch out.) At Christmas, she would pull down a round box from the top of her closet, which contained a close-fitting hat that looked like the top of a Christmas tree, with green crushed velvet leaves and elfin ornaments and a star on top. She wore false eyelashes to the Methodist church, where she caused a congregation-wide scandal by showing the iconic *Life* magazine photos of a human fetus as a visual aid to her Sunday school class on "the miracle of childbirth," after which she quit teaching, showily aggrieved by the gossip. She had a pink Pucci dress, with chandelier earrings to match. She could do the Charleston. Her laughter was high-pitched, often startling, especially in public. One summer she got an Afro and wore caftans. No one knew why.

Della and Georgia, the sisters, lived together in the giant Spencer family house until their death, except for the period when Georgia worked as a fashion buyer at a department store in Statesville, North Carolina. Della worked as a milliner and tailor after the Second World War, when everyone was still quite poor and even more relatives moved into the house. It was partitioned with heavy velvet curtains; clogged with too many velvet sofas and chairs, a pump organ, a piano, and lots of ferns; and had six fireplaces and a porch that stretched its length. It was dark and faded and sadly resplendent—which is how my mother would begin to seem when we'd visit. It appeared to make her melancholy. But not me.

Upon arrival I headed straight to the attic, which was full of flapper dresses, intricate hats, military uniforms, costume jewelry, books from the twenties and thirties (*Honey Bunch: Her First Summer on an Island*), and other things that seemed as exciting to unearth as dinosaur bones. But the dining room with its butler's kitchen was my favorite because of the rainbows the cut-glass windows threw on the walls in the morning and on the floor in the afternoon, and the pirate's chest full of cards and poker chips. I imagined Georgia and Della taking each other's money in lonely games of poker. Also, there was a dinner bell that hung on the wall, four chimes and a tiny mallet that you banged on to call everyone for mealtime. Della and Georgia were both about six feet tall and had long painted fingernails, wore lots of costume jewelry, hose, and dress-up pumps every day, and always seemed to be smoking a cigarette and drinking a cocktail or coffee. Their annual Christmas open house was one of our favorite Johnson City events as kids; all the other guests were old and breathed liquor breath all over us, but sneaking bourbon balls and little port wine cheese balls from the butler's kitchen, and trying to swallow them before we got caught, outweighed having to kiss all the old people.

Georgia was elegant, funny, and kind, and she laughed with a rasp like a cartoon dog; she claimed to be the first woman in America to wear a pantsuit. Della was bizarre, crass, and bitter; she once said to the room at large, including all of my preteen brothers and sisters, "I wouldn't marry Aristotle Onassis if his asshole were lined with gold."

I can't imagine it was very much fun for my nine-year-old mother to be left alone with Della, in spite of the fact that she made the most excellent pancakes, which were really like hoecakes because they were fried in too much oil (not butter) so they were crispy around the edges. She always had carrot and celery sticks in a lidded glass container in her old refrigerator, where she also claimed to be keeping poison to put in our food if we continued being so bad. Della once locked all five of us out of her house after telling us there were mad dogs roaming the neighborhood. "There is a woman down the street who has five children, too," she said to us after a particularly harrowing bout of badness. "She just died from exhaustion and everyone is worried sick about who is going to take care of those children." This spoke to my biggest fear, that we were killing my mother simply by existing. If the house was messy, she would rage in a way that made me feel sorry for her rather than rebellious. She would go into her room, close the door and lock it, and not come out or speak for hours, no matter how loudly we knocked. "I don't want to live," she once told me through the door. So I vacuumed and dusted the whole house.

●

My mother's childhood was not ideal, but Della and Georgia took her in and loved her the only way they knew how.

My mother grew up to be an excellent cook, which was a feat for anyone cooking for five kids. For a long time, she fed us enormous pots of shredded chicken and dumplings (the kind shaped like giant biscuits, soggy on the outside and bready on the inside); turkey tetrazzini with mushrooms cooked in wine, which I thought was so exotic; fried chicken that she first shook in a brown paper bag full of flour and paprika; tuna casserole with egg noodles; bowls of hot pinto beans that we'd top with a big spoonful of cold chow-chow, a cabbage relish; cast-iron pans of corn bread made with real buttermilk; barbecued brisket; roast beef that she took to the butcher after she cooked it, to have it sliced paper thin, served with the juices from the pot, drizzled over crushed new potatoes and chunks of carrots; green beans cooked to death with a ham hock—often with me by her side, chopping and stirring like a sous chef. I also mowed our giant hilly lawn on the riding mower, folded the laundry, and cleaned up after dinner to keep her from leaving us, or, worse, killing herself from the strain of taking care of us all, a tortured burden she reminded us of frequently and dramatically.

Some of my mother's favorite foods were boiled cabbage, creamed chipped beef on toast, corn bread dunked in buttermilk, or a big pot of butter beans, all of which I loathed, the cabbage especially, because she claimed it was what they had to eat during the Depression. Its awful odor of past despair clung to the air in the house for days.

After I'd grown up and moved to New York and put some distance between me and cabbage, I actually began to like it. Probably because I decided that rather than boiling it (why would anyone?), I would smother it (just like my feelings, but with better results). It was my way of trying to reinvent the past, to transform it into something more palatable.

I chopped a couple of slices of bacon together with four or five cloves of garlic and some rosemary, sautéed that resulting paste, called a *battuta* by Italians, in a large heavy pot until the garlic was pale golden and the bacon had browned, then threw in a whole head of sliced cabbage, salt, and pepper, and tossed to coat. I turned the heat down low, put a lid on it, and let it cook until very tender, about forty-five minutes, adding a half a cup of whatever was left of the jeroboam of dry white wine I was drinking, at some point early in the process (while there was still some left). Usually I made mashed potatoes and turnips, and ate the cabbage on top. However, this dish fell by the wayside after I discovered Jamie Oliver's red cabbage recipe. It's much, much prettier than my smothered green cabbage (which ends up a kind of drab military gray), because it retains its gorgeous garnet color, and the apple turns bright red, too. It's terrific with mashed potatoes.

Red Cabbage with Bacon, Apple, and Balsamic Vinegar

Serves 4

2 tablespoons olive oil

2 strips thick bacon, thinly sliced

1 tablespoon fennel seed, bashed in a mortar and pestle or with a rolling pin

1 medium onion, halved and sliced into ⅓-inch slices

2 medium apples (I use McIntosh, but any good tart eating apple works), peeled, cored, and chopped into 1-inch pieces

1 large head red cabbage, cored and chopped into irregular chunks (i.e., don't just slice or shred)

Sea salt, to taste

Freshly ground black pepper, to taste

¼ cup good balsamic vinegar

2 tablespoons butter

½ cup chopped fresh flat-leaf parsley, or more to taste

1. Heat the oil over medium-high heat in a large heavy pot.
2. Add the bacon and fennel seed; cook until golden. Add the onion and cook, with the lid on, until golden, about 5 minutes. Add the apples, cabbage, salt, pepper, and vinegar. Toss to coat well.
3. Cover, cook on low heat for about an hour, stirring occasionally. Stir in the butter, season with salt and pepper, and sprinkle with parsley.

My Mother's Cabbage

Serves 1 mother

1 large cabbage
Salt, pepper, and tears

1. Cut out the heart of the cabbage (or core it; however you want to think of it). Slice, chop, hack it—whatever—while staring off into space. If you cut yourself doing this, weep dramatically as if someone has died.
2. Place the cabbage in a giant pot as big as all your sorrows; fill to cover with water (or tears).
3. Bring to a boil, then lower the heat and simmer until the house smells like everything that has haunted you since the day you realized that you were completely alone in the world, despite your five children.
4. Serve in bowls with salt and pepper, and with a splash of cider vinegar at the table, if desired.

●

My gorgeous and dreamy mother had been an art and drama major in college, and she remained interested in living a life that was artistic and dramatic, especially for someone living in a small mountain town that had never given the world much in the way of "the fine arts."

The truth is, she brought the arts to Galax and changed the lives of a lot of people. Had it not been for her—she had herself been Miss East Tennessee State—my hometown would never have had the Miss Galax Pageant, which funneled the town's prettiest girl into the Miss Virginia Pageant.

The Miss Galax Pageant may not sound like much of an "arts" event, but it was a big deal to us. My mother managed to get women to do things that seemed entirely out of character not just for themselves but for just about anyone in Galax. One of the black competitors could sing—quite well—and chose to perform the Ike and

Tina Turner hit "Proud Mary." "Dance that way you do," my mother instructed her, meaning black people. Then my mother danced for her in the way in which she believed Tina Turner danced. The contestant then danced like my mother dancing like Tina Turner, all very confusing for me, at age ten.

In addition to the baton twirlers and the poetry reciters who sounded like Lou Ann Poovie on *Gomer Pyle* ("The year when I was twenty-one/(John that year was twenty-three)/That was the year, that was the spring,/We planted the white magnolia tree"), and the singers and modern dancers, the pageant gave everyone in town the chance to get a look at my mother, who'd given birth to five children but looked pretty damn fabulous, wearing a cherry-red velour hot-pants catsuit pantomiming a hit from the popular Barbra Streisand movie musical (originally a Broadway musical starring Barbara Harris), *On a Clear Day You Can See Forever.*

While she pranced around in her go-go boots lip-synching "Hurry, It's Lovely Up Here," in which Barbra used her psychic powers to coax flowers out of the soil, the contestants, who probably had believed they were the draw of the show, lined up behind her in their bathing suits, then walked down the runway and threw a little pot that contained a flower out into the audience. I'd helped make the flowerpots: Styrofoam cups covered in construction paper, with pipe-cleaner-stemmed fake zinnias poking through the bottom. The contestants popped the flower out of what appeared to be an empty pot, to simulate growing.

As a child, I was thrilled by my mother as impresario. Nobody else's mother could have multitasked like that—she was directing and starring in a beauty pageant, for Christ's sake. On top of it all, we got to go to pageant practice until late at night during the week and eat hot dogs with coleslaw from the pool hall downtown on weekends until the pageant was over and everything went back to normal, which in her case meant bouts of hysteria and indignation about the smallest things.

She was plagued by the kinds of neuroses that tended to shut down the entire show—and not just the pageant. She could bring anything to a screeching halt with her oversize, often inappropriate emotions, and her inability to cope with the unpredictable nature of everyday existence. If she got lost driving somewhere far from Galax, she'd start to cry and hyperventilate, as if there were no possibility of finding her way and you, the fourteen-year-old, were left to ask the filling station attendant for directions out of Raleigh. This made her all the more compelling as well as subconsciously terrifying. For example, I never knew if I'd make it to summer camp. "I'm having agoraphobia," she said breathlessly, as she drove me to rural Camp Cheerio, her knuckles white on the wheel, even though we were in the middle of nowhere. Camp Cheerio was only a half hour from Galax, but she turned around halfway there, sped home, and had our neighbors, the Oteys, take me in the back of their station wagon. And it was always a question if she'd remember to pick me up from my piano lessons, which were three miles outside the city limits; or if she'd snap out of depression and turn on the pizzazz when my homecoming date came to pick me up by trying to teach him to do the Lindy Hop in the driveway, as if he were *her* date. Or if we'd be subjected to her fits of righteousness and obsession that would last forever, over snatches of overheard conversation at a PTA meeting or party or on the street downtown, conversation that she perceived as rude or somehow a personal affront to her. She seemed unaware of the fact that she was not the center of attention in the world outside our house. She was always recently wronged, in a million tiny ways. And it was our job to tend to her emotions. Often, we were the ones who'd hurt her.

All this aside, I give the Miss Galax Pageant credit for teaching me at age ten about spoon bread. One of the pageant winners had a talent for making clothes, which she displayed in a giant book, as if for paper dolls. We went to Roanoke to see our winner in the Miss Virginia Pageant and I hung around the hotel watching the stiff-tressed, fabulously dressed ladies parade around with Vaseline on their teeth. Then I sat through the pageant, at which everyone stood up for the outgoing Miss Virginia as if she were the president of the United States, and I got to have dinner in the restaurant of the Hotel Roanoke, where we were staying.

The Hotel Roanoke is still renowned for its spoon bread. What was this stuff that made me want to push everyone out of the way in order to eat their serving? It was soft and custardy, like grits soufflé (which my mother made at Thanksgiving and called a casserole), but lighter, finer, and more buttery. I couldn't get enough of it or ever forget it. It was from another world, and I wanted to live there.

I tracked down the Hotel Roanoke recipe, which worked exactly twice. Every other time I made it, it separated into a layer of custard atop of a layer of cornmeal while baking. Such a disappointment. It may have been an altitude problem, but I blamed it on myself. (Was I not stirring briskly enough? Was I using the wrong cornmeal?) And for months, I stubbornly kept retrying this recipe, because it is traditional: it uses baking powder to give it lift. But I finally came upon a recipe by James Beard that goes straight to the stiffly beaten egg whites to do that job. I combined the two—my new version uses a lot of cornmeal and a lot of eggs, but it still has the corny flavor and eggy pudding richness that I remember from that trip to Roanoke. Sometimes it's good to give up. This new dish is exactly the way I want it.

Emily's Own Spoon Bread

Serves 10

1⅓ cups cornmeal

1½ teaspoons salt

2 teaspoons granulated sugar

2½ cups whole milk

4 tablespoons (½ stick) unsalted butter, melted

5 large eggs, separated

1. Preheat the oven to 350°F. Grease a large soufflé dish or 9-inch square casserole. In a large bowl, mix the cornmeal, salt, and sugar with a whisk or fork. In a small saucepan, bring the milk to a boil, reduce the heat, and simmer. Slowly stir in the cornmeal mixture, whisking until it begins to thicken. Remove from the heat and stir in the butter.

2. In a small bowl, beat the egg yolks by hand; in a larger bowl whisk the egg whites until stiff peaks form. Once the corn mush has cooled slightly, stir in the egg yolks. Next, gently fold in the egg whites.
3. Pour the mixture into the soufflé dish and bake for 40 minutes. The middle should be soft, but not loose. Serve immediately, with lots of butter.

●

I forgot about spoon bread for a long time. Many years later, when my life in Chicago had started to seem tenuous and I began developing lots of recipes for the online food community and recipe-contest website Food52 as an outlet, I invented this more modern version, which you can also make in a large soufflé dish. If you're a nervous wreck, it's extremely soothing.

Parmesan and Prosciutto Spoon Bread

Serves 6

2 cups water (more if needed)

1 teaspoon salt

1 teaspoon freshly ground black pepper

2 sprigs thyme

1 cup polenta, preferably fine mill

1½ cups buttermilk

2 tablespoons butter, plus more for the ramekins

1½ cups grated Parmigiano-Reggiano cheese

3 large eggs, separated

1 teaspoon baking powder

A few pinches of cayenne pepper

1½ ounces thinly sliced prosciutto (about 3 pieces), cut crosswise
    into ½-inch ribbons

1. Preheat the oven to 400°F. Grease six 12-ounce ramekins or soufflé dishes. In a large heavy saucepan, combine the water, salt, pepper,

and thyme; bring to a boil, then reduce the heat and simmer for 2 minutes. Bring it back to a boil and slowly add the polenta, whisking constantly, until you have a smooth porridge. Stir in 1 cup of the buttermilk, and continue to cook over medium heat for 2 minutes more. Remove the thyme; reduce the heat to low and continue to cook, whisking occasionally, for 35 minutes. It should bubble like a tar pit. If it gets too thick, stir in hot water as necessary. You want it to remain very thick, however.

2. Remove the polenta from the heat and let cool slightly. Stir in the remaining ½ cup buttermilk, the butter, and 1 cup of the Parmigiano-Reggiano. Beat the egg yolks; stir into the mixture.

3. Meanwhile, beat the egg whites in a separate bowl, until soft peaks form. Fold a spoonful of the egg whites into the polenta mixture; sprinkle the baking powder and cayenne into the polenta mixture and mix well by hand. Fold in the remaining egg whites.

4. Spoon the mixture (about 1 cup) into the ramekins. Bake for 25 minutes. Once the spoon breads have puffed and browned, sprinkle with the remaining ½ cup Parmigiano-Reggiano and the prosciutto shreds. Turn on the broiler and let the cheese brown and the prosciutto crisp. Let cool slightly before serving.

●

I loved my mother and father desperately as a kid, and couldn't bear to blame them for how strange my childhood would become, or even for their painful divorce, which felt like they had divorced me and my siblings, too, even though I was just fourteen years old. My mother was so beautiful, and my father was so handsome, and they were both funny and smart. All my friends thought they were ideal. I had no idea that neither of them was really bothering to raise the five of us, nor that it would come to the point that both of them would seem to wish, and act as if, they'd never had us.

"I didn't ask to be born!" screamed my sister Elaine, who in high school had begun to lash out at my mother in rebellious ways that I found shocking, impossible to imagine as a grade-schooler. My mother was heroic, my everything, and her life was so hard! I didn't know back then that other kids didn't feel like they were a millstone around their mother's neck.

"It's a good thing," replied my father. "I would have said no." Which was supposed to be a joke, but I wasn't really sure. I knew something stank, but I couldn't find the source.

From the outside, we probably looked exemplary, although my friends' more astute parents must have wondered what was going on inside our giant glass and stone house. They couldn't have known about my mother's depression, which at its worst took her away for treatment for weeks. She never seemed to have the slightest bit of physical attraction to my dad; I never saw them kiss or hug, and she always seemed scandalized by anyone who did. At home, in private, my mother was silent, depressed, or hysterical, but in public she was jazzy, charming, and entertaining, yet rarely interested in us.

And I never would have dared reveal to anyone, ever, that her happy and entertaining public personality was not the real one. I figured it just wasn't for us, because we didn't make her happy. In fact, we were upstaging her. Growing up in my family was like being in a movie in which my mother was the dazzling star. As children, we were definitely in the movie but we were supporting, supportive extras, always in the background. By the time I left home for college, we were in the back row of the audience. I felt both relieved to be away and unmoored, without a purpose: On whom was I now supposed to focus all of my attention and worry?

For his part, my dad was on the road during the week, never at home, and on weekends he didn't speak a word about what he did or where he'd been. He silently drank coffee, read a book a day, and went to the country club. (Once, I hid in the very back of the station wagon when I knew he was going golfing; I sprang out once we arrived at the club, and he let me ride along in the cart for nine holes.) He didn't talk to me about what he was reading but gave me books. He was amused by us kids, adored my mother, and he was always kind. Always. I'm just not sure he ever knew what he'd gotten himself into.

Although my mother mentioned that she and my father had incompatible blood types when she told the Lipizzaner story, the truth is, they were probably incompatible because neither of them had been raised in a family that stayed together or turned into anything better after it broke up. Which was exactly how things went with their own divorce.

●

I've never been sure where my father found comfort. But my mother found most of hers—thanks to lots of time in the spotlight—in the "magic of the theater," as she referred to it. She started the Galax Theatre Guild with Carol, a beautiful woman from Chicago, and one of her best friends, Millie Victor, who had moved to Galax from New York with her husband, Al, before I was born.

●

The Galax Theatre Guild still produces plays today. It brought the talented townsfolk out of the woodwork. The first play they produced was *The Music Man*, under my mother's direction (with me in another role my mother forced me into: the tail end of the horse in one of those two-person costumes; my older sister, Elaine, got to be the head). It was so successful, drawing a sold-out audience and boffo reviews from the big-city Roanoke paper, that the next year they decided to try something even fancier: the Rodgers and Hammerstein classic musical examination of race and wartime love, *South Pacific*.

After bringing the town fame from behind the curtain, it was only right that she hand off directing responsibilities to be the star of her next production. Somehow, she found Mallory, a real, live New York City choreographer who was working as a dance teacher in Winston-Salem, which was down a curvy road into North Carolina about an hour from the Virginia state line. Mallory had played Lucille Ball's nephew in *Mame*, had been in a McDonald's commercial, and was now teaching dance at Dorminy Dance Studio, in the very large stucco and green-tile-roofed house of an old dance instructor who walked with a cane and dressed only in black with her hair always in a bun.

Mallory appeared one day at our house like an elf, wearing tights and a leotard and character shoes, and aside from a short T-shirt pulled over it all, that was pretty much what he wore all the time. He was about five feet tall, cute as a button with dimples, but with a stomach that stuck out like a medicine ball on his otherwise fit body.

When he wasn't staying up at the Rose Lane Motel (whose giant neon letters slowly spelled out *Rose Lane,* over and over, every night, and could be seen from all over town) or down at the Midtowner Hotel, where we went to the Sunday buffet, he stayed with us in our five-bedroom house, where we almost never had guests because it was usually a mess. I never had friends over because it was hard to predict what the atmosphere might be like on any given day. But it got cleaner and more normalized once he arrived, even though he was not your typical houseguest. He taunted both of my brothers and changed the channel in the central playroom's TV between our bedrooms whenever he wanted, regardless of what hour of television we'd chosen to watch.

His favorite show was *The PTL Club* (short for *Praise the Lord,* but we called it *Pass the Loot*). He loved the evangelist-wife Tammy Faye Bakker's wide belts and drizzling black mascara. He would wait, almost breathless, until Tammy cried, and then he would scream with laughter until he fell out of the mod swiveling barrel chair he hogged. He called everyone a douchebag back in the seventies when nobody said douchebag, and he was the sort of guy whom small-town folks love to be scandalized by. If Mallory liked you, you were not only super-cool, but truly special. You were not a douchebag.

I found him disagreeable at times, but not every household in Galax featured a New York choreographer. I appreciated what had dropped into our laps: not just a glamorous stranger, but someone who seemed to make my mother happy. Thanks to Mallory, who took over as director of *South Pacific,* my mother could assume the role of the starry-eyed navy nurse Nellie Forbush, opposite the heroic plantation owner Emile de Becque, played by a prim and self-important local man from the next county over who had hair like a Chia Pet. I disliked him the minute I met him. My mother took her role very seriously. I had not realized how seriously until she appeared as a newly bleached blonde one afternoon while I sat at the breakfast table doing my homework. She and my father both have dark hair, but in the original Broadway show Mary Martin was blond and in the movie version of *South Pacific*, Mitzi Gaynor was blond, too. I was very disturbed by the flat yellow color but told her she looked great.

My mother had given me an earlier hair shock when she'd come home in an auburn wig that flipped up at the ends like Marlo Thomas's hair in *That Girl*. That change had been for no reason whatsoever. Back then, my mother and her best friends Millie, Lois, and my aunt Mariah did a lot of wild, glamorous things with their hair that you could think of as seventies-appropriate. They had twirling sideburns, big Jean Shrimpton-y heaps of curls, and falls, which are extra piles of fake hair they plugged on top of their heads for volume and curl. (While waiting in the station wagon, my mother would send me into the hairdresser holding a Styrofoam head to which a fall was pinned, to have it styled for her.)

But when she pranced in from her weekly psychiatric appointment in Winston-Salem with this new blond hair, along with a summer sausage, cocktail rye bread, and some Havarti cheese from Hickory Farms, the transformation just felt wrong, like a serious game changer.

As much as I liked him, I decided Mallory was to blame. In my kid's mind, his presence led not just to the hair thing, but also to my mother being up onstage night after night wearing tiny cutoff shorts and halter tops, singing some of Rodgers and Hammerstein's loveliest songs, dancing, shampooing her hair onstage with real water as she sang "I'm Gonna Wash That Man Right Outa My Hair," and passionately kissing an odious man who was not my father.

Most of us Nunn kids had roles, too, except for Oliver, who never appeared on the stage and avoided Mallory as much as possible. My cousins Toni and Susan and I were dancing, singing nurses, as were our friends. My sister Lisa was a native child, painted orange. Uncle John was in charge of the box office. Aunt Mariah was a stage manager.

I don't think any of us enjoyed seeing my mother necking with a man wearing a Panama suit and lots of pancake makeup—in front of the entire town of Galax. He was married with three kids, a local church minister, and the head, ironically enough, of the local alcohol rehab center. But my father, who had placed my mother on a pedestal of some remove, had no clue that she was falling in love with this stiff little version of Emile de Becque.

Whether I had a clue or not, I pretended it was Mallory who was responsible for my parents' divorce when it came, not long after the sets had been struck. I could never stand to blame my parents for anything.

I was always afraid she'd get rid of all of us, too, if we upset her. The same way she had ditched her best friend, Millie, not much earlier, after the big cast party for *The Music Man*. My mother's breakups seemed to mark the endings of theatrical productions.

Millie and her husband, Al, were native New Yorkers, who'd met my parents and John and Mariah during bowling league when a lot of us kids were still toddlers. Al had arrived in town as a textile designer for one of the factories. They were Jewish, neurotic, and fabulous in a way that made our world seem Technicolored for knowing them. Al played a silver cornet (usually in their downstairs powder room off his office, for the acoustics), and he was a cartoonist whose work hung in all of our houses. Millie was hilarious and creative and the most stylish dresser for miles around—her clothes were from New York! And best of all, they absolutely loved us. Their daughter Tracey was one of my closest friends, along with Toni; the three of us were together all the time, cackling and whispering like magpies. But before my parents got divorced, my mother had gotten mad at Millie, a woman she'd spent hours on the phone with each day, and with no explanation to any of us, without ever telling Millie why, my mother completely stopped talking to her. I remember Al coming over to our giant glass and stone house begging my mother to stop whatever this was, to take Millie back, to resume this valuable thing: a friendship. But she wouldn't. And if you tried to get her to explain, to talk about it, the threat that you would end up standing out in the cold with Millie was palpable.

In a town of six thousand, everyone knew about this inexplicable rift. It effectively ended my friendship with Tracey and made so many of our other social interactions at our high school of four hundred students odd and uncomfortable. It separated us from the other Nunn cousins to a certain extent, during holidays and parties—any social event. Because people who are true friends don't allow others to stay out in the cold unless they choose to. We began to have separate celebrations with my family before everyone else would go to Millie and Al's for Christmas. (They had the best Christmas parties ever, and made me want to be Jewish.) Even today, when I look at photo albums where we're all still together, during the holidays, it's wrenching. Our family would get smaller and smaller and smaller.

●

After my mother's request for a divorce, there was no discussion of counseling, or how it would affect the five children they'd produced, four of whom were still living in the house, trying to grow up. And she didn't ask for alimony or seem to have a plan for how she would support us, put us through college, or maintain our giant household, which began to deteriorate in symbolic ways: the wooden parquet tiles came loose from the floor, exposing large patches of concrete; the sliding glass doors leaked during rainstorms; and the hot water heater in the attic froze and burst in the winter, pouring water all over our playroom upstairs.

Elaine and I got clued in on this new direction our family would be taking, before Oliver, Michael, or Lisa were told, during my mother's next semiprivate performance: at the Roy Rogers hamburger restaurant in Chapel Hill, North Carolina, which had, to my fourteen-year-old palate, the best cheeseburgers in all the land—they toasted and buttered the buns, the meat was pink inside and juicy, there was lettuce, tomato, and pickles. Onion, if you asked.

Mother had taken me out of school, which she often did when she didn't want to do something alone (she took me along to the grocery store, the bank, to take the census one year—all of which

I considered a huge honor, by the way). This time I had gone with her to pick up Elaine for winter break during her freshman year at the University of North Carolina, where she'd joined a sorority and had apparently been consuming nothing but Tab. It would have been fine for Mother to have given us the news in a fast-food restaurant, but Elaine's preppy, clean-cut boyfriend, James, was with us, too.

"There's something I've needed to tell you for some time," Mother said, sitting next to me in the plastic booth, her hair piled up, red lips like a movie star, sipping iced tea through a straw.

She looked "theatrical," and that scared me. It was a look she got on her face: chin up, one eyebrow raised, very still, as if she were about to deliver Hamlet's soliloquy. Something meaningful was going to be said. (She had had this look a lot lately, followed by staring off into the distance, while fixing dinner.)

Great, I thought. I instinctively picked up my burger, took a big bite, and started chewing.

After a pause of excruciating length, she said, "Your father and I are getting a divorce." And then she was silent again. It wasn't until I was in my thirties and covering theater at the *New Yorker* that I realized she was a giant scenery chewer. Back then, though, this kind of behavior had a powerful effect on us.

She announced this to the table at large and anyone else at Roy Rogers within earshot, even though Daddy was not James's father. Why was he here? Elaine's eyes got wide, and then she broke down in sobs, which surprised me. I felt awkward. I'd always relied on Elaine's behavior for clues on how to behave myself, so I cried, too, although I was acutely aware that I had only eaten a couple of bites of my delicious, drippy cheeseburger, sitting on its tray half-wrapped in paper. And none of the fries.

I don't remember if my mother explained *why* they were divorcing. "Is there anything you want to ask?" she said, after we'd had our little breakdowns. This felt like a booby trap. I certainly wondered why she wasn't telling Michael, Oliver, and Lisa—all of us at the same time—but I didn't dare ask, because I knew that if I asked a question (or uttered a statement) that made her feel blamed for something, I'd get either the full-on silent treatment or the long-winded hurt tirade about her own feelings that never enlightened me and left me feeling empty and full of guilt. So I shook my head no.

James, the boyfriend, looked utterly stunned. He put his arm around Elaine and tried to be conversational. "I'm very sorry, Mrs. Nunn. This is a very difficult thing for a family to face." Poor James. I felt bad for him, having to be there with us.

We left our food unfinished—it seemed incorrect to continue eating a big meal—and dropped off James at his frat house before starting back to Galax.

Until this point, the only couples I knew who'd gotten divorced in our town were the hopeless, clownlike drunks who wife-swapped and crashed their cars and whose children became so fucked up that they talked openly about their parents' antics ("My father is seeing his whore on silk sheets in Los Angeles this weekend," my friend Sally said, baffling me at age ten) and smoked cigarettes at age twelve, which my mother had always condemned as "tacky."

•

I don't remember Daddy packing anything or any further discussion about the divorce. One day, he simply didn't live in the house he'd built for all of us anymore. He'd been ejected from his own life.

Not long after the divorce was out in the open, my brother Michael came home from a Friday night out with some of his basketball friends and found Daddy asleep in his Tornado, parked in our driveway next to one of the stone and cedar lanterns that cast fairylike circular patterns of light on the grass and pavement. This was stunning and confusing. Michael, who was crying when he told us, went upstairs to his room and didn't come out for what felt like days. My mother seemed to feel that Michael and Daddy were doing something intended to hurt her.

"Go knock on your brother's door," she told me, looking as if every moment of his silence and solitude were killing her soul, as if she were the person who needed consoling rather than my brother.

Very soon Emile de Becque began to slyly move into our house, leaving his pipe and tobacco in my father's antique lap desk that Oliver had given him for his birthday, telling us to turn off lights we weren't using, making remarks about how we needed to help our mother and the fact that girls who played sports were tomboys (this, directed at me, when I came home with trophies). But we were never allowed to acknowledge the fact that my mother had divorced our father to be with him, despite the town gossip. We had to pretend, along with her, that it was just a coincidence, and defend her. Even if it was just to ourselves. To do otherwise, to ask questions, meant being crushed by her silence and hurt and anger over being confronted with the truth. We knew we had to go along with the unreality.

Mom started adding the spice mixture Beau Monde to the scrambled eggs in the morning, which turned them green. This was for Emile. His three nerdy and rather mean-spirited kids started coming over on the weekends, the two girls (who saw themselves as extremely talented vocalists) singing in their dog-whistle voices, turning my only home into theirs. Sometimes, Emile played the guitar and sang, too. Excruciating.

Later, after I got my driver's license, I was forced to drive them back home after their visits. I would pull into the driveway of their mother's house and she would come out and stare at me with hateful eyes, as if I had stolen her gross husband who my mother insisted looked like Robert Goulet, as if that were good, when in fact he looked like Karl Malden.

"He fills my cup," she actually said to me, while I was waiting for a friend to pick me up for Saturday tennis practice. Way too much information. Emile de Becque was patting her hand.

"Okay, bye, I'm leaving," I said, over the patting. "Enjoy your squalorous intimacy." I had just learned the word *squalorous* from a J. D. Salinger book.

This other family soon got so comfortable in my father's lovely house that they forgot it was already occupied. One afternoon, I took my math book way down to the bottom of the hill, where the yard met a big grassy field, to do my homework in the Pawleys Island

Hammock that Daddy had hung between two locust trees. I could lie there with my Scottish terrier in the hammock and work on math problems while the sun set over the rolling hills that fronted the Blue Ridge Mountains. As long as I could recall, it had been my habit to stay outdoors until the very last minute, until dark, to delay being home. Home was chaos.

Sometimes I could hear Billy Spivey practicing his trumpet across the highway and down in a little valley. I fell asleep in the hammock, and when I woke up it was dark, and the lights were on in the house. I walked up the hill and opened the door, and Emile and his kids and my mother were having dinner at our large square breakfast table, big enough for our original family of seven, made of pink Formica to match the floral wallpaper in the kitchen. Elaine was at college; I don't know where my other real siblings were. But these people had forgotten to call me in for dinner. I was not a part of their group, apparently not a part of my mother's plan anymore. She didn't really have one.

But long before my mother had even asked my clueless and perhaps careless father for a divorce, the gossips in Galax had determined that my mother was having an affair. Except rather than with Emile de Becque it was with the dancer and director Mallory from New York City. That was the best they could do. You'd almost think nobody in town had ever seen a gay man. Or ever admitted to knowing or being one. I believed that Mallory had a big heart, but I also believed for a long time that had he never shown up in Galax, my parents would have been a happy couple.

It was no surprise that people wondered about my mother's relationship to Mallory. He was at our house all the time and became, very casually, a large part of our lives. He cussed when we weren't allowed to and even had a say in what we ate.

"Susan," he'd say to my mother, in his nondescript accent, "make me some of that purple shit." And she would. He was referring to this Jell-O salad. Everyone—not just Mallory—raved when she made it, including the people at church potlucks. It was a signature dish.

Purple Shit

Serves 10 to 12

2 (3-ounce) packages grape Jell-O (or blackberry if grape is not
   available)

1 teaspoon unflavored gelatin

2 cups boiling water

1 (15.5-ounce) can crushed pineapple

1 (21-ounce) can blueberry pie filling

1 (8-ounce) package cream cheese, at room temperature

1 (8-ounce) container sour cream

½ cup granulated sugar

1 teaspoon vanilla

1. Dissolve the Jell-O and unflavored gelatin in the water. Stir in the
   pineapple and blueberry pie filling.
2. Cream together the cream cheese, sour cream, sugar, and vanilla.
3. In a 7 x 11-inch clear ovenproof glass dish, spread half the Jell-O
   mixture. Put it in the refrigerator and let it set. Once this happens,
   spread the cream cheese mixture on top, pour on the rest of the
   Jell-O mixture, and gently spread it.

●

I found the recipe and made it once in the California desert, when Elaine came out to pick up Maggie the rescue dog, and after taking a couple of bites we decided that it might not be that good after all. Maybe I'd screwed it up or maybe we'd outgrown it.

But we both liked the sour-cream-cream-cheese-layer concept, so we decided to change the Purple Shit into this elegant recipe for spicy layered aspic. It's really lovely served in parfait dishes or molded in custard cups or other similar molds that you can slip the gelatin out of and serve prettily with a cold shrimp on top and an edible leaf of some sort underneath.

Elaine and Emily's Bloody Mary Aspic

Serves 6 to 8

3 cups tomato juice, V8 juice, or a mix of the two

½ cup finely chopped red, yellow, or orange bell pepper

½ cup finely chopped cucumber, peeled and seeded

½ cup finely chopped shallot

½ cup finely chopped celery (include leaves)

2 jalapeños, finely chopped

2 garlic cloves, crushed

⅓ cup lemon juice

2 tablespoons olive oil, plus more for the mold

1 tablespoon cider vinegar

1 tablespoon plus 1 teaspoon salt

½ teaspoon smoked paprika

1 teaspoon cayenne pepper

2 tablespoons Tabasco sauce

2 envelopes powdered unflavored gelatin

1 (8-ounce) package cream cheese, at room temperature

1 (8-ounce) container sour cream

1. In a large bowl, combine 1 cup of the tomato juice, the bell pepper, cucumber, shallot, celery, jalapeños, garlic, lemon juice, oil, vinegar, salt, paprika, cayenne, and Tabasco.
2. In a small bowl, pour 1 cup of the tomato juice over the gelatin; stir and let sit while heating the remaining 1 cup tomato juice to a boil in a small saucepan. Pour the heated tomato juice over the gelatin mixture and stir until all the granules have melted. Mix the gelatin mixture into the vegetable mixture.
3. Meanwhile, cream the cream cheese and sour cream.
4. Lightly oil a mold or several small molds. Divide half the aspic mixture among the chosen containers; refrigerate until firm. Spread the sour cream mixture on top of the firm aspic, then top with the

final layer of aspic mixture. Refrigerate for at least 4 hours before unmolding.

●

I love this recipe, not just because we created it together from a shared food memory, but because it felt like something was coming untangled, being released—turning into something delicious and modern without destroying the original completely, something updated to suit the life I'd begun to allow myself to imagine. The purple salad became funny and endearing rather than a sign of something broken and sad, the pivotal salad served during a time when my mother began to realize she'd made a terrible mistake by having us at all. Or that's the way it had seemed to me. It was just a dish that suited us back then, a dish that we had loved and thought of as very fancy, but a dish that suited us no longer.

Seven

THE IDEA OF A FAMILY

In many parts of the country and the world, overcooked food is ruined food. You, as the cook, might choke it down, but you'd never serve the results to a guest. In the South, though, the line between cooked enough and overcooked is very wide. Stewing goes on much longer here, with little or no complaint. Which is to say it was the right place for me to stay for a while. I had believed my Comfort Food Tour was on hold, but the longer I was with Toni, the more it became apparent that the South, my family, and my quest were all a part of me, unfolding naturally, with a life of their own. That seemed right.

As Toni and I drove away from Courtland toward Atlanta, we went over the only solid plan I'd made: staying with her until it was time to go to the Old Fiddlers' Convention in Galax, the second weekend in August.

When it was time for lunch, we pulled off the interstate in Henderson, North Carolina, and found Nunnery-Freeman Barbecue, a bare-bones roadside joint, with low ceilings and packing-plant decor. The minute we slid into an empty vinyl booth with a view of the other diners' run-down pickup trucks, a waitress brought over a little bowl of hot crispy hush puppies—not the balls, the oblong fingers.

We ordered North Carolina–style barbecue, which is vinegar-based and the best.

Actually, Addie asked for an entire chicken dinner, because she didn't want *just one leg*; the three sides it came with arrived on a separate plate because the giant fried breast, wing, and leg needed their own. My pulled pork sandwich, on a white bun with a scant spoonful of vinegar coleslaw and a generous squirt of vinegar sauce from a sticky red bottle on the table, was just like a million other pulled pork sandwiches eaten daily throughout North Carolina. The food is almost always good at places like this.

After we'd eaten, Toni grabbed a pair of the leftover hush puppies that were stuck together in a permanent grin, a set of extra-puffy, golden-brown, deep-fried corn bread lips. She placed them over her mouth, to make a big hush puppy smile, which made me burst into laughter. Joy again. It felt like having an arrow removed from my chest.

I decided then to throw myself into the life of Toni's family, as if it were my own. Hoping to learn by example. Thinking of ways to use the enormous crop of tomatoes ripening in Toni's raised vegetable patch kept us busy in the kitchen when we got back to her home in Atlanta. We took Addie and Mariah to the pool and watched them leap bravely from the high diving board, flying through space in their cute bathing suits. Their wet eyelashes stuck together in dazzling fairy-child clumps, and they turned purple and shivered until we rubbed them with beach towels, even though the sun was scorching the top of my head like a crème brûlée.

We took the girls to the nearby branch library to check out stacks of books about horses (Mariah) and cartoon dogs (Addie), to horrible, age-appropriate cartoon movie musicals, to get haircuts in a salon where the chairs were shaped like race cars, and down a long gravel road to riding lessons, where Toni and I ceased to exist once the horses were in sight. A familiar instinct was coming back to me the more time I spent with the girls. "Addie, you have to put your helmet on *before* you get on your horse," I called. Their skulls were as fragile as eggs! Addie turned around, put one hand up, a stop sign, and whisper-yelled back, "Yeah, yeah, yeah, Emily. O-kaaaaaay."

We picked sun-warmed tomatoes and carried them to the kitchen in our shirts to make sandwiches. My friend John once told me that you don't need a recipe for a sandwich, after I'd just given him a recipe for a sandwich. This is not true with the tomato sandwich. At the very least, you need a strict guide. I couldn't let Toni eat an ordinary tomato sandwich if I could make a perfect one for both of us.

Here is the only way to make a tomato sandwich, ever:

You need a perfectly ripe red tomato that is heavy with juice. It is my experience that the yellow ones do not have the acidity necessary to create the tart spark of contrast to the preposterous amount of mayo you'll also need, along with salt, pepper, and white bread. I prefer Pepperidge Farm Very Thin Sliced Bread, but you can use any white sliced bread as long as you don't include focaccia or a bun or a bagel in that category. Never toast it. Use real mayonnaise—no Miracle Whip, which is, according to the jar, a dressing. If that's all you have, just don't make the sandwich.

Slice the tomato with a sharp knife into quarter-inch slices. Slather *both* pieces of bread with so much mayonnaise that you can't see the texture of the bread through it; think of it as a main ingredient rather than a condiment. Sprinkle one side liberally with sea salt, the other with freshly ground black pepper. Place a few slices of tomato on one side of the bread. (If you're lucky, you'll have tomato slices that match the size of the bread.) Here you may add some shavings or a slice of extra sharp cheddar cheese. Assemble and slice on the diagonal, never crosswise. Eat it. Make another one and eat that, too.

Toni couldn't believe how good it was. "I never thought about putting cheese on it," she said.

"Bea taught me that," I replied, meaning our grandmother, who also insisted on Pepperidge Farm Very Thin Sliced Bread.

"You mean when she wasn't eating candy?" Toni asked.

That made us miss her and start telling Bea stories.

Beatrice Mercedes Messer Nunn was the daughter of my mean great-grandmother, Augusta. We often called her Tippy (which we'd come up with as kids, when we decided to give everyone dog names). She loved sweets and had candy dishes all over her house, allegedly "for the kids," since she was a diabetic. It was cheap candy, too: lemon drops, Brach's Bridge Mix, cream drops, jelly beans, and a few wrapped things, like Kraft Caramels. Which was A-OK, because we weren't picky.

Tippy read millions of books, grew orchids, and watched reruns of *Murder, She Wrote* ("I love my Angela Lansbury").

Since she couldn't eat the candy, she made delicious bowls of ambrosia and kept small cans of apricot nectar on hand. As much as she loved fruit, its preservation didn't interest her. "Remember the bananas?" Toni said, folding one hand over the other. If Bea wanted just a *bite* of a banana, she'd have it, then casually fold over the loose flap of peel, as if that had some preservative power, before putting it back in the fruit bowl for later. These half-eaten bananas, which she insisted were "self-sealing," gathered up, as did other evidence of her fruit habit—half an orange turned facedown on a plate in the living room, next to a teacup, a pear positioned the same way on her nightstand.

All of these things endeared her to me.

"I wouldn't have called her a hoarder," I said to Toni. "But when it came to food, she kept a lot of things around that no longer identified as food."

"The bar of almond paste," Toni said. Every few months, one of us would pull out an ancient square bar, the label on its tinfoil wrapper eroded beyond recognition, and try to throw it out. "I might need that," she'd say, and we'd leave it to find again.

Bea did whatever she wanted. Despite her fat-cat industrialist father's furious disapproval, just out of college she had married an extremely handsome railway man she'd met while teaching school in nearby Austinville. "I thought he was the strong, silent type," she loved to say, "but he was just dull." They had three children before deciding enough was enough. While waiting for the divorce to go through, she took Daddy, his brother, John (Toni's father), and sister, Judy, to Florida temporarily. They rarely saw their father after that; he disappeared to his hometown a couple of hours away. After raising her children (she sent the boys to military school), she spent the rest of her life alone, without the comfort and companionship of a husband, playing bridge with a gang of old ladies in Galax, down the hill from Aunt Mariah and Uncle John's house; traveling around the world (she took me and Toni to England and Scotland when I was in the ninth grade, and the entire family on the *Queen Elizabeth 2*'s Christmas cruise before my parents got divorced); growing her precious lilies, the scent of which instantly brings her back to me; baking hams; working as a professional studio photographer; decorating cakes with ornate icing flowers, which we received on our birthdays; and painting quite well (I own one of her egg temperas of apples, which has hung in every kitchen I've had). Toward the end of the golden years of her father's furniture and mirror plants, she staged a coup and took charge of them herself before selling them off. Despite the fact that she was not exactly an experienced businesswoman, I am told she was quite a hard-ass during her brief reign.

Bea, who was only five foot three, had a giant Great Dane named Midi who was always accidentally knocking her over. She clipped the dog's ears so late they wouldn't stand up, so the vet told her to re-splint them with hospital tape and something stiff. The dog ran around the neighborhood with tampons Bea had found in the downstairs bathroom taped to her ears.

Back then the only clue I'd had that she might not have been an ideal mother was the fact that she stiffened up, just like my Scottish terrier, when you hugged her. But she was a wonderful grandmother. She wasn't perfect. For one thing, she wasn't crazy about Jews, even though her father, John Alvin Messer, was Jewish, a fact that her daughter, my aunt Judy, later documented in two large and impeccably researched genealogical histories of the Messer family, Russians who arrived in the United States from Kiev.

"Well. Are all my granddaughters going to shack up with Jews?" she asked me during a holiday visit. I was the only one living with a Jew, in New York. Elaine and Lisa had married theirs. We had a natural affinity.

"God, Tippy, be an anti-Semite why don't you?" I said, taken aback.

"I don't dislike Jews," she replied.

"It's a good thing, 'cause you are one," Oliver told her.

But she'd been taught to pretend otherwise, and those kinds of things, preconceptions about what you should and should not be ashamed of, stick with you. By the time Aunt Judy, an excellent writer, historian, and keeper of family history, had produced several large books documenting the true history of the Messers and the Nunns, Bea had passed away. The day before her funeral, Toni, Susan, Lisa, and I took a bag of lemon drops and a box of candied almonds to the funeral home and placed them in her coffin.

Bea laughed all the time and she was never dull. And, as a grand-mother, at least, she was very clear: you never had to wonder how she felt about you, what she thought. If she criticized you, it was because she was worried about you, rather than about how you might be making her look. Because she wasn't worried at all about what anyone thought about her. I valued that fact and missed her desperately when she was gone.

One of my very fondest memories is of going with her and her sister Gertie (Gertrude Augusta) to the beach for a week the summer before I moved to New York. They played bridge and wore muu-muus and I took them to get their hair done at the mall. We roasted a chicken one night and made sandwiches from the leftovers with farm stand tomatoes and this mayonnaise, which she jotted down on a pad for me right there; I still have it somewhere. Even though Duke's brand is pretty great, there is absolutely nothing like home-made mayonnaise.

Bea's Blender Mayo (verbatim)

Makes 1⅓ cups

1 egg

½ teaspoon dry mustard

½ teaspoon salt

2 tablespoons vinegar

1 cup of salad oil (by this she meant Wesson)

Break the egg in a blender and add the mustard, salt, vinegar, and
¼ cup of the oil. Cover and turn the blender on low speed. Immediately uncover, with the blender on, and pour the remaining ¾ cup
oil in a slow, steady stream. Cut off the motor (this means "turn off"
in southern) and stir. Turn on blender briefly. Be sure the blender
is dry when you start.

●

One thing Bea didn't mention in the recipe was that you should have
everything at room temperature before you start. Obviously, you can
use different oils, such as olive or walnut or grapeseed or peanut (just
make sure it's fresh, and make sure the egg is super-fresh, too). And
you can add garlic to make aioli, or soft herbs. Don't keep it longer
than two days in the fridge. And don't leave it sitting out on the
counter, like a crazy person.

●

Richard and Toni were thinking about selling their house, so the two
of us labored in the Georgia sun like members of a chain gang: we
cleaned out the garage and weeded the giant sandbox where a swing
set and a fort on stilts were located. This was absolutely exhausting—
it was so overgrown it was like pulling up the yard. Toni had sprayed
it with some kind of poison that I was sure was seeping into my
garden gloves. We trimmed the hedges, picked up all the sticks in
the yard, and stared at the asparagus plants, pretending they would
produce something edible this year.

We took walks in the evening, looking for blackberry bushes in
the dark to remember for later. I went to Toni's hellish 6:00 a.m.
boot-camp workout class a couple of times, which nearly killed me,
but seemed to pep Toni up.

Toni and I cooked and cooked. She produced a batch of her famous tomato sauce, I made my dough, and we threw a pizza together
to slip onto the hot stone: slices of soft buffalo mozzarella, garden
tomatoes and basil, paper-thin slices of red onion and garlic. The girls
didn't eat it. It didn't look like pizza to them, with its gorgeously mis-

shapen crust, all bumpy and bubbled, slightly burnt rings of onion, and the green herbs blighting it all.

We split and roasted a load of her plum tomatoes with tons of garlic and handfuls of fresh basil that perfumed our fingers when we tore it, letting them roast on very low heat for hours until they were transformed into a savory caramelized jam. We tossed that, still warm, with hot pasta, more fresh basil, and chunks of buffalo mozzarella, which melted just enough to bring out its sweet mellowness. Sometimes Toni added chopped jalapeños from the garden, which made the dish something else altogether, painful but invigorating to eat.

For Richard (because he loves it), we made a giant banana pudding the traditional southern way, with vanilla wafers and slices of banana studding the sweet creamy pudding; it looked like a Wayne Thiebaud painting in its glass trifle bowl.

Richard is strictly a carnivore, so Toni usually grilled a steak for him when he got home from work each night, along with making whatever she was feeding the girls, which was very different from what she liked to eat. She loves spicy food, but she gets exhausted from cooking several different meals; often her own dinner got short shrift. So I showed her how to make a zesty dish that you can have ready in a snap because almost every ingredient was canned (scandal): kidney beans, tomatoes, coconut milk, and Thai red curry paste—the kinds of things you might overlook in your cupboard when you think you have absolutely nothing left to cook, nothing left to give to people you love, nothing left for yourself. It is absolutely delicious.

Spicy Beans with Coconut Milk

(adapted from *Southern Living* magazine)

Serves 4

1 small onion, finely chopped

2 tablespoons olive oil

4 garlic cloves, minced

2 to 3 tablespoons Thai red curry paste (the kind in a can is
   always more potent than the jarred)

2 (15-ounce) cans kidney beans, rinsed and drained

1 (14.5-ounce) can Italian plum tomatoes, preferably San Marzano,
   with their juice, crushed with your hands over the pan

1 (13.5-ounce) can coconut milk (you can use light, but it's better with
   the real thing; just so you know, it has 900 calories in a single can)

1 teaspoon salt

2 tablespoons maple syrup

Zest and juice of 1 large lime

4 cups hot cooked basmati or long grain rice

TOPPINGS

4 scallions, chopped (optional)

A handful chopped fresh cilantro (optional)

1. Sauté the onion in a Dutch oven with the oil over medium-high heat until translucent, about 5 minutes.
2. Add the garlic; sauté for 1 minute.
3. Add the curry paste, sauté for 1 minute. Stir in the beans, tomatoes, coconut milk, salt, and maple syrup. Bring to a boil, reduce the heat, and simmer for 30 minutes.
4. Add the lime zest and juice. Serve over rice and sprinkle with toppings, if using.

●

Every day we sat together around their breakfast room table, our positions established by place cards the girls made. I felt at home, like I belonged at that table, and not just because I had helped make the things we ate there. Occasionally I felt joy, which took me by surprise. We baked corn bread and drank tons of coffee, and Toni drank a little red wine at night after our walks, sometimes with a single mini Snickers bar, sitting out on the back deck, looking at the stars.

Even though I didn't go to meetings for a while after I left California, I never thought about having a glass with her. I felt so much better—physically, at least—that it held no allure for me. No one ever believes that, of course—even if, like me, you have always been very open about your drinking; in my case specifically, about having been in rehab before, being in AA, and about relapsing.

And thanks to an email Toni received, I understood that Elaine was not a believer, in either my sobriety or my responsibility, especially when it came to the luxurious gifts I had received from her. Although I'd only left Santa Barbara a few weeks ago, I started to get the awful feeling that she was now furious about giving them to me. But most of all I got the feeling that I had managed to overdraw my "family" account, financial and emotional.

In our family, needing help or a little compassion when you were unlucky or afraid rarely turned out well. It was part of the reason I'd spent most of my IRA on our household back in Chicago when I'd taken over the stay-at-home stepmother role. I couldn't run the risk of letting the Engineer think I was trying to *get* something from him, such as care and comfort I might not deserve.

At this point, if the bill came due, I apparently owed Elaine more money than the Engineer had finally given me as a sort of alimony, to get rid of me. I owed her not just for the clothes, the salon makeover, meals out, and Betty Ford, but for letting me stay in the desert house with no rent or utility bills, among other things. It had been a very expensive visit. And now half my belongings were out in California, too.

I had no home, no idea how to get one, and no job, a fact that gnawed at me: How do you look for a job when you don't live anywhere?

Our communication, or miscommunication, was now so fraught that it was never clear whether Elaine actually intended for me to repay her for all these things—or the exact balance of my debt to her. I just didn't know. What I knew was that I felt ashamed, as if I *had* actually been drinking and tried to fleece my own sister. I felt that I was failing Elaine somehow. And maybe I was. But I also remembered what my young psychiatrist told me back at the hospital in Chicago: I might become a scapegoat in my dysfunctional family now that my brother was dead. They would need someone to blame their tangled feelings on. "Make sure you don't internalize that," she said.

I did anyway, but I was also so relieved to be with time. She made me feel normal and strong, like I was a lucky s rather than a guilty broken mope who was the cause of everyone pain, simply because I'd fallen apart. "You may have to rethink your idea of who your family is," Toni said to me, more than once.

With that, instead of beating myself up, I decided: *Time to make bread*. I made the dough for the famous no-knead Mark Bittman–Jim Lahey bread, but for the first time in years, it didn't rise. I have a picture of it straight out of the oven: a flat biblical loaf that would not feed multitudes because nobody wanted to eat it. "Maybe we should do the rolls," Toni said, holding it over the trash.

The rolls. I had once believed the rolls could cure everything. This is not as absurd as you might think after you've had them. According to Aunt Mariah, they're not Parker House rolls, even though they look like it, shaped like little purses. "They-ah just rolls," she says.

After Aunt Mariah cuts the soft baby-flesh dough into circles, she dips each one in "buttah" and folds it over gently, so as not to bruise it. She lines them up in one of her old aluminum baking pans or cookie sheets, snuggled together so that they touch one another, and bakes them until they turn the yellow brown of a newly ripe acorn. They are like brioche, almost—not as coarse but sweet and slightly yeasty and tender with a bit of crisp on the outside. When you put butter on them, you might as well up and die right there.

These rolls, I recalled, had been an early catalyst for my wanderings, the spring before Oliver died. The Engineer and I were at a low point; the silence between us punishing. But I was beginning to realize that accepting dysfunction was a choice, one that my upbringing had led me to, but perhaps not the right choice.

Rather than check into a hotel room and drink a bottle of wine, as I had done before during the bouts of silence, I decided to do something that would make me feel good instead of punishing myself even more, and asked Aunt Mariah if I could come down to Galax for a cooking weekend.

And it had worked beautifully. Toni came, too, with the girls; Kello cousin Martha came, and Uncle John even video-recorded the lesson

128 · EMILY NUNN

on the rolls. But he put the camera on top of the refrigerator, aimed it at Toni, and left the room, so it is just a record of Toni reacting to her mother making rolls she'd eaten all her life, as if she were on a cooking show. After our lessons, we made them three more times in a row, at Aunt Mariah's insistence. "It takes practice," she said, but then we realized she was just stocking them up in her freezer for the holidays.

During this trip, Toni and I also made a broad but random investigation of the amazing community cookbooks Martha had brought along from Tidewater, Virginia, which are unlike a lot of Junior League, Lions Club International, or church group cookbooks, which always seem heavy on fluffy Jell-O-mold delights identified as salads, macaroni salad recipes, and the kind of run-of-the-mill party food and hors d'oeuvres made with sausage and canned crescent rolls that people think they want when they're drunk. We made photocopies from them, and from Aunt Mariah's several recipe boxes—actual wooden boxes filled with index cards, some with handwritten recipes to which a clipping from a magazine or newspaper had been taped or glued. Some were fancy index cards for recipes, decorated with a picture of an old-fashioned stove or a border of tiny cooking tools and ingredients dancing together, printed with such headings as "Here's What's Cookin' _____" and "Recipe from the Kitchen of _____."

There were three different recipes for sweet potato pie, and several versions of both Tea Time Tassies and Texas Sheet Cake. Dumplings in several guises turned up, as did various incarnations of cobblers, pies, and corn bread. I found a recipe for something terrific called Easter Pie, which I'm definitely making someday: it uses two pounds of ricotta cheese, six eggs, a pint of cream, just half a cup of sugar, and it is baked in a crust in a "modest" oven.

My mother's delicious "vegetable" soup was in there (a pound of lean boiling beef is the first ingredient; it serves fifteen), in her familiar, perfect handwriting. So was Bea's Baked Custard and her Magic Salad Dressing—everyone's favorite—that she chilled then used to drench nothing more than chunks of peeled tomato, onion, and roughly chopped blocks of iceberg lettuce. It was somehow perfect. Now that Bea is gone, Aunt Mariah's salad with crumbled blue cheese, pine nuts, and her raspberry vinaigrette is our new old-fashioned favorite.

Grandmother's decadent recipe for Coconut Icing (coconut, sugar, sour cream—that's it) was folded into the lid of one recipe box. On the back of the recipe was one of her absurd lists: radio, alarm clock, presents, bathrobe, sweater. She always had a list like that in her kitchen, and it always seemed to have an alarm clock on it.

It was like going on an archaeological dig, back into a past where my mother still spoke to everyone in the family and all of her Galax friends she'd parted ways with, and even gave them recipes, had parties with them, and held luncheons. When women still had to write everything down and they saw one another in person—just dropped by. They needed lots of recipes for the kind of food you served at garden club meetings. Aunt Mariah's Lemon Sponge Cups (which I jotted down right on the spot, even before Toni and I photocopied everything) were the very thing after a lunch of chicken salad (served in a tomato) and sweet iced tea with mint.

Aunt Mariah's Rolls

Makes about 4 dozen rolls, depending on the size biscuit cutter used

¾ cup plus 1 teaspoon granulated sugar

¼ teaspoon ground ginger

2 packages dry yeast

2 cups warm water

½ cup powdered skim milk

3 large eggs, well beaten

4 tablespoons (½ stick) unsalted butter, melted

6 cups all-purpose flour, plus more if needed

1. In a very large bowl, preferably a ceramic or electric-mixer one, dissolve the 1 teaspoon sugar, the ginger—do not leave out the ginger; no excuses—yeast, and water. Set aside. In another bowl, mix the milk, eggs, the ¾ cup sugar, and the butter and add to the yeast mixture (make sure this has begun to foam slightly; if not, you

may need new yeast). Slowly add 2 cups of the flour to this, mixing well. Gradually mix in the remaining 4 cups flour; if the dough is still sticky, add more flour, a bit at a time.

2. Cover the bowl with a clean dishcloth and put in a warm place to rise. Once it has risen to its full glory (meaning when it has doubled in bulk, which takes about 1 hour), punch it down and knead gently for a minute or so on a floured board. Roll out the dough to ¼ inch thickness and cut out circles with a 2¾-inch biscuit cutter. Dip them in the melted butter, fold over (pinch them down a bit so they stay folded), and place on baking sheets very close together but with the sides not touching. Cover and let rise again, for about 1 hour, by which time they will have doubled in bulk and their sides will touch. In the meantime, preheat the oven to 400°F. Bake for 12 to 15 minutes, or until golden brown. If you plan to freeze them, bake only until they are very lightly browned.

Bea's Magic Salad Dressing

Makes 4 cups

1 cup water
1 cup vegetable oil
1½ cups cider vinegar
Pinch of salt
Pinch of freshly ground black pepper
Pinch of granulated sugar
½ cup tomato juice
1 teaspoon dry mustard (optional)

Shake the water, oil, vinegar, salt, pepper, sugar, tomato juice, and mustard (if using) in a large jar (I think she used an old applesauce jar) and refrigerate. Before serving, swish a few ice cubes around in the jar; discard them before they've melted.

I told myself that no matter what happened to me in the coming weeks or months or decades, I would always have Bea's Magic Salad Dressing and Aunt Mariah's Rolls, something more valuable to me than my platinum and diamond engagement ring from Tiffany. I was so pleased by Aunt Mariah's Lemon Sponge Cups that I shared the recipe on the internet, on Food52, rather than by index card.

Much later, when I had left Chicago for good and was staying in Atlanta, after Toni and I had finished running a million errands in the heat and the girls were across the street playing, I logged on and found out the recipe was a Wildcard Winner (meaning a recipe chosen by the editors rather than by community vote) on Food52, and would be published in the website's upcoming print cookbook, more than a year after I'd posted it. Google the words *Aunt Mariah,* and you'll see she has become a bit of an internet sensation.

Aunt Mariah's Lemon Sponge Cups

Makes 4 to 6

2 tablespoons unsalted butter, at room temperature

1 cup sugar

4 tablespoons all-purpose flour

Pinch of salt

1 lemon, zested and juiced

3 large eggs, separated

1½ cups milk

1. Preheat the oven to 350°F. In a large bowl, cream the butter. Add the sugar, flour, salt, lemon zest, and juice. In a separate bowl, beat the egg yolks; stir in the milk. Slowly add the egg mixture to the butter mixture.

2. Beat the egg whites until stiff; gently fold into the mixture. Pour into 4 to 6 ramekins or individual soufflé dishes (depending on the size; I use four 12-ounce dishes) and place in a pan of hot water.

Bake in a "moderate" oven (350°F, in my case) for 45 minutes. You
will have a layer of lemon custard, with gorgeous, lightly browned
sponge on top. Let cool a bit.

3. Turn out and serve with whipped cream, or serve still in the dish.
   You can also bake this in one large soufflé dish; you'll know it's done
   when the puffed dome is browned and firm. Aunt Mariah likes to
   garnish the puddings with a thin slice of lemon.

●

In my whole life I had never spent this much time with Toni, my
oldest friend, and yet here we were, peacefully coexisting for almost
five weeks, from early July through the first weekend in August.

Toni had no time to waste dwelling on slights. "We never get mad
at each other," she'd say after we got annoyed with each other about
something.

Aunt Mariah's house has always been the same way. No guilt; easy
forgiveness. When we were nine years old, Toni drove us around the
block in Aunt Mariah's Oldsmobile Vista Cruiser. As we pulled into
the driveway, Aunt Mariah ran out, mad as a hornet, screamed at us
for a minute, and tore the keys out of Toni's hand. But we still got to
have a cookout that night, with both hot dogs and hamburgers. At
home, my mother would have sent me to my room for the rest of the
summer, to write essays about automobile death statistics. We'd have
been punished because we had scared *her*.

At Aunt Mariah's, we were always playing or laughing (shrieking)
at something. No stunned bouts of anxiety. And best of all, we could
eat whatever we wanted. Toni *buttered* Pop-Tarts and put them in the
toaster oven. We'd steal a ten-pound paper sack of pistachios from
Uncle John's bar and eat them while reading Archie comics in the
dark basement rec room, even though it was a perfectly beautiful day
and we should have been outside.

Like Aunt Mariah, Toni had set up a guiltless household, where
being a family was just something you *do,* where you were always
welcome just because you happened to be there. Nobody had to die.
Nobody had to be mentally waterboarded. In my family, there was

always some crisis, my mother had been wronged, we were ingrates, and silence was our punishment.

One night, the girls balked at several of Toni's attempts to get them to go to bed. They kept appearing around corners, staring at us as we watched HBO or thumbed through magazines.

"Drag us to bed!" Mariah yelled. Toni had once threatened to do that, and they'd gotten excited and said, "Okay!" So she grabbed them by their ankles and pulled them in their pajamas down the carpeted hall to their bedrooms.

I had thought it was hilarious and fun when my mother commanded one of us to "Slap yourself in the mouth," after cussing, lying, or being critical. After doing something she didn't approve of or being a disappointment . . . as long as it didn't happen to me. We would actually *do* it, lamely, at first. She threatened to do it for us if we didn't slap harder, but it never came to that. We had to punish ourselves so she didn't have to. One night at dinner, Oliver got the command and slapped himself so hard he fell out of his chair, as a joke. Love, breakups, humiliation, choking: everything happens at dinner.

Eight

BELLY OF THE BEAST

All too soon for me, it was time to go back to Galax, Virginia, for the Old Fiddlers' Convention. It was the last place I'd seen Oliver alive; I was pretty sure everyone there would know he was dead, that since his death I had fallen apart, and my life had come crashing down around me.

Toni talked me into going, even though I was nervous about being back there, and she persuaded me to make the trip to Galax in one of Richard's two prop planes. They took me out to the hangar one night to get me used to the idea.

"Emily, it's so safe," Richard said to me, standing near one of his giant metal things—a couple of industrial kitchen refrigerators with a propeller—and throwing out statistics on things that are more dangerous, like getting out of the bathtub.

"Addie flies this plane," he said. I looked over at Addie, who said, "Yeah!" and then pantomimed steering a car off the road.

When the time came, I did it; I even sat in the front, wearing the giant audio headphones Richard, Toni, and the girls immediately donned, so we could hear one another over the engine roar. Once we'd been pulled up into the sky, I felt as if I were being gently pushed down a hallway of puffed clouds in a delicate Tilt-a-Whirl car, slipping and sliding along. It was wonderful. I stopped worrying about the little door to my right flying open, sucking me out into the clouds, and sending me tumbling through the air.

I felt safe, and maybe it was because we were all willing to accept the same fate—just as long as we were together. I think this meant . . . I trusted them. Galax came into view after we came down from the clouds, heading toward the little airstrip north of town.

We could see the Old Fiddlers' Convention already underway, visible as a blotch of campers crowded onto a misshapen oblong of brown earth along Chestnut Creek. It's the oldest and largest old-time and bluegrass (there's a difference) music festival in the country, the home of claw hammer style banjo.

Every year or so, anyone in the extended family still speaking to one another has traditionally traveled back, as a sort of reunion: it used to include my two brothers and two sisters; Toni and Susan and their sister, Kathy; and Jayne and Tracey (my mother's ex-friend Millie and Al's daughters), among others. Aunt Mariah and Uncle John's tremendous Williamsburg-style house, which is set down in the woods with a big deck attached out back, is always the location for dinner and drinks and lot of stories and jokes before we go down to Felts Park, the fairground where the competition takes place onstage, in front of concrete bleachers. We like to wander around the rest of the park, where the campers are parked, and the musicians hang their wash where you can see it, fry chicken out in the open, practice for their time onstage, or just pass the time jamming. People gather in circles around the best bands as they play their hearts out right next to all of their personal belongings.

We do this until two in the morning, steeping ourselves in the damp mountain air. We eat a lot, of course: sweet corn on the cob, which you eat by pulling back the husk and using it as a handle, strawberry shortcake with whipped cream, hot fudge cake with vanilla ice cream, pinto beans with onions, fried catfish, fried pork tenderloin, biscuits, hush puppies, pork-chop sandwiches, watermelon, fresh lemonade (for the vodka), Chinese food (at your own risk), corn dogs (which I happen to love), curly fries, and giant fried funnel cakes coated in confectioners' sugar.

Aside from music and food, the Old Fiddlers' Convention is also the place to catch up on small-town gossip, some of which I myself starred in when I was in my thirties, when I drank too much wine from the big plastic college cups everyone carries past the gate to disguise their alcohol; late in the evening I began flirting in an obnoxious way with a handsome Dobro guitar player—while he was jamming in the parking lot.

Everyone in my family thought this was hilarious rather than pitiful. It made the guitarist's oversensitive (in my opinion), country-fried girlfriend angry; I can still see her face screwed up with fury as I stood very close to her man, flatfooting (or something like it) and grinning at him. She reported me to the town police, and they arrested me for being drunk in public. Which I was.

While I was in a holding trailer at the edge of the park near the horse stalls, I caught up on old times with one of the policemen, whom I'd known forever; he was one of my brother Michael's friends. Meanwhile my cousins and siblings, also probably intoxicated but in a less obvious way, were trying to get me released on the grounds that our family was tight with a local judge, who was also known to enjoy a drink or two.

At around 1:00 a.m., Toni called Uncle John, asking him to get in touch with the judge to throw his weight around. "Toni, he's been dead for six years," said Uncle John, who drove down to spring me from the pokey.

The next morning at breakfast, of course, the fun had not seemed worth the self-inflicted humiliation. I showed up in the kitchen in my pajamas, wearing one of the robes that hung in each room for guests, and started crying. Aunt Mariah gave me a cup of coffee and a bran muffin. The rest of the family laughed at me and turned it into a story that they have threatened to tell to every man I brought back to Galax thereafter. No one ever said, *Gee, Emily, you sure are an alcoholic.* In fact, the only person to take a drink out of my hand and pour it down a sink drain had been Oliver, years later, when he had been sober for years.

This year I wasn't bringing a man, or anyone. I was alone, broke, and sober, the latter of which made me proud. But I'd learned not to announce it. Tell someone you don't drink: they're scandalized. Get so drunk you wear a lampshade (or tinkle in your hostess's lettuce crisper, as a member of my parents' social set had done, back when they and John and Mariah were very young), people think you're a riot, even if you do it every time anyone throws a party.

Not that I have been perfect, as I've said. But as someone who has relapsed, I know that alcohol will do nothing but make me feel bad, almost immediately. Nothing ever feels as good as *not* drinking feels. I've had to accept the surprising fact that because of my honesty, my trustworthiness is in question (particularly with closet alcoholics, who tend to throw the public off their own trail by implying that any questionable behavior you display, as an openly sober person, must be because you're drinking in secret, like they do). Once you've been to rehab a second time, it's a bit like being accused of being defensive: you can't really defend yourself. I know that if I'd been more faithful to AA, I probably could have exited Chicago a lot more gracefully. No one has to remind me.

The important thing is that bran muffin I mentioned; it made me feel better that morning after my incarceration. I had eaten them throughout my childhood and they made me feel sure, falsely, that my incredibly childish behavior would be forgotten someday. These are unforgettable muffins. First, they are true muffins, rather than cupcakes masquerading as muffins. They taste like the bran of oats—nutty and wild as long as you don't obliterate them with too much sugar. Nobody in the family has any idea who Father Tracy is, but to me it sounds like a recipe that might have come out of *Reader's Digest,* attached to an article about Catholic salvation. Or maybe he was somebody's actual father, who baked. Whoever he was, I am much beholden to Father Tracy.

Father Tracy's Bran Muffins

Makes 2 dozen large or 5 dozen very small muffins

1 cup boiling water

1 cup Kellogg's All-Bran Buds

½ cup plus 1 tablespoon Crisco

1½ cups minus 1 tablespoon granulated sugar

2 large eggs, beaten

2 cups Kellogg's All-Bran Original

2 cups buttermilk

2½ cups all-purpose flour

1½ teaspoons baking soda

1 teaspoon salt

1. Preheat the oven to 400°F. Grease a muffin tin.
2. In a small bowl, pour the boiling water over the All-Bran Buds. Set aside.
3. In a large bowl, cream the Crisco with the sugar. Add the eggs, All-Bran Original, and the buttermilk. Sift together the flour, baking soda, and salt. Add to the buttermilk mixture. Stir in the soaked bran buds. Beat well. Bake for 15 minutes.

Note: Must use the 2 types of bran. Makes 2 quarts of very thick batter; will keep in a covered container in the refrigerator for 6 weeks. A cup or so of raisins or chopped dates will make a sweeter muffin.

●

The first thing Toni and I did when we got to Aunt Mariah and Uncle John's house was head directly to the apple-green kitchen. Aunt Mariah was at the far end of the island using the worst knife in the world, her favorite, to slice an Edwards country ham into *sli-vehs,* as she calls them. After she had a pile, we helped her place the slivers on mini biscuits, for appetizers, while she gave us the lowdown on what we needed to do to help.

By the way, I just gave you the recipe for a country ham biscuit, and you probably didn't notice. You slice some ham and you place it on a biscuit: no type of mustard, no condiments of any kind. There's no such thing as a country ham sandwich. Country ham is not for sandwiches. I've had the biscuits with a little butter spread on them, and they were not bad.

Uncle Johnny, who is well over six feet tall with a deep voice, came in with a large McDonald's iced tea and put it in the overpacked refrigerator for Aunt Mariah, who is just over five feet tall, with a sweet, girlish voice.

"Would you like me to make a pitcher of iced tea?" I asked, after John had hugged us and wandered out. But she said no, she liked to get it at McDonald's now.

"Why?" Toni asked.

"Toni, I *don't know*. I just woke up one morning and I couldn't make good iced tea," she said.

"Oh no!" I said. Everything changes.

The house started filling up with family, and I could feel myself floating up in the air like a kite on a string. My brother Michael and his son, Charlie, walked into the kitchen after we'd brought our stuff in. Daddy was somewhere in the house now, too, because Michael had picked him up in Knoxville.

I hugged Michael way too long. And I felt so sad, seeing my only living brother, that I started crying a little bit. He stepped back from me, with his eyebrows up and a curiously amused smile on his face, a look I was extremely familiar with. "What did I do?" he asked. But he knew why I was crying.

Not that we were going to talk about Oliver's death . . . ever again, probably. It was okay to make fun of one another, and rehash absurd stories from our childhood. But it was not okay to talk about or admit things that were truly sad. It was not okay to tell the truth.

I had always been considered the contrarian. If my mother had told the whole family at dinner that we were eating a unicorn casserole and don't forget to try the salad made of rainbows, no one would question her. "But . . . wait a minute," I might say. And all my brothers and sisters would scowl at me and put a finger to their lips: *Shhhhhhhh!*

At least, that's the way it had always felt.

I wandered around the house, looking for Daddy. During Fiddlers' weekend the year before, when Oliver was still alive, Daddy had arrived rattled and disoriented, having driven his old Jeep by himself the four and a half hours from Knoxville, because he knew that all of his kids, except for Lisa, would be in one place. Even after a big scotch, he was shaken. "Phew! I'm never gonna do that again, buddy," he said to me when I sat down next to him. "I damn near killed myself."

This year, it quickly became clear he had no business living alone. "Where's Elaine?" he asked when I popped my head into the library. He was sitting by himself in the robin's-egg-blue leather chair next to the window looking onto the patio, with a scotch in his hand. He was eighty-one, looked older, and was on oxygen at night after smoking for many years.

"She's not coming this year," I said. Through the window, I watched Toni's kids playing on the patio, distracting myself from the thought of him sitting there in the library drinking alone.

"I just saw her," he said. "She got here before I did."

What ho?!

I leaned in to look him directly in his brown-gold eyes, which had gotten a little milky since last year's Fiddlers'. I spoke in a loud voice—perhaps we'd misheard each other?

"No, Daddy. Nope. You're thinking of last year. She can't come this year," I told him. She had canceled our hotel room and sent an email about being sick. And she still wasn't speaking to me since the weird email to Toni back in Atlanta.

"Well, I just saw her," Daddy insisted, triumphantly but with little conviction.

"Are you sure? I want you to think, okay?" I felt tired. I felt like running away. He looked up at me now, as if he had just met me. And I felt the same way about him, to a certain extent.

"Well, okay, wait . . . I'm thinking," he said, in his soft, gravelly voice. "Yes. I'm sure." And then he added, ever the rim-shot comic, "But you all look alike to me!"

And then he knocked himself out laughing, almost choking, that giant laugh I'd always tried to elicit from him when I was a little kid, when he was still around. Being funny, knowing a good joke or story, was the only way to get his attention.

My most triumphant moment in this arena had been one early fall morning as he was driving all five of us to school, dropping Elaine, Michael, and Oliver off at the high school at the top of the hill before driving me and Lisa back down the hill to elementary school. Oliver, who was a know-it-all, was arguing loudly with me—I was wrong about something, as usual, and he called me a dumbbell.

"You know everything, Oliver," I told him. "You're such a prophet. Matthew, Mark, Luke, and Oliver." Daddy's laugh—a cannon shot that echoed—scared everyone in the car, which he'd pulled over to the side of the road. He turned around and zeroed in his focus on me, however briefly, in the back seat, grinning at me as if I were some pre-adolescent comic genius whose act he'd never caught before. I smiled at him and asked, "What?"

He had told this story, off and on, many times since. I never thought it was that funny, but I held on to that moment for a long time. And I didn't think his joke about not being able to tell us apart was that funny, either—because it was probably true.

I walked back to the kitchen and reported his memory lapse to Aunt Mariah, who is always right about things like this. She takes her role as the matriarch and excellent hostess very seriously.

"He's not using his oxygen tank, and it's affecting his brain," she said, in her Tidewater drawl, which always made things seem less awful than they might actually be.

Not long afterward, I headed into the kitchen again. The house had gotten more crowded with visitors who knew the Nunn kids were back in town. My nephew was playing the piano quite expertly and loudly in the formal living room, even though he'd never had lessons. He just figured it out.

"Daddy just asked me how Oliver died," I said to Aunt Mariah, noting that he had picked me, in particular, to ask this question. Perhaps my own propensities showed, although he knew nothing about my recent downfall.

"Well, that has to stop," Aunt Mariah said, cutting up a cantaloupe.

So I took Daddy aside and reminded him that we weren't talking about death at this year's party.

"Oh, okay," he said, again, raising his eyebrows with less conviction than before. For someone who had always made me furious, he was a pretty agreeable guy. At some point, he handed me a piece of paper with handwritten figures delineating the state of his bank accounts. Some of his money was missing. I stared at it, although I had no idea what his notations meant. "We'll take care of this, Daddy. Don't worry," I said, feeling pity, love, and protectiveness at once, an uncomfortable emotional combo for me.

How in the world was I supposed to take care of him, when I was living my own life as fecklessly as Tess of the D'Urbervilles?

Luckily, Jayne showed up. She's a lobbyist in DC and a very bright light wherever she goes.

"All right!" she yelled at all the kids, almost as soon as she arrived. She was wearing her signature fuchsia lipstick and crisp white shirt. "Who wants to go to the Walmart?" It had become a tradition for her to take the kids to pick out atrocious Walmart clothing and baubles to wear, or toys. She was like a magical queen to them. The year before, she'd guided them to the women's underwear department, where the enormous brassieres and underpants scandalized them.

This time Toni and I went, too. When we were leaving, I told her I was afraid I was going to have to shop there soon, since beyond my two suitcases I had nothing.

"You have things, Emily. You have so much," she replied, her hand on my arm, looking me in the eyes. I nodded my head. "Just not things people can touch," she added, which started out as genuinely heartfelt and ended up making both of us laugh until tears started running down Toni's cheeks, which made her blue eyes turn Technicolor.

Aunt Judy, sister of John and Daddy, arrived. That was going to be the extent of our reunion this year, aside from some friends who'd drop by or we'd bump into or visit.

Over the next several days we occupied ourselves the way we always had before it was time to go down to the fairgrounds at night. At least once, we met a group at the Dairy Bar, one of the drive-ins where the waitresses come out to your car. We liked to go inside and order, and then take our hot dog baskets, onion rings, and thick chocolate milk shakes out to the patio right off the road overlooking the Fiddlers' crowd lazing around their campers and playing a little music. We walked up and down Main Street downtown, where the buildings had once been department stores, hardware stores, ladies' dress shops, banks, car dealerships, shoe stores, soda fountains, a movie house, a post office, churches, and a city hall, but were now either closed or transformed into antiques and consignment shops, a computer place, a bookstore, and a good barbecue restaurant. Even the post office building had been abandoned, replaced by a restaurant none of us ever went to.

The music was almost over by the time we arrived for the Fiddlers' final night, the only one I attended. I'd volunteered to babysit the kids, and spent the evenings watching children's movies. I just couldn't do it: immerse myself in a crowd whose collective past contained mine and Oliver's, his life gone forever and mine obliterated, all of that mixed up together, set down in a place that I'd returned to practically every year since I'd moved away—with music? I had an hour or so to wander around while everybody else socialized. I listened to a man playing bass fiddle throw his head back and wail the song "Ruby," which was not the ridiculous Kenny Rogers song but a baleful, gorgeous old ballad about love.

The year before Oliver died, he and I were standing alone side by side at the Fiddlers', looking at the stage from the edge of the crowd with harsh football lights shining on us. Oliver turned to me and said, irritated, "What are we doing here?"

"Here? At the Fiddlers'?" I asked. He frowned his Oliver frown—*your questions are idiotic*—and replied, "No. Just here." It made me mad, so I walked away. That summer was the last time I saw him. He was gone by November. Goodbye, goodbye, goodbye.

•

That final day, I woke up after everyone had already placed their bags downstairs on the Karastan rug in the entry hall near the front door, the goodbye cue. Time to go back home. But I didn't even have my temporary home now that I was no longer welcome back in the desert, where all my clothes and cookbooks and cameras remained.

Since I had no plans and none of my belongings (other than two suitcases and a laptop) I asked Aunt Mariah if I could stay with her and Uncle John for a couple of weeks until I got some things figured out.

"Why, Emily, you can stay as long as you want," she said. We drove Toni, Richard, Mariah, and Addie back to the landing strip to watch them take off.

"Bye, Emily. I'm going to miss you," Toni said, hugging me hard, before running across the tarmac to get into the plane packed with her family. I ended up staying in Galax, my original home, for almost five months.

Nine

DELIVERANCE

"Pick any room you want," Aunt Mariah told me after everyone except Aunt Judy had left. Judy was sticking around in my cousin Susan's Delft blue bedroom with the twin beds for a few more days, doing research at county libraries for a book about the original families of Galax.

That left Toni's giant Queen of the Universe Room or the other bedroom with the four-poster, which was so high off the floor it had a step stool. I assumed Toni and her family would need her room when they came back for the gigantic Labor Day Hillsville Flea Market, so I chose the four-poster—the room with *the dolls*.

Everyone else loved mean Great-grandmother's antique doll collection, of which these were a very small subset. They were treasures. But they scared me when I was a kid, and they didn't comfort me now, arranged on a marble-topped dresser with their painted ceramic heads, lobotomized expressions, and too-tiny ceramic hands poking out of their elaborate Victorian costumes. They looked like small, taxidermied women.

I settled into the otherwise sunny, welcoming room, with its antique furniture, red and pink floral chintz, ruffled bedclothes, and piles of decorative pillows. Like a stuffed and mounted teenager, I slept in that bed, high off the ground as if on display, frozen. It was already mid-August and I still had no idea what was going to happen to me or how I was going to change my life; I felt like a burden, which was not a new thing.

But whenever I was bedeviled by such practical worries, I found my hometown was a great distraction. A great place to be in complete denial. I went to Horton's Supermarket, a country grocer that has been on the edge of town since I was a kid. On one visit, I noticed a lady was standing in the back, past the country butter, pigs' feet, and pickled eggs, and to the left of the produce, frosting a row of cakes. I couldn't get over the fact that she was baking cakes from scratch, in a grocery store. "Yeah, I'm here pretty much all the time," she said. I bought a yellow cake with chocolate icing and it was fantastic. Horton's also has an in-house butcher, which is almost as rare. I was filling a bag of snap beans from the produce bins when a man who was inspecting bunches of giant-leaved watercress said, "I won't go to that damn farmers' market downtown. I don't want apple butter. I have to have my fresh vegetables." I might have been visiting a grocery store in a foreign country.

I borrowed Aunt Mariah's car one Friday afternoon and drove the twelve miles to the library in Hillsville, to see what kind of old country cookbooks they might have. From back in the stacks, I heard someone tuning up a guitar. I walked around the corner, and there was a bluegrass band, with microphones, setting up for a jam. *In the library.* When I whispered a polite inquiry, the gray-haired librarian said loudly, "Ee-yeah sure, they'll play here every third Friday," not looking at me because she was *trying to enjoy the music.*

They were wonderful. One of the female librarians picked up a banjo and joined them, singing in a sweet high voice songs that seemed to be pointed comments about both my emotional status and the logistics of how to put my life back together. "Your Little Cottage Is Not Here Anymore," "Like a Prodigal Son, I Wandered in the Darkness," and "I'm Back in the Saddle Again."

With that, I put some change in their basket and drove toward Galax in a state of mild alarm. What the hell did I think I was doing? You can't just quit life. You can't go back home and climb in your cousin's bed and pretend her parents are your parents. I had to get a job at some newspaper or magazine, get it together, be presentable. Have a reason for existing. Be a valid human being. Get back on the horse. But these thoughts overwhelmed me. I could not imagine how to start.

By the time I got back to Galax, my green hilly familiar drive— past the Amish grocer, the quilt shop that was really just somebody's house, the turnoff for the Joy Ranch orphanage, the Shetland pony farm, my elementary school, and all the old houses of all my old friends that looked exactly the same except for the taller trees and different cars in the driveways—had lulled me into thinking every- thing was fine. My alarm now buried, my only concern was finding scissors to cut herbs from Aunt Mariah's garden. I'd decided I needed to make Mark Bittman's pasta with garlic and herbs, an impossibly delicious dish for the amount of effort it takes. Each day, my mind was like a feather on the wind, blown up and down and all around, before coming to rest, on dinner.

After you chop up a cupful or more of mixed herbs (I used basil, parsley, some mint, thyme, and a couple of sage leaves), you heat some olive oil, add chopped garlic, let it barely color and become fra- grant, then remove it from the heat to let the garlic flavor meld with the oil. You can leave all that sitting there, which I did until Uncle John came home, passed through the breakfast room where I was reading, smelled the garlic, and said, "When's dinner?"

"Hi. Whenever you want," I said.

"I'll tell Mariah. You want to say half an hour?"

"Fine by me," I said, even though it was only five thirty in the afternoon.

When the pasta is al dente, you drain it, put it back in its pot, pour the garlicky oil over it, add a plug of butter if you wish (and we did), throw in the herbs, and toss it all together. John and Mariah raved about this and eventually began requesting it.

"Emily," John said (more than once, as time went on), "you can stay here as long as you want . . . as long as you cook."

"Aw, Johnny, thanks," I said. Almost immediately I thought, *What if that happened? What if I stayed here forever cooking dinner?*

Dinner seemed to be the only thing that I was capable of. I loved *mise en place*—chopping, measuring, mixing, and assembling ingredients in a way necessary to make the final execution go smoothly and for the dish to turn out perfectly. There was no longer any other area in my life that I executed with such focus, nothing I did so deliberately.

I worried that I was overstaying my welcome. "Are you sure it's okay?" I'd ask my cousin Susan, an excellent cook, when she'd call from Rye, New York, to talk to her parents (which would remind me that they were not *my* parents.) "Yeeeesssssssss, Emily! Of course! They love having you there," she said more than once. "I'm so glad you're cooking for them."

Not that I wasn't trying to head toward a new life that took advantage of my old skills. I was working and writing, and I got a freelance assignment from the *Art of Eating* to review Michael Ruhlman's latest cookbook. Mariah, John, and I became devotees of Ruhlman's luscious shrimp and grits, a dish that requires very few tricks beyond simmering bacon and onion in a bit of water until the water evaporates, before adding the grits to cook in more water. The shrimp get poached separately and slowly in a bath of butter that has been emulsified by slowly beating it, chunk by chunk, into a small amount of simmering water. After you remove the shrimp from the butter, you pour about a third of it into the bacon-enhanced grits.

Ruhlman's roast chicken was revelatory for us, too, just perfect, and all you do is place a lemon inside the bird, sprinkle it with an alarming amount of salt, and cook it for one hour in a cast-iron pan. No pepper, nothing. I had a hard time convincing the editors at *Art of Eating* that this recipe worked, but it did. It was miracle chicken.

One of our favorite dishes began as a giant green salad topped with leftovers from this roast chicken. We liked that so much that Aunt Mariah began to poach or broil some breasts and tear them into shreds expressly for this dish. I would wash and dry the greens, put them in the fridge, and chop up an enormous bowl of assorted vegetables: cherry tomatoes, carrots, cauliflower, celery, avocado, a sliced English cucumber, and some broccoli slaw and red onion slices, all of which I'd soak in half a cup or so of my mustard vinaigrette. When we were ready to eat, out came the big wooden salad bowl: greens on the bottom, the marinated vegetables next with maybe a splash more of the vinaigrette, and a pile of the shredded chicken on top, with a grind of black pepper and salt. If I'd made corn muffins in the last day or two, John and Mariah would split and toast them. And that was dinner.

Six o'clock became our regular suppertime, but on a few weekends I made my long-cooking, particularly rich version of Ragù Bolognese. Mariah would freeze some, but usually the leftovers became lunch the next day. I liked that.

Emily's Ragù Bolognese

Makes 7 cups, which serves 10 people (it freezes very well)

4 tablespoons olive oil

2 tablespoons unsalted butter (you can leave this out and
    substitute more olive oil if you insist; I think the butter helps
    the browning process)

2 medium onions, finely chopped

1 large carrot, scraped and finely chopped

2 celery stalks, finely chopped

4 garlic cloves, minced

1 pound ground veal

1 pound ground pork (or use all beef/veal)

½ pound ground beef

¼ pound pancetta, minced or ground (or you can use bacon, but
    less)

2 cups heavy cream, half-and-half, or milk (or use a combination)

1 (14.5-ounce) can whole peeled tomatoes, chopped, with their
    juice

1 cup dry white wine

2 cups chicken stock

Salt, to taste

Freshly ground black pepper, to taste

Pappardelle, for serving

1. In a very large heavy-bottomed saucepan, heat the oil and butter over medium heat. Add the onions, carrot, celery, and garlic, and sauté over medium heat until the onions are translucent. Add the veal, pork, beef, and pancetta to the vegetables, and brown over high heat for 15 to 20 minutes. You really want it to brown; stir it often, breaking up clumps of meat.

2. Add 1 cup of the heavy cream and simmer until almost dry, about 15 minutes. Add the tomatoes and simmer, breaking up any large pieces, for 15 minutes. Add the wine and stock, bring to a boil, then lower the heat and simmer for 2 hours. Add the remaining 1 cup heavy cream; simmer for another ½ hour or longer, until the flavor has intensified, and it has become somewhat dry. It is not a very "saucy" sauce. It's a meaty sauce.

3. Season with salt and pepper.

4. Serve over pappardelle; better yet, toss the pasta and sauce together before serving; pass freshly grated Parmigiano-Reggiano at the table.

•

One time I made a pot of creamy polenta and spooned Ragù Bolognese leftovers over it for a luxurious dinner, with my pale green salad (thinly sliced cucumbers and celery, avocado chunks, a little finely chopped red onion, and the vinaigrette).

Doing the dishes after dinner with Aunt Mariah turned into regular late-night talks over cups of decaf. "The only reason I cook is because I get hungry," Aunt Mariah said once. It seemed understandable, after her years of mandatory cooking, but it wasn't quite true, as she was unflaggingly generous.

When Toni and Richard brought the girls for the flea market, Aunt Mariah made the most wonderful pork loin by covering it with fresh sage leaves that perfumed the tender meat as it roasted. We had Toni's delicious tomatoes in fat slices; corn bought from the farm truck near Horton's; sliced baked sweet potatoes; and her special fried apples, with the peel on, cooked to death in butter and brown sugar and cinnamon. The only thing I did was whip the cream for the sliced peaches we had for dessert. "Announcement," Aunt Mariah said, trying not to be bossy. "I like sugar in my whipped cream." So I put more in.

The next morning, while Toni and Richard and I were in the library on our computers, Aunt Mariah was napping in the sunroom. I saw Addie and little Mariah looking for her. "How did you know I was in here?" I heard her whisper, in a tone of voice that implied being shaken awake was delightful. They wanted her bran muffins, so she went with them to the kitchen to fill the tins with batter. All this family in the house, and yet so much peace! How was this possible?

More than once during my stay, Mariah reminisced about the days when her house was filled with people to feed.

"My tables were laden," she said one night during dishwashing time, out of nowhere, recalling how natural it had been to have people over—sometimes at a moment's notice. "I'd have a smoked turkey, a ham, a broccoli salad. I would just decide that very day to have the girls' friends and their parents over—Marie Walker, Joyce Wilson. And then have the party that night." Once, the hostess of a party she and Uncle John were invited to got sick. "Just bring it all over here," Aunt Mariah told her, and that's what happened.

Uncle Johnny, who usually fled the dinner table long before we'd started these talks, came back in for a slice of Horton's cake and lingered long enough to tell me about soup parties he and Aunt Mariah would throw in the winter. "Buck Higgins loved Mariah's black bean soup so much. I was in my Chinese cooking phase, and one time I fixed barbecued spareribs instead. He was so bitterly disappointed, he said he wasn't coming back if there was no soup."

"I've had these place mats for twenty-five years," Aunt Mariah said, another evening as we were setting the table. She'd used them as long as I could remember—they were nothing fancy, just white ovals with a pretty scalloped edge—along with her olive-green pressed-glass goblets, wooden salad bowls, and copper-bottomed Revere Ware pots and pans, which she washed by hand, rubbed with copper polish, and dried after every use. She also had fine linens stacked away, relics of the dinners and parties she'd once given in this house, including the funeral receptions and the reciprocal baby and engagement showers that require a lot of silver polishing, crystal cleaning, and chafing dishes, which are at the center of social life in that part of the South.

"'Twenty places were laid for the bridal guests'—that's how they wrote it up in the paper. That was the proper way to put it. Not 'twenty people were invited.' And you had to play bridge back then, which required a light lunch," she said. I wanted to have that kind of house, where people gathered and you shared with them and it was not a big deal.

Each time I decided I would get started on that plan right away, it seemed more important that I do something much less constructive. I would go outside with a book and sit on the deck in the sun, then head into the azalea- and hosta-filled yard and through the woods looking for the local cardinals, blue jays, song sparrows, finches, and white-breasted nuthatches, as well as what was either a yellow-bellied sapsucker or a red-bellied woodpecker. When I reached the murky lily pond, I would sit in a hammock wondering how I'd ended up in yet another place I'd never pictured myself.

I would drive around the back roads of Grayson County, along the slow-moving New River, which is only slightly younger than the Nile, and into Ivanhoe, an old half-empty mining town where only the brick facade of the decayed old school still stands, with trees growing through the windows, and the ornate houses look like churches. Along curvy roads through Max Meadows and Fort Chiswell, signs announced Wednesday night prayer meetings, and the hills along the road—a stage set between performances, with gorgeous old red barns and no signs of humans—were so steep that the grazing cows' balance seemed acrobatic. Sometimes I drove across the state line seven miles away into North Carolina, along winding, frightening roads where the rocky mountainsides were so close to the car you could hit a hanging rock, roads I'd never been on, past country stores with Mountain Dew signs and giant gracious farms with stone gates, until I was completely lost, even though I was just a few miles away from John and Mariah's, which was down the street from my grandmother's old house, and barely a mile from the stone and glass house where I'd grown up, on a hill overlooking the highway that led out of town. A highway that I'd always viewed as a getaway. And it didn't scare me, getting lost this way, because this place that I'd once avoided—Galax, after all, was where my family had disintegrated, a place of long-ago pain—was becoming my home, and Aunt Mariah and Uncle John's house was becoming the peaceful nest I'd never had here.

While I was living in their house, John and Mariah went away on vacation twice. The first time, there was a small but definitely perceptible earthquake that made the wrought-iron lantern hanging from a chain on the front portico swing for twenty minutes, after which Carol, the woman who'd started the Galax Theatre Guild with my mother and now lived next door in the enormous house that she continued to own after divorcing the man she'd come to Galax for, rang me up to make sure I was okay. The second time, a tornado swept through the mountains, a pretty unusual thing, and took out a long curving row of trees on the public golf course that had once been the country club. Another one of my mother's friends called to check on me, even though I'm pretty sure she knew my mother and I had been estranged. "I'm going to have Clark come and check on you," she said, meaning her son, the town vet, whom I'd gone to high school with and whose father had been the town vet when I was a kid. It was as if Galax had not noticed that I had rejected it so many years ago. Or didn't mind.

Aunt Mariah had been hinting since I'd arrived that I might expand my horizons: "Don't you want to go see Becky's gallery?" and "Mary Margaret asked about you at church."

So, like a kid heading to kindergarten, I had lunch at the coffee-house on Main Street with Mary Margaret (we both had the tuna, egg, and pimento-cheese salad plate, with Captain's Wafers, a buttery southern cracker). I'd known her since kindergarten, and she lived right down the hill from John and Mariah. It was a little weird, not seeing her for so long then seeing her again. But later we went to see a movie, and soon I was heading to her house to pop in on her husband, Bernie, and their dog. Mary Margaret and I began to hang out and she became a treasured friend. This seemed like an unimaginable windfall. When my friend Lucinda, who'd been the society editor at the *Chicago Tribune*, came to visit, the three of us spent an afternoon talking by the lily pond—my kindergarten friend and my grown-up friend together in Galax.

I participated in the life of the town by filling in at the desk at the art gallery owned by my friend Becky, who'd been my tennis and basketball teammate. Ginger, who was the head of the city arts council, asked me to plan a menu for the annual gala.

"I've always wanted to apologize to you for breaking up your parents' marriage," she said, after I slid into the booth across from her at the Mexican restaurant we'd chosen for our meeting. She had been my high school's drama teacher and the assistant director of *South Pacific*.

"What?" I asked.

"I was the one who made your mother and [Emile] go into the band room and kiss until it seemed natural," she said.

"Oh, I think it was more than that," I said. And I apologized when she told me that Mother had stopped speaking to her, too, after she'd told her that her shorts in the shower scene were too short for a small-town audience. I was happy to plan the menu for the gala, and was glad Galax was still speaking to me.

I did these things while hiding a secret that made me feel like an impostor abusing the generosity of people who loved me: I was not okay. I was not finished with the past; I had not even begun to be. It had been seven months since my ex-fiancé had left me at the hospital in Chicago, since I'd flown away, longer since Oliver had died. I should have been long over my multiple losses.

But my darkest secret was that my heart and brain would not let me access Oliver—would not let me truly think about him much at all except when I was asleep in the dark, in the pink bedroom, in the middle of the night. The next morning, I would remember what seemed to be a dream in which I had cried until the tight, burned-out place in me was soothed. If I remained numb, obsessed with things I couldn't say out loud, the things I couldn't tell, the things I should have done differently, the mistakes I should have fixed, I had no right to the solace I'd received so far, nor to any in the future. I was like a snake eating my own tail.

The best I could do at the time was to pretend that I believed this state of mind would end. And I had to make sure I was openly, lovingly grateful and kind to the people around me. And finally, at some point, something did change—even though the two catalysts were slightly nutty. First, I had become keenly aware of one large, beautiful cardinal that was plainly antagonizing me during my time outside on the deck. A few cardinals would flutter down onto a branch in the dogwood off the deck, look around, be all striking and totemic, and fly away, like normal cardinals. But this one persisted, even though it knew I was on the deck. I would mentally dare it to come closer. It would step onto the deck railing, jump onto a piece of wrought-iron furniture, and then the deck itself, pretending to be interested in a bug or a crumb. But I had this cardinal's number.

I had become completely convinced that this gorgeous red bird was Oliver. This kind of projection is not unusual for people when someone close to them dies. But I also began talking to it every once in a while, telling it that I missed it, and loved it, and that I was sorry that I had not been there for it, and, eventually, that I couldn't spend any more time with it. After this went on for a while, I told the cardinal that it was time for it to leave now, go to where it was meant to be.

The bird still came around, but at a certain point I became able just to talk to Oliver, whether the cardinal was there or not. Mostly I'd talk to him at night. I'd go outside, lie down on one of the wrought-iron deck chaises, and look up at the stars, which in rural areas, without the ambient light of excessive commerce and prosperity, seem close enough to pluck from the sky. One night, the moon was full, as bright as a klieg light on a movie set. I was completely convinced that Oliver was there, too, and my proof was that the wind chime tinkled and clinked even in the absence of any wind.

Naturally, I kept this to myself.

The second agent was an old cat: at about ten o'clock one night, while I was just sitting on a bench off the carport, near the herb garden, I noticed a ratty old orange-striped cat stretched out on the hood of Mariah's car. I could see that he had a large open gash on his head; it looked like the scalp between his ears had been torn off, and the dark bloody wound didn't look like it was healing. The cat stood up, slipped down off the car, and wandered far enough away from the lighted carport that I couldn't see him anymore.

I forgot about him and his wound until early one morning a few days later, after I'd come back from a walk, made my coffee, and sat down on the same bench, where it had become my ritual to drink the coffee and worry that I was going to become one of those broken people, like Delta Dawn from the eponymous song, wandering around Galax in a flowered dress, carrying my suitcase in my hand.

But on this morning, a giant pileated woodpecker with a big red cap, which is a pretty rare sight, started tapping away in the dead pine tree right next to the deck. A dog started barking and didn't stop, and the striped cat came skulking across the driveway from the far end of the house somewhere and began a slow amble up the steep wooded hill that was John and Mariah's yard, toward the street, stopping near a rhododendron, where he sat down facing the house, not moving at all, just staring straight ahead, not noticing me.

I could feel the enormous force of this small animal's suffering. It felt limitless and universal, connected to me—connected to anyone who might bother to notice it, which sounds ridiculous, I suppose. But I did: I experienced this cat's dreadful pain and its aloneness, its saying goodbye to the world and walking toward death. I wondered how anyone could ever say goodbye to the world on purpose. I never saw him again.

The striped cat had cracked, ever so slightly, the bell jar under which I had been stewing for so long. Because of this cat, I began to become someone slightly better than the person I'd been before, someone awake, able to be more aware of other people.

It did occur to me I might be bugging out again. But I went along with this mystical gift, rather than throwing it away as if it were no good. Saying goodbye to the world *alone* was not something I ever wanted to do.

After I'd made him one of my fantastic tomato sandwiches, John started coming to the house at lunchtime every once in a while, rather than going to the diner or the Smokehouse or the County Line. ("I told Johnny after we got married, I married you for better or worse, but not for lunch," Aunt Mariah has said many times.)

He and I were sitting in the library eating (which was not really allowed) a couple of tomato sandwiches and drinking Diet Cokes with the news on. I looked up and he had fallen asleep in his chair, which produced in me an almost unrecognizable form of contentment.

He and Aunt Mariah and I had become a new family, fallen into a routine of living together in which I cared for them and they cared for me (although they had been doing that all along; I just couldn't see it).

Actually, I had fallen madly *in love* with my aunt and uncle, in the most devoted way. They were *mine*. And they weren't going to hurt me. I needed to take very good care of them. But I couldn't make them my whole world.

I knew it was time to plan the next stop on my Comfort Food Tour, even if things might be different when I came back. I couldn't continue to be surprised when things went wrong in my life if I also continued to just let that life happen to me. I had to reach out, connect with a world outside my very recent past, and take responsibility for finding comfort elsewhere.

After two months in Galax, John took me to buy a big American car. The guy who sold me my used vehicle was in AA, which he told me right off the bat. After we talked about that, I guess I got a pretty good deal on the car.

When the time came to decide whom I'd visit, I decided on three college friends. It seemed like the natural next step in trying to understand how I'd become so lost. Surely old friends would help me remember who I'd been, as we'd moved together into adulthood. My plan: stop for a few days in Atlanta to visit Toni and the girls again (and help turn their house into a haunted one, for Halloween) then travel way back into my past, to see my long-lost friends Portia, Dot, and Wyler—college friends I'd neglected but who'd never really given up on me, I felt sure.

These were women I'd known long before I'd left the South to live in New York City, long before I'd given up my great friends and job in NYC to move to Chicago.

When I had gotten back in touch with each of them, Portia, Dot, and Wyler had sounded balanced and happy. But they were three very different people. Portia had been as much of a loose cannon as I had been in college, but now she was many years sober, living on a farm in Georgia, painting and cooking, a mother and wife, and, not surprisingly still a lovely kook but also a very vocal proponent of AA. Wyler had always been the kind of passionately loyal friend you wanted on your side; she had become a naturopathic doctor, and had come out of the closet, and was now living an openly gay life in the Deep South. And Dot was a photographer, returned to a small town in North Carolina after life in big cities like Atlanta and New York, the kind of person for whom friendship was second nature; she had kept more lifetime friendships than anyone I've ever known and steadfastly refused to participate in the kind of tangled stonewalling that marked my family, in spite of the fact that her parents had divorced, she'd recently divorced, too, and was raising two children. My hope was that if I studied how friends I'd entered adulthood with had made their lives work, maybe I could learn by example.

I made my arrangements, printed out my maps, and packed up. I admitted to Aunt Mariah that I was a little scared, so before I left, she showed me how to make her pot roast, which she'd told me long ago was her supper of choice when she needed soothing. I love this pot roast not just because it is delicious but also because Aunt Mariah makes it by heart. It's just a part of who she is.

Aunt Mariah's Pot Roast

Serves 4

Use a cast-iron pot with a lid because it's cooked on top of the stove and then in the oven.

Corn oil, about 3 tablespoons (or enough to thinly coat the
    bottom of the pot), plus more for the meat

1 (2-pound) chuck roast or sirloin

Salt, to taste

Freshly ground black pepper, to taste

1 large onion, cut into 8 wedges

2 to 3 plugs of butter (where I come from a plug is about a
    tablespoon; the word implies that measuring isn't important)

1 cup all-purpose flour

3 big stirring spoons bacon grease (meaning the big spoon you're
    stirring with; use about ½ cup)

1 cup hot water

4 large carrots, peeled and cut into 1-inch chunks

8 to 10 small new potatoes, scrubbed

1. Preheat the oven to 350°F. Heat the cast-iron pot on high, add the corn oil, and let it get hot enough to make a droplet of water sizzle but not so hot that it smokes.
2. Rub the meat with oil, then generously sprinkle with salt and pepper.
3. Lay the roast down in the pot and do not move it for 4 to 5 minutes. Do not turn the roast until it releases from the pot. It should be the color of black coffee and dry—no juiciness. ("Now that's what I want it to look like," Aunt Mariah says. She scrubs the small potatoes while I peel and chop the carrots.)
4. After it's dark brown on all sides, remove the meat, scrape up the bits from the pot for a minute, and don't really pay any attention to it.
5. Turn down the heat just a little bit, and throw in the onion. After it has cooked for a minute, throw in the butter. (Aunt Mariah says the butter is really for the color as much as it is for the taste. And sure enough, the onion starts to get darker around the edges than it would have with just the oil. It sizzles a while longer.)
6. After 6 to 7 minutes, once the onion is brown around the edges and is beautiful, remove it to a bowl and make the gravy.

7. Add ½ cup of the flour to the grease in the pot, and stir on medium-high heat to make a paste for the roux.

8. Plop in the bacon grease. ("I just did that because it was close," Aunt Mariah says sheepishly. "You can use butter.")

9. Stir in another ½ cup of the flour, sprinkling it over the top and into the mixture, and continue to stir over medium-high heat. ("See, it's starting to brown," she says.)

10. Drizzle in 1 cup or so of the hot water. (Steam rises, and it smells so good I can't wait to try it. The gravy is the color of café au lait, which worries Aunt Mariah, but this smell, the steam, and the entire activity cheers me immensely. "I didn't let it get brown enough," she says. "So here's a secret." She pulls out a bottle of Kitchen Bouquet and drizzles some in. This is not for "flay-vah." It is for "cullah." She splashes in a bit more and the gravy turns darker. "Some people just use coffee," she adds, looking at me over her glasses. She continues whisking while it bubbles briskly. "I don't want any lumps." She dips in a spoon and holds it to let it cool. "I haven't put in any salt or peppah," she says, " 'cept on the meat." She tastes it and makes a hilarious face. She salts and peppers it, tastes it again.)

11. Plop the roast back into the bubbling gravy, then scoop in the onions and add some hot water. ("How much?" I ask. "You do it by looks," she says. "You don't want it to be thick as a paste.")

12. Put in the carrots. Then put on the lid and place the pot into the oven. (It is 4:55 p.m. Aunt Mariah tells me to check to make sure it is not too thick and drop in the potatoes at 5:45 p.m. "But when do you take it out?" I ask. "When I'm ready to eat it," she says, laughing. "You can keep cooking it for a long time without hurting it.")

13. After 50 minutes, check the roast, which is making a rumbling noise that I can hear through the door of the oven. Put in the potatoes and add some more water, almost up to the top.

14. Cook for another 1 hour 15 minutes, when you should check for doneness. (Or, as Aunt Mariah says, "If I put it in at 3:00 p.m., I cook it until dinnertime. If it's not ready, I cook it some more."

15. Serve in bowls, making sure to give each person a couple of nice chunks of carrot.

•

That afternoon, before we sat down to our magnificent pot roast dinner, I found her mother's wedding invitation in an old cookbook I pulled off a shelf in the library. When I gave it to Aunt Mariah later that night, she smiled at me like I was some kind of magical cardinal, gave me a hug, and said, "I love you, Emily."

But it was really nothing. In all the years that I have been cooking, I have collected cookbooks from thrift stores and antiques shops or received them as hand-me-down gifts. And good things that have absolutely nothing to do with me have always fallen out of the pages.

Ten

RINGING BELLES

The only good way to get out of Galax is to take Route 89 down the mountain into North Carolina. I know the twisting curves of this road so well I could almost drive it blindfolded. But then I'd miss the New River Valley and Blue Ridge landscape, which was now lit up with fall colors but in spring and summer is almost painfully vivid with Queen Anne's lace, morning glories, blackberry bushes and goldenrod, violets and buttercups, cornflowers and sweet peas, the brilliantly colored azaleas and rhododendrons and redbuds, the black walnut and dogwood trees scattered throughout the white piney woods, the thick green moss covering the silver stone outcrops hovering along the road, some so close they're etched with car-colored rainbows.

Galax had always seemed cut off from the rest of the world when I was growing up, so driving down this mountain road has always thrilled me. You're not on your way to freedom until you're going downhill fast, almost out of control, barely knowing what's around the next loop in the road, with some jackass dogging your tail, and WATCH FOR FALLING ROCKS signs to give you one more thing to worry about.

I was going from one safe nest to the next, but also into the unfamiliar; my brain was in several agitated states at once. So before I hit the interstate, I very nearly killed myself and a bunch of other people while trying to pass the car in front of me, even though it was going sixty-five. In a snap I knew I'd made a mistake; an oncoming car came hurtling at me so fast I had to veer off the two-lane road into an unlucky family's scruffy lawn. As soon as my car came to a stop, the man who'd been driving behind me was at my car door, screaming at me, asking me what in the world I'd been thinking.

I got out to face him, feeling like I was going to faint, as he threatened to make me stay right there until he called the police.

"I have *kids* in this car!" he said, pointing toward a minivan, where the faces of three children stared out at me, along with their mother.

I said, "I'm so sorry, I'm so sorry, I'm so sorry, I've never done anything like that," and added that I certainly wouldn't blame him. My legs were so weak I had to sit down in the grass.

He shook his head. "Are you all right?" he asked in a normal tone of voice, looking down at me.

"Yeah, I'm just shaken up."

"Well . . . *just stop it!*" he yelled, and went back to his car where everyone inside scowled at me as they pulled away. Both of us had left deep, long ruts in the yard, but nobody seemed to be at home in the ranch house. So I sat there next to my car, in the strange October sun, wondering if I had a right, after all my nutty behavior, to be driving something so big and heavy anywhere but up and down the hill of John and Mariah's driveway.

My mere presence was capable of destroying someone else's family. In a way I'd believed that all my life.

I wasn't sure which of my fears were valid, or if they were rooted inside me or out. But they were becoming an issue, which seemed to matter more than ever now, a few nights after Aunt Mariah had told me—quite explicitly—that she was "never scared."

This barely computed. She'd had open-heart surgery, for one thing, was a scout leader who fended off snakes, had deterred a hotel room robbery in Charleston, and once slept through a tornado. Yet when I tried to conjure a memory of her getting hysterical when I was growing up or making *me* feel afraid because she was afraid, the way my real mother always had, I couldn't do it. In fact, just being with her had a lulling effect—what could be so bad that we couldn't handle it together?

"It just doesn't make sense," she said, regarding being "'fraid," during one of our late-night conversations that always began in the kitchen.

Many nights after the dishes were done we parked ourselves at the lazy Susan captain's table in the breakfast room off the kitchen, the same table I'd sat at ever since I was a kid, eating corn on the cob and Pop-Tarts and spaghetti and Grape-Nuts, drinking Kool-Aid and iced tea, playing checkers. I'd try to get Aunt Mariah to talk about what it was like growing up on a working farm, on an actual dirt road. Especially the food, which had always made far-off Courtland seem like a storybook place.

"We ate a *lot* of fried fish," she said one night. "Not much breading, with cornmeal. Perch, trout. And we had spots, fish with one little black spot on each side. We *never* would have eaten a catfish—it was a bottom-feeder. When the herring and shad were running, the men would go seining at night and get them in nets. It would be the men from five families. Rockfish was another, but that came out of big rivers, like the James. The Nottoway River was right behind the house. There was squirrel hunting. But none of us liked deer. And we would kill hogs every January. We made sausage. We smoked the links and canned the patties—we called them pork chips. We smoked the hams and the shoulders. You'd go down to the smokehouse to chop off some meat to flavor something," she said.

"We always kept sweet potatoes in the cellar of the house," she continued, in a lilting voice that sounded like a lullaby late at night. "There was pine straw on the floor, then you spread the potatoes out and put more pine straw on top, to keep them from freezing in winter. Pinto beans were not in our vocabulary. We didn't ever have them. That doesn't mean they weren't there. But we had fresh beans. We didn't dry anything in Courtland; we put it up. In the summer, everything was fresh. Butter beans. And corn and of course lots of tomatoes and cucumbers, green beans, and potatoes."

Until I asked her about her favorite meal I hadn't considered the actual farmwork.

"My favorite was fried chicken and butter beans, with fresh corn and tomatoes. She killed a chicken every Sunday," Aunt Mariah told me.

"Wait—*she* did? *Who* did?" I asked. As a kid, of course, I'd had no concept of what went along with living on a farm. I just thought about the sweet freshly churned butter melting on a hot biscuit.

"Matt," she replied, meaning her paternal aunt Mattie, whose parents had left her the farm and the house, Rose Hill, where Aunt Mariah's parents and siblings lived, too. "She chopped the heads off and pulled the feathers. She also raised turkeys, but that was for extra money."

They always needed extra money. Edith, Aunt Mariah's mother—who had come to town to teach at a one-room schoolhouse—went into the hospital with pneumonia around Christmastime in 1937, near the end of the Depression. While she was there, Richard, her husband, fell ill and entered the hospital, too. When Edith recovered, after two long months ("Remember, we didn't have antibiotics," Aunt Mariah said), she was met with the news that pneumonia had killed her husband, he'd been buried, and she now had to raise her four children—Aunt Mariah was two, sister Glynn was just nine months old, brother Richard was fifteen, and Francis was ten—without him. And she had a farm to run with her late husband's sister Matt.

"He only had a $1,000 insurance policy," Mariah said.

Once she was strong enough, Edith got to work. "She was smart, and she wasn't afraid of tough jobs," said Aunt Mariah. She talked the hospital and other places she owed into letting her pay a little at a time and keep $1,000 from what she owed them, for seeds and other supplies. During World War II, the school board asked her if she wanted to drive a bus, and she took the job to support her family. She began to do everything she could think of to keep the family afloat and the farm—a thousand acres of peanuts, cotton, tobacco, corn, and grain farmed to sell—operating through the hard times to come, during the war, when all the men began to disappear, with the exception of the tenant farmers who lived and worked the land and helped Matt and Edith learn to do the same: "Mama felt responsible for keeping it up."

When Mariah's older brother Richard was a medic in a naval hospital during World War II, Edith contacted his commanding officer and said, "We do not know how to work the planting machine. Could you let my son Richard come home?" Instead, he sent a busload of seamen. They came every year until the war ended to plant peanuts, cotton, and tobacco. And after the war was over, that officer and his friends came back to hunt on the family property along the Nottoway.

"We also had a big garden for food, many fruit trees—pears, plums, early apples, late apples, damson peaches, berries. Huckleberries were the same as wild blueberries. There were always wild grapes to make jam. We grew squash, butter beans, cucumbers, green beans. And raised pigs and cattle for milk and butter."

I asked Aunt Mariah if she ever worried that they'd all be taken to the poorhouse (which I'd learned on my visit to Courtland was not just a figure of speech; they existed), that her mother was going to work herself to death, or that she'd die of sadness over the death of her husband. Was she worried she'd go hungry? Maybe I was projecting.

She gave me a steady look, accompanied by a gesture that I'd become familiar with over the last few months—the head tilt, shoulder shrug, and delicate foot stamp that indicated a certain amount of incomprehensible absurdity in what I was saying.

"I never *knew* we were poe-wah. I thought I didn't have roller skates because we lived on a dirt road. You can't skate on a dirt road. When I went along with other families to the beach, on their vacations, I didn't think it was because we couldn't afford trips together. I thought it was because everyone liked my company." Through all the trials Edith endured, she had always made her children feel loved and safe in their home.

"I was never afraid, except that the Germans were going to drop out of the air. The planes from the base were practicing over non-populated areas. And I never remember seeing Matt or Edith afraid. Never. My mother was having some timber cut once—back then they brought the sawmill to the farm and took it away after they finished cutting. I remember some wood was being stolen. My mother went up to the sawmill, and she had her hand in the pocket of the apron, like she might have a gun, and she told them that if any lumber was stolen, they would be reported to the police.

"There was a farmer who'd get drunk, Plummer. Plummer and his wife, Doree, had ten girls and a boy. He would get drunk on Saturday night and Doree would come down to the house. 'Miss Edith, Plummer got drunk and he's going to kill me.' 'No, he's not.' Mother would go to the house. 'Plummer, you can't kill Doree.' She'd take his gun and give it back to him after he'd sobered up. Sunday he would come over and get the gun, and go hunting."

Aunt Mariah and Glynn were never enlisted to work during the war or otherwise ("We were protected from labor"), even though Matt and Edith were desperate for help—especially when it was time to get the crops in.

"She was brave," I said.

"And she wasn't afraid of hard work. You couldn't have a nervous breakdown back then," Aunt Mariah replied. Which shamed me a little, although that certainly was not her intention: one of the ways you stayed above that sort of thing was to reach out, to ask for help.

Sitting by the side of the road after my nearly fatal car accident, I thought about all of this. As soon as I'd stopped shaking, after the angry family was out of sight, I got back in the car. But first I told myself, *You have not killed anyone, damaged them irreparably. You are not guilty of a terrible crime and you never have been.* When I finally hit the highway, it was nice to be driving on my own for the first time in months, heading out on a path to some other way of feeling.

But I also began to get nervous about how my old friends would feel about my barging in on their happy homes and wanting them to help me remember who I used to be, just so I could factor that person into the person I'd become and come up with a workable solution to my life. I'd brought hostess gifts. But even so, it still seemed like a lot to ask. I had to keep reminding myself that they'd invited me.

●

Portia, in fact, had invited me to visit her in Georgia several times toward the end of the last year in Chicago, surely the most unproductive time of my life. But my excuse had been that I was way too busy to take a trip: I had to stay in the unhealthy zone as punishment for being so willing to be punished. And maybe, just a little bit, I avoided her because I suspected we were alike back in college; we'd met freshman year during sorority rush and she was one of the funniest, wildest, most offbeat characters I'd ever met; like me, she was a big boozer who didn't quite fit into sorority life but didn't quite fit anywhere else, either. She was petite, with ice-blue eyes and curly hair, a laugh that verged on unhinged, and a perverse sense of humor: Portia has always loved to make prank phone calls. You picked up, heard the bizarre Burl Ives voice she always used for this purpose, recognized that it was Portia on the other end, said so, and she'd laugh but keep going until you hung up on her. But the phone would ring again: Burl Ives calling you back.

I adored her. Her present-day dedication to AA was part of the reason I'd made her the first stop on this trip. She was the only one who knew what I'd been through.

Portia had been in rehab, too, and back when I had just arrived at Elaine's in Santa Barbara, I finally got in touch to ask her opinion about the Betty Ford Center. She sounded exactly the same, bluntly honest behind her Gracie Allen persona: "I don't know about those places where they play spa music and give massages as part of the deal." (Betty Ford does not do this, by the way.)

Her husband, Buddy, had dropped her off at a hard-core recovery institute in Florida, where she had to stay for seven months and work a real job at a diner when she wasn't being yelled at and broken down like a military recruit. She told me she had to carry a suitcase full of bricks for miles into a nearby town and leave her husband and son for more than half a year to do it. Going to Betty Ford sounded like medical school in Grenada.

She had struggled for a long time before finally giving in to Buddy's scary ultimatum about her drinking: your family or booze; rehab or divorce. He'd set his cap for her the minute they'd met during our freshman year and had never given up on her. The brave, painful things that loving people do to help one another always amaze me.

After years of living in Atlanta, Portia and Buddy moved to a farmhouse in Mansfield, Georgia, with their son. It's forty miles east of Atlanta, but the outskirts get rural pretty fast. The population is about 370, so there's no real town.

I drove through their gate, across a little bridge, and up a hill to find Portia standing in the middle of the long dirt drive, skinny as a broom, dressed in jogging tights and shoes, a long T-shirt, and her wild curly hair under a baseball cap. I was nervous, sure the last time I'd seen her she'd been wearing a sundress and cotton-candy-pink lipstick with hot-rollered hair and lots of gold jewelry, holding a red plastic cup full of beer. We had turned into different people. But after I got out of the car and we stood hugging, we fell back into being comfortable, close friends, just like that, after more than twenty years of silence. We'd each put ourselves through a lot in that time, but however much life changes you, the people who truly recognize you always will.

While Portia was in rehab, their Buckhead home was destroyed in a flood, and after her rehab neither Buddy nor Portia cared as much about living their old Atlanta lifestyle. Their son, Payne, was approaching college, so they moved full-time to the farm, which immediately seemed like my idea of a playground, especially after their dogs, a goofy-looking German hunting dog named Harley and a cairn terrier named Angus, came leaping and skittering over to greet me.

And from there, the weekend was a bit like visiting Willy Wonka's chocolate factory if Wonka had been a food network star. My friend Portia, it turned out, had become an incredible, creative cook.

Before she fed me a thing, she took me and the dogs zooming off in an all-terrain buggy to see the land. Portia had decorated the woods, as if they needed it, in bright colors, with pots of flowers and hand-painted signs telling you what to do in each of the areas. We sped past the barn, which held, along with farm equipment, Buddy's big gas-fueled pot for making boiled peanuts.

Portia and Buddy raised goats—brown babies, fat white ones, and black ones—whose rough fur felt like my childhood Scottish terrier's coat. When we opened the pen, they merrily trotted over to Portia, following her as she introduced me to her exotic chickens in a wide variety of psychedelic colors. "That one is named Emily," Portia said, pointing to one that had escaped the pen, chased by one of the dogs.

Inside the henhouse, which was within the goat pen, I saw the café au lait brown eggs laid by one of her Black Copper Marans, which French chefs have always loved. "I've been selling them to some restaurants in Atlanta," Portia said, handing one to me, still warm. "We're going to eat some of those."

In another fenced red building, a lean-to, lived the donkeys. They ignored us. The lower-class laying chickens lived here with them. "Why do you have donkeys?" I asked.

"Because they're cute," she said.

By the time Buddy got home, I'd barely gotten to look around the house, two large, very old log cabins connected by a new addition, with red brick walks leading to several outbuildings. "Welcome to the Funny Farm," he said, hugging me as if he'd seen me yesterday, before immediately leading me down one brick path, followed by some chickens, to a large kitchen garden behind a red picket fence and surrounded by pots of geraniums, full of cabbages, corn, peppers, butternut squash, lettuces, and herbs. We were there to pull up sweet potatoes, something I'd never done. I watched how he did it, then found my own potato, grabbed on, and pulled a whole connected network of sweet potatoes along with it, like that bomb in the movie *The Hurt Locker*—except, of course, sweet potatoes never hurt anyone.

Every bit of each of these things—including the warm Georgia sun—made me feel like a kind of compass was still alive in me, and it had led me back to Portia and Buddy at just the right time in my life. I was glad for the hundreds of tiny accidents mixed with purpose that had allowed it to happen.

Portia and Buddy had prepared for my visit in ways that touched me deeply; it was almost too much to bear. Portia had a lady in Mansfield make matching aprons for the two of us, embroidered with THE COMFORT FOOD TOUR. I had assumed that we were going to cook together, but she'd already baked an apple pie, two cakes, pecan bars, and some kind of chocolate bar, which were on domed cake plates.

"You're insane," I said.

"I know," she responded.

And we talked for the rest of the afternoon, about our shared past and everything that had happened in the years we'd been apart, with the dogs piled against us.

The full extent of Portia's TV-chef personality didn't really reveal itself until supper. I helped her make a robust salad—she called it slaw—of salted cabbage, chunks of apple, roasted sweet potato cubes, and candied, spicy pecans all tossed in a mysteriously wonderful dressing she produced from the refrigerator that I had to learn how to make. It is good on a lot of other things, including citrus fruit.

Sweet Chipotle Salad Dressing

Makes 2½ cups

1 tablespoon chopped onion

1 tablespoon chopped garlic

2 tablespoons Dijon mustard

½ teaspoon ground cumin

2 teaspoons chopped cilantro

⅔ cup balsamic or rice vinegar

1 teaspoon kosher salt

Freshly ground black pepper, to taste

1 to 2 canned chipotle peppers in adobo sauce, seeds removed, chopped

2 tablespoons honey

1 cup plain Greek yogurt

½ cup olive oil

Mix the onion, garlic, mustard, cumin, cilantro, vinegar, salt, black pepper, chipotle pepper, honey, yogurt, and oil and serve over the cabbage slaw with cubes of roasted sweet potato and apple with candied pecans.

•

There was ham on sweet potato biscuits, which were as tender and rich as cake, and Brunswick stew made with tomatoes, shredded chicken, and real creamed corn (Portia uses a scraper that extracts almost all the good milk from the cobs; we all need one of these).

After dinner, Buddy made Italian coffee with his giant, fancy espresso machine, which we drank on the screened side porch, sitting in a deep soft sofa, and we ate homemade apple pie full of butter, cinnamon, and brown sugar, simple and perfect, more like a green apple dumpling.

"I don't do complicated," Portia said, when I complimented her wonderful dinner and the dessert. "Like, I won't do latticework crust." She had put on a pair of giant wax lips, the kind dropped into our childhood Halloween bags; they were our dinner-party favors. Buddy had a wax mustache.

"But Portia, you spelled *Comfort* in crust letters on this pie," I pointed out to her.

"Yeah, but . . ." was as much as she'd say. Her ridiculous refusal to acknowledge that, yes, she clearly does "do complicated" made me recall the utter perversity of her humor, and that she could be incredulous and hysterical about someone else's strange behavior while doing something equally absurd herself, but with a straight face.

Portia and I stayed up late, blissed-out from dinner and being together after so much time, and talked about college. We kept looking at each other and saying, "I can't believe it. I can't believe you are here." Both of us should probably have died in a ditch since college.

Even the room where I slept, in a dreamy four-poster reclaimed-wood bed covered in patchwork quilts, was filled with food; it was off the kitchen, where an old pantry with screen doors was filled with kitchen utensils, pots, molds, and jars of Portia's homemade soups and preserves.

Portia had placed a little basket of presents on the trunk at the foot of my bed, including an envelope that contained pictures of us in college, two scrawny, bright-eyed twenty-year-olds, all dressed up and wearing lipstick, drunk as two skunks.

I woke up the next morning and wandered into the kitchen in my robe. Along with more of Buddy's coffee, Portia had put out fresh plain homemade yogurt and homemade granola with honey, a lovely breakfast by itself. She lined small soufflé dishes with slices of a homemade brioche that had caught my eye on the kitchen counter when I arrived, to which she added a thin layer of prosciutto, and then cracked and eased a just-laid egg on top, with lemon zest and chives, before baking.

The prosciutto became barely crunchy and the warm farm egg, from one of the Black Copper Marans, soaked the brioche and coated the inside of my mouth with a texture and flavor matching the color yellow; it was slightly sweet in contrast to the chewy, salty meat. I looked up at Buddy with my eyes really wide. He smiled and nodded his head.

"Yeah, how about that?" he said; he seemed, at that moment especially, to be a person who understood how much good there was in his life. He was proud, but he'd clearly fought for all of it—for Portia. I imagine he'd recognized how much good there was to be saved despite the hell she'd admittedly put herself and her family through, and then executed a plan. Buddy had stood by Portia; it made me absolutely adore him.

I felt uncomfortable about taking so much, having given so little. And it would be a long time before I could repay them. Or anybody.

In fact I could feel my guilt trying to wrestle the loveliness of all these gifts into submission. But they gave me all this generous comfort so freely, *so happily,* that I just decided to sink into it; outside, the birds were singing and inside, the dogs were nuzzling their noses on my leg, the signal for me to drop something into their mouths.

When Buddy left to go hunting, Portia informed me that he was a terrific cook, too. "When I'm away, Buddy will make gnocchi," she said, outside on a screened porch where we smoked a cigarette, which I hadn't done in years, and which we did a lot over the next couple of days, along with drinking way too much coffee.

In spite of our not having seen each other for such a long time, she had no trouble picking up on my worries about starting over. She talked about how it was to feel alone in the world and how you can get "dragged into listening to other people's opinions," as she put it.

"The people who do love you matter," she said, "and the people who don't love you do not matter."

Portia told me what it was like to be the daughter of two alcoholics who'd gotten married when they were teenagers. Her dad had been a college football hero who could do no wrong and both her parents expected her to continue to keep all the secrets that went into maintaining that image. Her siblings, who were much older, had left home, so she was on her own for the day-to-day onslaught. One memory made me particularly sad: Portia was never allowed to be in the kitchen because it was where her mother drank. She and her mother and father never sat down to have dinner together, even though her mother was known to all her friends as a great southern cook. Instead, her mother would take a tray in for her father, and Portia ended up eating "Pop-Tarts and other junk." (Obviously, those days were over.) Once she ran away and told the neighbors that her parents were acting strange and that she was afraid. The jig was up.

"After that, every time I went from one room to another, or went to the bathroom, they'd say, 'Where are you going?'" She did a pantomime, took two steps, tiptoed toward an imaginary escape, and then yelled, in a deep parental voice, "Where are you going?" A very early lesson in what can happen when you out an alcoholic against his or her will.

Both of her parents had died years earlier, and at this point so had the older sister she'd loved so much and relied upon during her childhood, lost to cancer.

In spite of their neglect, and Portia's sad losses, she was still happy, able to find humor. And she still had tremendous, unwavering love for all of her family. "My mother made me wear her muumuus with tigers on them while everyone else was wearing go-go outfits," she said.

"Oh my God," I replied. "I had to go to school in my older sister's sizzler set."

"Her what?" Portia said.

"It was a short dress from the late sixties with matching underpants, like an ice-skater's costume, when everyone else was wearing maxi skirts. And my mother didn't even drink."

Portia remembered a pretty tasteless game we'd play in college called Who Am I Now? using our dinner napkins folded in various ways to represent the pope, a hostage during the Carter administration, a KKK member, a sorority girl (giant bow), a Playboy Bunny.

"That's the way my life had been," Portia said. "Who am I now? Am I country club wife? A Junior Leaguer? A drunk? A hysteric? A child? A wife? A teacher? An artist? We've both asked those kinds of questions a lot of times since college, and it wasn't a game. But in a way it was. You keep trying on outfits."

Both of us had been told we were hysterical when we'd cried for help. In fact, that had happened to me just recently.

"You realize what we've been doing is having AA meetings, don't you?" Portia said, laughing, meaning all the revealing, honest, even liberating conversations we'd been having. We did in fact go to an actual local AA meeting, but I realized as the weekend unspooled that for Portia these sorts of conversations had become an absolute way of life. In the years since she'd gotten sober, she'd become a professional counselor and was very involved in the recovery community. She wears an AA ring, which looks like a college ring and seems to carry just as little stigma for her; she'll tell strangers all about it if they ask, and even if they don't. Because she's not embarrassed, she's proud. And amusing.

When she'd decided to start an AA meeting at one of the local churches near the farm, the minister announced one Sunday, as part of the regular church business before the sermon began, "Anyone who believes they may have a drinking problem, please see Portia Hendrick." It didn't bother her at all that he'd blown her anonymity. Which was part of the reason it felt so easy to be with her: total acceptance.

"How did we get through it and come out on the other side?" I asked. We just looked at each other. And on that note, we cooked a little bit.

We cut some rosemary from the garden, and while we toasted pecans in the oven, Portia placed the rosemary in a pan on top of the stove with brown sugar and melted butter. When the pecans came out of the oven still hot she tossed them in the rosemary mixture and spread them on parchment paper to cool.

After we finished the minor pecan project, we headed out to gather more eggs from the chickens, including one who regularly deposited hers not in her henhouse hay box but in a dark crevice between some large boulders a few yards away. "Go ahead," Portia said, so I stuck my hand into the hole; I felt around, worried about spiders and snakes, but came up with my prize, a beautiful, delicate, almost-blue egg—totally worth the leap of faith. I'd grown up in the country and never touched a chicken. Portia had grown up in suburban Dunwoody, Georgia, and was now selling eggs.

Afterward, on a long walk in the warm autumn light, we ended up at the pole barn, where Buddy was using an electric log splitter, just setting wood down and buzzing through it like butter. It looked like fun. "You want to do a few?" Buddy asked, from behind his goggles. But I wanted to leave with good memories and all of my fingers, so I declined.

When we finally got hungry for some lunch, we had this fabulous soup, which contains all that is good in the world: smoky bacon and ham, white beans, chipotle—and collards, which are like a restorative sixth food group for southerners, along with corn bread, pinto beans, country ham, and other dishes we couldn't live without.

Portia's Collard Soup

(adapted from *Southern Living* magazine)

Serves 10

"I make a double stock, meaning I use my own homemade chicken stock and then add a ham bone with meat to the chicken stock and simmer it for an hour," says Portia.

2 strips bacon
Smoked ham, cubed, about 2 cups

1 onion, chopped

½ cup high-quality barbecue sauce

Ground chipotle pepper, to taste

Sea salt, to taste

Smoked paprika, to taste

4 (15-ounce) cans navy or other white beans

Splash of maple syrup, to taste

1 (6-ounce) can tomato paste

Fresh or dried thyme, to taste

Freshly ground black pepper, to taste

Tabasco sauce, to taste

8 cups chicken stock total for finished soup

1 ham bone

6 cups collard greens, ribs removed and leaves chopped (or
  more; I like a lot)

1. In a very large Dutch oven, cook the bacon until crisp, then transfer to a plate. Reserve 2 tablespoons of the drippings. When cool, crumble the bacon.
2. Sauté the ham in the drippings with the onion and barbecue sauce; sprinkle with chipotle powder, sea salt, and paprika.
3. Add the beans, maple syrup, tomato paste, thyme, black pepper, and Tabasco to the same Dutch oven with 4 cups of homemade stock and enough water or canned broth to make 8 cups. Toss in the ham bone.
4. Bring to a boil over medium-high heat. Cover, reduce the heat, and cook for 1 hour, stirring occasionally. Stir in the collards. Cook for 10 minutes, or until really tender. Serve hot, garnished with the bacon and hot sauce at the table.

●

One of the sweetest surprises that Portia gave me was not a special dish but a person, Eileen, who had encouraged me, back on that cold dark day when I was at my wits' end in Chicago, to make comfort food visits to my long-ago friends and write about it. Sunny, beautiful, tennis-playing, jam-making Eileen showed up dressed in slim pants like Laura Petrie (although she's more of a Doris Day), bearing jars of homemade jam and other gifts, and spent an afternoon lazing around with us over an al fresco lunch of rustic butternut squash tarts, promising to send me the recipe for her crab stew.

It's a stupendous old-school receipt, as they call recipes where Eileen grew up, in Savannah. For Eileen, it naturally came attached with memories of family gatherings that took her back to the rivers and marshes of her childhood, even though she has lived away from the ocean for a long time. Memories of her grandfather teaching her to open an oyster by inserting a knife into the keyhole, the image of her tiny grandmother standing over a table piled with boiled crabs after everyone else had eaten their fill, always come rushing back when she needs them. It's all in there and can't be taken away by something like distance or time.

She also sent a terrific cocktail sauce, which is so good I will eat it by itself, after whatever delicacy it's meant to accompany has been consumed, spooning it straight into my mouth like a bracing sorbet.

Eileen's Savannah Crab Stew

Makes 9 cups

4 tablespoons (½ stick) salted butter

1 cup chopped celery

2 (10.25-ounce) cans cream of celery soup

6 cups half-and-half

2 pounds lump crabmeat and claw meat mixed together (best if fresh)

Old Bay Seasoning, to taste

Worcestershire sauce, to taste

Salt, to taste

Freshly ground black pepper, to taste

½ cup good sherry

4 tablespoons chopped fresh chives

1. In a large heavy pot, melt the butter and add the celery. Sauté until tender. Add the soup and mix well. Slowly pour in the half-and-half, mixing well again. Incorporate the crabmeat. Season the stew with Old Bay, Worcestershire, salt, and pepper.
2. Cook on very low heat for about 1½ hours, until it has thickened to a chowder consistency. Add the sherry and chives and stir well. Serve with extra sherry on the side.

Minnie's Cocktail Sauce

Makes about 3 cups

2 bottles Heinz Chili Sauce
Worcestershire sauce, to taste
Tabasco sauce, to taste
Horseradish, to taste
Fresh lemon juice, to taste

Mix the chili sauce, Worcestershire, and Tabasco sauces in a large bowl. Add the horseradish and lemon juice. I use about 6 ounces of horseradish and a liberal amount of Worcestershire and Tabasco. We like it spicy!

•

After Eileen had waved goodbye and pulled away in her car, going back to her inland home in Griffin, Georgia, Portia took me into her art studio in the low red barn past the kitchen garden. She hadn't been an art student and I'd never seen her draw so much as a circle in college. Yet all over her messy, bright studio were in-progress examples of the same beguiling, mystical pieces hanging in the house. I'd had no idea they were her work. She showed me dreamy, religious, otherworldly paintings she'd done when she was in her cups, some commissioned by her church. Another surprise.

The dinner that Portia served on my last night at their home felt particularly special to me because I knew it would be my last with her and Buddy for a while. They had made me feel welcome. I knew remembering this meal could help me recall what that felt like.

We started in the kitchen with peel-and-eat shrimp that Buddy had smoked, and then, rather than eating in their breakfast room as we had all weekend, we sat down at their dining room table for squash soup, made with ham stock, accompanied by rouille-slathered croutons.

Portia's Roasted Winter Squash Soup

Serves about 6

2 pounds pumpkin, acorn, or butternut squash, peeled and
    cut into chunks
1 pound ripe tomatoes, coarsely chopped
6 garlic cloves, unpeeled
1 to 2 sprigs rosemary
2 sprigs thyme
1 red onion, cut into 8 wedges
4 tablespoons extra-virgin olive oil
1½ quarts hot stock
Juice of 1 lime, or to taste
Dash of maple syrup, or to taste
Pinch of cayenne pepper, or to taste
Salt and freshly ground black pepper, to taste

1. Preheat the oven to 425°F.
2. Put the pumpkin, tomatoes, garlic, rosemary, thyme, and onion in a roasting pan and coat with oil.
3. Roast, turning occasionally, for 45 minutes, until the pumpkin is very tender.
4. Discard the herb stems. Squeeze the garlic from its paper skin. Scrape the rest of the contents of the roasting pan along with the garlic into a food processor or blender. Add the stock and process until smooth.

5. Pour into a large soup pot and reheat before serving. Add the lime juice, maple syrup, and cayenne. Season with salt and pepper.

Rouille Croutons
Makes 12

Small pinch of saffron
1 tablespoon warm water
1 garlic clove
1 red chile, seeded and chopped
Salt, to taste
Freshly ground black pepper, to taste
1 large egg yolk
1 tablespoon red wine vinegar
¼ cup extra-virgin olive oil
½ cup sunflower oil
12 croutons, made with a day-old baguette
Grated Gruyère, for sprinkling

1. Soak the saffron in the warm water. Using a mortar and pestle, grind together the garlic, chile, salt, and black pepper. Slowly incorporate the egg yolk and vinegar. Mix the olive and sunflower oils, then drip them into the mortar, whisking constantly. When one-third of the oil is incorporated, increase the flow of oil to a trickle. Stir in the drained saffron and adjust the seasoning.
2. To serve, reheat the soup. Put the croutons, rouille, and cheese on separate plates to pass around, letting diners spread the rouille on croutons to place in their soup bowls and the cheese to sprinkle on top. Make sure the soup is steaming hot.

●

We ate garden greens with shaved Parmigiano-Reggiano, the pecans, and, naturally, a poached farm egg on top—I was getting used to this. I was going to have to buy my own hen at some point. And, finally, a dish of creamed corn topped with plump, sweet scallops that Portia seared perfectly, accompanied by lime-cilantro butter and just a little bit of smoked sausage. For dessert, Portia produced pumpkin pots de crème, topped with homemade whipped cream and maple-flavored shortbread cookies. "When did you make these?" I asked Portia. "You were napping, I think," she said.

One major thing that I relearned in assisting with the soothing meals Portia made is that the freezer is not just your friend, it's your best friend, especially if you want to eat at the level she and Buddy do, and even more especially if you wish to stockpile a form of unconditional love—once given, food can't really be taken back—to have around if friends drop by. She makes sure to freeze bags of fresh corn with its milk, good slabs of bacon, assorted homemade stocks, her favorite dough for pies or the terrific rustic tarts she also makes, both savory and sweet. Also, she refreshes her supply of homemade granola frequently. I kept asking what I could do, but aside from stirring or chopping I just absorbed her grace in the kitchen, which is unstressed, and unembarrassed by mistakes. If you drop a chicken, you pick it up and rinse it off. You keep going. This scallop dish is the best example of this: giant luxurious payoff with very little effort on Portia's part on the actual day she made it.

Portia's Scallops on Creamed Corn

Serves 4 to 6

16 large scallops

Kosher salt, to taste

Freshly ground black pepper, to taste

¼ cup all-purpose flour

2 tablespoons vegetable oil, a bit more if needed

4 cups hot creamed corn

4 ounces (1 stick) butter, at room temperature, cubed

¼ cup lime juice

1 teaspoon or more lime zest

Cilantro, for garnish

A handful of clover sprouts, if you can find them, or use any
    pretty sprouts

Smoked sausage, chopped into very small pieces (about 8
    tablespoons), for garnish (Portia uses Conecuh Sausage
    Company brand)

1. Pat the scallops until very dry and wrap in paper towels.
2. Unwrap and season with the salt and pepper. Lightly dust with the flour.
3. Let the scallops sit for 1 minute or so on a plate, so they become totally dry.
4. Heat the oil in a nonstick skillet on medium-high heat.
5. Add the scallops to the skillet. Leave 1 inch between them, so they will brown and not steam.
6. Cook for 2 minutes without moving them. Then use tongs to flip the scallops.
7. Put the hot corn on plates.
8. Cook the scallops for 2 minutes more.
9. Put the scallops on the corn. They will cook a bit more on their own.
10. Melt the butter in the skillet. Scrape up any brown bits from the pan. Stir in the lime juice and the zest and pour the sauce over the scallops. Top with the cilantro and sprouts and sprinkle the sausage around each plate.

●

After dinner, Portia and Buddy submitted to a goodbye photo session with me, a game that I have begun to call the Many Emotions Of . . . I say *sad*: you make your sad face and I photograph you. I say *shocked*: you make your shocked face. Portia didn't have to be pushed; she was vivid and precise in each of about thirty different photos, a combination of Meryl Streep and Lucille Ball.

Buddy, on the other hand, had about three slightly varying expressions, all executed with his hands on his hips. "You two are so perfect for each other," I said, as we reviewed the photos. Buddy smiled and nodded his head, then raised his eyebrows.

Portia hadn't gotten the best parents in the world, as much as she had loved them. But something about the way she was raised led her to Buddy, who had helped keep her alive and helped her thrive.

Even their dogs seem perfect for each other. Angus is small and cuddly and impish, running in circles and easily excited. Harley is tall and languid and reserved, until something interests her, and then her laser focus is inexhaustible. Which reminded me, of course, of Portia and Buddy.

Portia had brought Angus into the mix.

"I knew Harley needed a friend. The goats have their friends. The donkeys have their friends. And even the chickens have a close community," she said, quite seriously. "But Harley didn't have a *friend*. So I said to Buddy, 'I'm going to get Harley a friend,' and he was against it. 'Portia, she's a dog. She doesn't need a friend,' he said.

"'Why do you think they put them in twos on Noah's Ark?' I asked Buddy."

We all took a moment to think about this.

"Well, it was actually to mate," I said, even though I liked her idea.

"Yeah, but still," Portia replied and scratched Harley's head.

●

To be attached to a home and a person, animal, or a job—even the animals on this farm have that. It's so wonderful, so natural.

I wanted that again. Someday.

In the meantime, I had not just been fed—I had not just *feasted*—I had been genuinely comforted. I felt like a prodigal friend come back home.

Eleven

WYLER

When I was in college in Athens, Georgia, my friend Wyler's tiny town of Watkinsville, about thirty minutes away, was where the hard-core hipsters and hippies lived. Because Portia and Wyler and I were in a sorority, we didn't go there much. We lived in a giant antebellum mansion with ornate wrought-iron balustrades and two of the largest and oldest magnolia trees in Athens. We ate our meals in this house, before which we sang the sorority blessing, and did things that you do in a sorority, many of which were very good (make dear friends, socialize, volunteer, etc.), and many of which never felt suited to me but were an unspoken norm (dressing a certain way, having a limited social circle, maintaining a faux-virginal facade, getting engaged at twenty), and many of which remain dubious for just about anyone (drinking before lunch). Wyler, who was my "little sister" in the sorority, had had more of a traditional southern upbringing than I. She had been presented at a cotillion in Columbus, Georgia, and had a much more stable family growing up. But she was always extremely curious about other people, other cultures, and the world outside her own.

Visiting her at home in Columbus one weekend during college, I saw a side of Wyler beyond sorority cocktail parties. Her architect father had designed their house on Lake Oliver, where she and I canoed for hours, surrounded by dense woods through which chimney smoke from hidden houses rose in lovely gray curls. She was a really good canoeist—something that had little value back at the sorority house but impressed me greatly. And she introduced me to the wonderful scramble dog, at the Dinglewood Pharmacy. A scramble dog requires a rectangular dish into which two hot dogs are sliced, covered with chili and beans, topped with pickle slices and oyster crackers, and squirted with mustard and ketchup.

After two years, I dropped out of the sorority, stopped straightening my wildly curly hair, which made me look like a dandelion, and began buying all my clothes at Potters House (which was like Goodwill, but smellier). I got a job at the vegetarian, wheat-head Bluebird Café, where none of us brushed our hair), smoked rolled cigarettes, and started doing radio at WUGA, the alternative radio station, where I met my friend Tripp.

I moved into a grubby little house at the bottom of a big hill, near the sanitation plant and close to a kudzu-covered rail trestle, with Tripp and an accounting professor/Ultimate Frisbee freak, who was so handsome that more than a couple of my friends ended up sleeping with him (we'd play cards, it would get late, I'd go to bed, and the next morning my friend would still be there), and who was best friends with Mike Mills, of the then-exploding band R.E.M.

I began to avoid my old sorority friends, as if trying on personalities to see what fit, but also because I told myself that I didn't trust that they'd understand why I needed to remove myself from a restrictive way of living—or why doing so meant my not remaining friends with them. I didn't understand it myself. The truth was my parents weren't paying for my college. I had no money left for classes or sorority dues, and I was sure I couldn't wait tables and be in a sorority. So I spent the rest of my six-year college career dropping out, working to make enough money to pay for a class or two, and dropping out again—over and over, until I had only one Spanish class left, at which point I got a real job and dropped out for good.

Wyler had always gravitated to life beyond our little community of beer parties and spring dances. She collected interesting people, was drawn to artists, fell in love with and actually became friends with her coolest professors—and she had wild hair, too. When she finally moved away from sorority life, she did so in a much more graceful way than I had. She didn't deal in absolutes just to save face. She didn't pretend she'd never been that other person in order to become someone new.

A few times while I was living in New York, many years later, I called her or maybe she called me. She had settled down after years of traveling and working around the world and was in Arizona, where she told me she was studying to become a naturopathic doctor at one of the only certified colleges at that time.

A witch doctor, I thought. We caught up a little bit, and before we hung up, she said, "Emily, it seems like every time you call me you're drunk."

"I know," I replied, and didn't call her again for years.

After she moved back to the Athens-Watkinsville area, Wyler had been among the first of many people who'd posted a variation of this on my Facebook wall: "Come here, we have room, let's cook."

We decided that while she worked, I'd spend the day exploring Athens, driving around, and taking pictures of places I'd lived in, including the dump, the Taylor-Grady House, a landmarked antebellum mansion with giant Ionic columns and a formal garden, where I had lived in the basement off the garden and been caretaker one year.

When we finally met up, she looked ten years younger than she was: slender and athletic and completely natural, her pale blond hair still untouched by man-made lighteners, her ice-blue eyes sparkling.

When I got out of my car, she yelled, "Emily Nunn!" Which startled me, but it was also flattering, like being called onstage for an award. She's petite but has this gigantic gravelly voice, which I'd forgotten about. When she's excited or enthusiastic, which is often, she sort of yells, and she says *fuck* a lot. Which makes whatever you're doing seem like it must be the most wonderful thing ever. Even if it's buying some okra. Wyler doesn't just live in each moment, she *lives!* in it. How had I gone so long without her in my life? More important: Why had I?

"I have to go to the greenmarket!" she said, almost immediately, so we ran across the street, in a slight drizzle, where the baskets of organic vegetables were nearly empty at the end of the day. "Fuck!" she said. "No brussels sprouts!" Instead, she bought some beautiful deep garnet-colored okra, which I'd never seen before, only the green ones.

On the way over to Chef Hugh Acheson's the National, a restaurant I'd been curious about (I'd worked at the Athens's haute cuisine restaurant when we were in school, and it was pretty awful; the Grand Marnier soufflé was a big deal), Wyler found a large purple beet lying on the sidewalk, with the stem and pretty leaves still attached. She picked it up and put it in her bag. "Somebody lost a beet," she said, as if this were a commonplace way to get your produce.

We shared appetizers at the bar: a plate of marinated anchovies with pickled chiles, caper berries, and tomato-garlic toasts; some stuffed Medjool dates with celery and manchego cheese; and a pizzette with butternut squash, Fontina, bacon, almonds, and arugula, all of which were completely delicious and satisfying.

Athens had sure changed since I'd worked at the Bluebird Café, where we served wonderful but predictable vegetable plates at lunch (your choice of three or four vegetables, with a whole wheat biscuit; apple butter on the table) and tofu with vegetables and nutritional yeast at breakfast, as well as morning custard, which I have thought about longingly since those years, and for which I tracked down the recipe, from the Culinary Institute of America grad Chef Carol Babb, who still lives in Athens and happens to have become a friend of Wyler's. After I visited Wyler, I got in touch with Carol for the recipe, feeling nostalgic. Since then I have made this many times, and it is the most soothing thing, and not just in the morning. As the world around it changed, it lost none of its power. That fact alone is comforting.

Morning Custard

(adapted from *Joy of Cooking*)

Makes about 4 cups

4 cups milk, scalded

4 egg yolks, lightly beaten

½ cup honey (you may substitute sugar, in an equal amount, but
   the Bluebird was pro-honey)

½ teaspoon salt

1 teaspoon pure vanilla extract

Heat the milk until it begins to steam and small bubbles form at the edges. Reserve 1 cup of the scalded milk and transfer the remaining 3 cups milk to a double boiler. Slowly stir the reserved milk into the egg yolks, then slowly stir the egg mixture into the milk in the double boiler. Add the honey and salt, and continue to cook over medium-low heat until the mixture has thickened, about 20 minutes, being careful not to allow the egg to overcook and curdle. Add the vanilla. Cool in the refrigerator. Serve in parfait dishes or custard cups. Sprinkle with nutmeg.

Note: This is not the same as baked custard; the consistency makes it perfect for serving over fruit or pound cake, but I like to eat it with a spoon, which is how we served it at the Bluebird Café, in a little soup cup with a bare dusting of nutmeg. So wonderful.

●

Catching up over our fancier meal at the National, it was not surprising that Wyler had changed, but it felt as if she had changed into a concentrated truer version of someone she'd always been, with whatever possible false parts fallen away.

Had I known in college that she was gay? I can't remember; she dated plenty of cute men and always had a date to all the dances, but now she was happily out and planning dinner the next night for her girlfriend and me. And she wasn't fooling around with the naturopath thing, which was probably why she looked so great.

After she'd finished a doctorate in naturopathic medicine in Arizona, she told me, she got a master's in acupuncture. While she was living in Durham, practicing at an alternative medicine center, she lectured at Duke University School of Medicine and the University of North Carolina's School of Medicine. During this same time, I had some pants hemmed, as my younger sister liked to say, in response to the dazzling achievements of others.

We were both exhausted, so I followed Wyler, who drove too fast in the dark, to her charming old house, the kind of groovy, art-centric place we'd dreamed of living in during college. After meeting her dog and talking for about twenty minutes in the kitchen, which, like the rest of her house, was filled with her huge collection of beautiful art pottery by local artists and UGA professors, she startled me when she said, "I'm so fucking upset! I have to go to bed. I have to work tomorrow!"

She put me upstairs, in an attic room whose walls, dormered windows, and ceiling were completely paneled with beaded heart pine tongue and groove. Her cat, Gregory, slept with me (against my will, frankly, and way too close to my face), and when I woke up Wyler had showered and was in the kitchen placing a beautiful fried egg on toast.

"You don't want one?!" she said. I really wanted a giant coffee, or for her to put the speed on the perfect cappuccino she was making—I'd forgotten how methodical and intense she was about any task she was executing. She's exactly the kind of person you'd want to be your doctor.

Or your psychiatrist. "You know, Emily, I was thinking about you and what's happened in your life. And I think you're the sort of person who seems so okay all the time, so laid-back and flexible, that people who've gotten dependent on that part of you might get upset and not be able to handle it when you can't be that way anymore, when you have to stop." I knew she was talking about my breakdown, and how abandoned I'd felt by the people closest to me, but we just let it go at that. It was enough to hear it. I didn't need to talk.

I heard a little bit about the patients she was seeing that day, during the cappuccino ordeal, and how they were doing. She mentioned that coconut water is "the same pH and osmolality as your blood. In patients dying of dehydration, you could IV it right into the veins." (I jotted this down, just in case.)

And then she sped off. While she was at work, I visited friends in Athens, explored the huge district of landmarked architecture in nearby Madison, a town spared by General William Sherman on his March to the Sea because it happened to be the home of a senator who was friends with his brother, and spent the rest of my time working on her screened back porch, where her dog, Riley Mae, ate from a big bowl of pecans, just cracked them with her teeth and used her tongue to delicately lift out the meats.

Just as I had with Portia, I took long walks with Wyler. Important conversations always seem to come during walks, and I got up the nerve to ask Wyler about coming out. Was it hard? She stopped in her tracks and got an expression on her face that I recalled from college—which was essentially no expression at all but a moment of utter stillness, hands at her neck, as if grabbing a string of invisible pearls left over from sorority days. "Emily, are you fucking kidding me? It was *the* hardest thing I've *ever* done in my life. It completely blew me away." I thought about this; I started crying. "I know I don't really have the right to say this after such a long lapse in our friendship," I said, "but I'm really proud of you."

"Emily, thanks, but what difference does it make how long it's been?" she said. That felt true; it also felt kind of miraculous.

Even though Wyler had been terrified to tell her family, they were great about it; they love her. They wanted her to be happy being her authentic self. I wondered how different Wyler's life might have turned out had she not come out, or if her family had not fully accepted her when she had: Would she be as vivid, as true, as healthy? How would it have distorted the beautiful person I was seeing?

I wanted that for Oliver; maybe he'd still be alive.

I wanted it, too. I wanted the people I had chosen to love and who claimed to love me to accept rather than reject me if it turned out I was not exactly who they wanted me to be, or if I fell down, faltered, needed them desperately.

If only the two of us—Oliver and I—had been strong enough, under pressure, to know that who we were was not just okay but pretty great; if only we'd been able to accept ourselves when others disapproved. He was gone, but I had the chance to build my own compass, to lead myself back in the right direction: toward self-respect, despite the fact that we'd never been taught to continue, to survive. We had to learn that on our own. I knew that finding my friend Wyler again was a part of that compass. She had gone through enormous, transformative changes and thrived.

•

When I finally went to visit her office, I realized the reason I wasn't getting to see her more was not, of course, because she was a witch doctor working out of a secret teepee in the woods but an extremely busy professional who, by the way, could remain immune to misperceptions about her discipline, even from friends who never should have doubted her.

I worried, however, about how her healthy ethos would figure into the kind of dinner Wyler was going to make for me, since a fairly large part of her practice involves diet—the idea being that our bad reaction to food is less allergic than it is chemical. She's gluten-free, low dairy, and, of course, completely organic. "GMO foods are the worst!" she said more than once. "We're going to lose the recipe for nature!" All of which I completely agree with or, at least, admire—the fact that Wyler *had* picked up a beet someone dropped on the sidewalk notwithstanding.

After she'd made dinner for me and her girlfriend, I was really more worried about her losing the recipe for her broiled okra, a simple and practically life-changing dish that I would like to eat every day.

It didn't even seem like the same vegetable I'd had in stewed until it was soggy, stringy, and flavorless, or sliced, and salted until it could have been any other deep-fried thing. Wyler's treatment was crisp and hot, salty and sweet, and impossible to stop eating. Okra was much better as its own self, rather than pretending to be every other vegetable or overdressed like some floozy.

We had it along with brussels sprouts and delicious salmon cakes made with a brand of canned fish that sponsors naturopathic physicians, and a giant green salad, sprinkled with something purple. "What's that on top?" I asked Wyler as we sat down to eat.

"That's the beet I found. I just grated it on top."

•

Wyler's Organic Okra, as dictated by Wyler

1. It's not really a recipe. I use fresh okra, preferably organic and freshly cut, so that you don't have to wash it at all. Washing okra just doesn't work for this. I guess it's kind of like washing mushrooms—you just don't want to do it. Wipe them off if there's a need.
2. Do not cut them; rather, put them whole in a bowl and pour in enough good extra-virgin olive oil to coat them. Be careful not to drench them.
3. Add some coarse sea salt, toss, and place them in a single layer on a shallow tray.
4. I have convection roast on my oven and that's what I use, but when I cook these at anyone else's house I broil them until they just start to brown a little. That's it.

•

People eat them like candy. And I always tell folks to eat them with their fingers. The half inch or so of stem is a perfect handle and can be discarded (as I do) or eaten. Okra gets a bad name for its sliminess, but this takes the slime factor out completely. And it's a great side dish for a brunch.

Wyler's Pure and Simple Salmon Cakes

Makes 4 to 6

Wyler says: "My salmon cakes, I'm afraid, are a bit boring—not to eat, but as a recipe. And I never measure a damn thing, but these are pretty good guesses, I'm hoping."

> 1 (14-ounce) can red (must be red, not pink) wild salmon,
>   completely drained
> 2 large eggs
> ½ cup finely chopped sweet onion, preferably Vidalia
> 4 tablespoons finely chopped celery
> 1 good squirt prepared mustard
> 2 teaspoons finely chopped fresh dill
> ½ cup bread crumbs, or more if needed
> Olive oil or coconut oil

1. Put the salmon in a bowl, add the eggs, and mix well.
2. Add the onion, celery, mustard, and dill, and mix again.
3. Stir in enough bread crumbs to make the mixture stiff enough to form a patty.
4. Heat a cast-iron (imperative!) skillet, before adding enough oil to coat the bottom of the pan. You want it quite hot but not smoking.
5. Add the salmon cakes and turn them after they have browned and crisped a bit. Repeat for the other side. This is great to serve with Crystal hot sauce or a sauce made of yogurt with chopped dill.

•

Wyler's measurements were spot-on, but this is the kind of quick-fix supper that you can make without even thinking about it, once you've made the salmon cakes once or twice. Obviously, when you can get good, fresh, organic, wild-caught, morally pure salmon, you can use that instead in this recipe. I've made these patties using left-over poached salmon.

●

Wyler got up and made absolutely luxurious gluten-free cornmeal pancakes topped with plain yogurt the morning I left, and we finally got around to why I was on my "pilgrimage" when Wyler asked me about Oliver; she'd known him when we were in college, because we'd run into him on campus, and he'd grab me and mess up my hair or just shove me off the sidewalk without saying anything. He was a great dancer, so my sorority girlfriends got a lot of his attention when we had a mixer with his fraternity. He danced with me, too, but he'd always let go of my hand at some point and let me go reeling off across the dance floor. "I remember that," Wyler said. "He was so fucking funny."

To hear someone I cared about remember the funny, happy Oliver, his public persona back then—it broke my heart. I might have gone reeling across the dance floor, off into space, but unlike Oliver, I still had a chance to be who I was supposed to be. I realized my trip was as much about Oliver as it was about me: my obligation to find out what went wrong for both of us, and, for me, how to fix it and find a way back to a happier, fuller life. I needed to do this for no other reason than to prove that it could be done—not just to people who'd given up on both of us, but to myself.

In the years that we had been apart, Wyler has turned into someone who believes in who she is. As our friendship has revitalized, I've noticed that she never stops questioning how to be a better person, her true self. "I want to learn how to be more honest," she said one day, over the phone. And she meant it on a level that resonated with me.

I packed up my car and she got ready for work, and then we acknowledged how great, how easy, how wonderful it was to see one another, and how this wasn't the last time, it was the first time; it seemed to be too good to be true. But it was true, simply because I had reached out I received these giant gifts in return. Neither Portia nor Wyler allowed me to drive off alone. Each one was afraid that I'd get lost and made me follow her in my car, so she could show me the way out of town.

Twelve

DOT

I had known my photographer friend Dot since college, when she was the longtime girlfriend of my college roommate Tripp. But the last time I'd seen her was back in New York, when I was working at the *New Yorker* magazine and going out almost every night to see a play, scout a restaurant, or drink; she was in town for her birthday. It was early in the evening, but I was already tipsy, so accidentally left her present, a copy of Maira Kalman's *Max Makes a Million,* in the taxi I'd taken to her mother's apartment near Lincoln Center (her mother is a concert pianist). Now, decades later, Dot was having her yearly girls' reunion, which I was crashing, at her late grandparents' house in Linville, North Carolina, a nineteenth-century community located in the High Country, not far from Asheville and Pisgah National Forest. This time, I remembered her present, a hand-carved wooden condiment spoon I'd bought at Becky's gallery in Galax.

Dot lives in Linville, too, but the get-together was planned around closing up the house for winter, which made sense once I saw the size of the house, a place that made its majesty known even in the dark as I arrived. When I found the right set of stone stairs and walked inside, nervous about coming upon a crowd I didn't know, Dot, who is slim from biking, with shiny chestnut hair and a timeless cool-kid style, greeted me with a hug as if I'd seen her the week before, accepted my little gift, and said, "Now go upstairs and pick a room." So before I met anybody, I wandered from room to room, looking for a place to put my stuff, counting thirteen bedrooms of various sizes and moods, before I found a room at the north end of the house with pretty twin beds and lovely antiques.

Dot's grandparents bought the house in 1946, and since their passing her family has maintained it for family gatherings, mostly during the summer. Built in the square shingle-and-crossbeam style that is part of the Linville architectural vernacular, its size and grandeur also made it special. Made of chestnut inside and out, it gleamed like a giant piece of burnished antique furniture. But it was as cold inside as it was outdoors—I could see my breath—because the house was built as part of a summer community and not winterized.

The fact that Dot would still be there as my friend, in this other part of the world, in spite of my neglect, seemed spectacular. I never would have believed it was possible when we sat together in a café in college so many years earlier, listening to a tall stand-up bass player with long red hair talking about where we'd be in twenty years. Dot had said, "I know we'll still be friends." It seemed ridiculously hopeful, the idea of friendships or any kind of relationship continuing into the future, building strength and love rather than deteriorating and eventually falling apart. I found that for Dot, keeping people she loved in her life was a policy she'd maintained as much as possible. And she seemed to live her life by the adage that there is no greater way to show love than through good food: Dot is a blast to cook with.

I warmed up pretty fast after I'd eaten leftover soup in the kitchen and joined everybody around the vast fireplace to do what southerners do: tell stories. One of the women, Weedie, had gone to college with Dot and me, and two of them, Katherine and Lynn, had gone to high school with Portia.

It was a nice mix of eccentric and sensible (leaning toward eccentric), and I felt lucky to be there in this amazing house, just listening and drinking tea around the fireplace. As tales unspooled over cocktails, I learned that in our small group alone, our families had been affected by a half dozen suicides, more when we included close friends and untreated family alcoholism with its peripheral dysfunction. These beautiful, smart, athletic, talented women discussed friends who were drinking themselves to death over bad marriages, step-in-laws addicted to pornography, a friend from college who got amnesia while studying in Paris and was never seen again, close relatives who refused to show up to weddings, and relatives who hadn't communicated in thirty years. Our conversation mellowed out and turned back to nostalgia and tamer southern tales, but it stuck with me: no one lives unscathed for long.

Stories, and stories, and stories about circumstances bizarre, grotesque, tragic, and funny. It's an oblique method southerners employ to teach themselves to live right. Or maybe it's just the way they tell one another, without getting too maudlin: *We've all been there, others have it much worse,* and human beings come through the most absurdly soul-killing events and live to tell, refracted through the kind of humor only survivors are privy to. Telling people your stories and listening to theirs was the way my southern friends had always had of helping the people they loved carry their load, no matter how heavy or light it might be.

I felt so cozy that I started to nod off. "I'm going to bed," I said apologetically, even though I wanted to hear more. I could tell this party wasn't ending anytime soon.

"Why leave? We used to sleep right in front of the fireplace," said James, a charming southern lawyer who'd known Dot since they were teenagers and had dropped by later in the evening. I could hear him beginning another story as I climbed the stairs to sleep.

Even though I had been the first to go to bed the night before, I was somehow the last one to get up in the morning. Time for a big hike. In fact, any time was time for a big hike with this group. Everyone in attendance was a hiker, runner, or biker, and they all loved being outdoors in the mountains.

First, of course, somebody took over making sandwiches while others were downing breakfast, including fresh eggs that Portia had sent along, which were delicious on a piece of buttered toast with salt and pepper; we loaded up and drove toward one of the medium-difficult trails below Grandfather Mountain.

I'd missed hiking in the mountains, being with a group of people, not really talking, just taking in the scent of the forest, the changing light, the birds and streams and all of it while trying not to hurt myself by tripping over a branch or falling into a ravine, being alert for bears. You can't do this with a group of virtual strangers without a certain amount of genuine affection for everyone and everything welling up in your heart, even if you're the last one in line, and especially if you have to be helped onto that last giant step that gets you to the rocky peak, where it feels like you can see the whole world.

We did two different mountain trail hikes in about four hours, and ended up having our sandwich lunch in the sun, all of us stretched out on a dock attached to a mostly empty boathouse on a still, slate-blue lake. The sandwich Lynn passed over to me was the best sandwich I'd ever eaten. *Another best damn sandwich.*

"Who made this? What in the world is in it?" I asked, holding the wheat bread apart and staring at it.

"Kosher salami, pancetta, cheese, and roasted peppers," Katherine said kindly, as if she were talking to a blind person.

"Here," said Dot, passing me a bag of sea-salted almonds and chocolate. "Hypothermia food." But I wasn't cold. I focused on my fabulous sandwich and listened to other people talking, the boats bumping against the dock in the breeze, and the chatter of birds.

●

If you think that you cannot cook, but you would like to make something to eat for people you love or people you wish to bring into your life and keep them there forever, consider starting with a sandwich. Everybody likes sandwiches. In my opinion, making a sandwich is cooking. Especially if you cut it on the diagonal and put it on a plate. I'd suggest starting with pimento cheese, which I've served all my life, and which everyone loves. But I'm also recommending a strange sandwich my mother used to make, because it is a fine example of how making just a little effort—throwing together things you like and pressing them between slices of toast—can lead to further exploration and possibly a whole new life in the kitchen. Making sandwiches can be the culinary gateway to making friends, joining the world, bringing people together, keeping them in your life.

Every time you make a sandwich is a new opportunity to give someone else the best damn sandwich they ever had.

Emily's Pimento Cheese

Makes much more than you should consume in one sitting

1 pound very sharp or sharp cheddar cheese, grated
½ cup mayonnaise (more if necessary; it's just to bind)
1 (4-ounce) jar pimentos, drained (juice reserved) and finely
   chopped
Lots of black pepper (but probably no more than ½ teaspoon)
A few shakes of Tabasco sauce

Combine the cheese, mayo, pimientos, some of their juice, black pepper, and Tabasco. Adjust the seasoning to taste. I usually use about half the pimiento juice from the jar. It helps to let this sit for a while before eating, so the flavors can blossom. You can eat it on saltines or on toast with more mayo. Some people, ridiculous ones, eat it on celery. Never ever add things like pickle relish, diced onions, or herbs in an effort to jazz up your pimento cheese. It doesn't need your help.

My Mother's Southern Salami Sandwich

Makes 1

Jewish rye bread (with seeds)
American cheese (you can use sandwich slices of cheddar if you're
   going to be a snob about it, but it won't be the same, trust me)
Hard salami
Chunky blue cheese dressing from a jar (I like Marie's)

For each sandwich, toast 2 slices of rye bread. While it is still hot, lay
on 2 slices of cheese and 4 to 6 slices of salami. Quickly spoon on
a few tablespoons of the blue cheese dressing. Press together, cut,
and eat immediately. While I suggest that this sandwich be eaten
right away, it is also good in a lunch box, because the dressing
soaks into the bread.

•

I was so thankful to be among this group of friends who'd stayed
in touch for so many years, who were letting me in, pulling me up
steep rock faces, and feeding me, that I decided I'd make them something more than sandwiches. I'd make dinner that night. A familiar
feeling—I adore you so now I will feed you—had awakened in me
again. I remember thinking, *Oh, there it is*. I wanted their connection
to rub off on me.

•

Dot made an enormous salad—she turned into my salad idol over the
weekend; she adds chopped dried fruit and nuts and makes dressings
that are not overpowering, the way I often do. Her mellower dressings
may be a reflection of her personality.

Not that long ago, if I'd had more than six people in my house,
I would have been a wreck. To Dot, it was no big deal. She was
comfortable with her home and her life. Otherwise known as being
comfortable with who she was.

Dot's Fantastic Salad Dressing

Makes about 2 cups

SHAKE TOGETHER IN A JAR WITH A TIGHT-FITTING LID:
⅓ cup seasoned rice vinegar
⅓ cup balsamic vinegar
⅓ cup cider vinegar
¾ cup olive oil
1 tablespoon Dijon mustard
1 tablespoon red miso (to give it depth)
2 garlic cloves, pressed
Freshly ground black pepper, to taste

Dot's Salad

Butter lettuce, or a mix of red and green leaf lettuce (not bagged
prewashed mixes)

**THEN GRAB ANYTHING THAT IS IN THE FRIDGE,
SUCH AS:**
Cucumbers, carrots, celery, and/or avocado
Apple or orange (see Note)
Pecans or slivered almonds, toasted in a toaster oven (watch
them; I myself am a notorious nut burner)
Cheese, whatever you have (feta, goat, blue), crumbled, or some
ribbons of Parm, shaved
Some basil or mint leaves snipped into thin strips, to add to the
top (optional)

*Note: Peel both, then, if it is an orange, cut between the membrane
sections to get only the pulp (do this over the lettuce that is already
in the bowl to catch the juice); if it is winter, use pomegranate seeds
as your fruit.*

Pour that yummy dressing over the salad 5 to 10 minutes before you plan to eat it.

•

I made Marcella Hazan's roasted pepper and Italian sausage on pappardelle, which is both hearty and fancy enough for company. However, you absolutely have to peel the peppers for this dish; otherwise the textures are off and the peppers don't meld into the other flavors the way they should. So please don't bother making it if you're not going to do this.

Red and Yellow Bell Pepper Sauce with Sausages

(adapted from Marcella Hazan's *Essentials of Classic Italian Cooking*)

Serves 4

3 meaty bell peppers: 1 red, 2 yellow

4 tablespoons extra-virgin olive oil

2 tablespoons chopped onion

4 sweet sausages (without fennel seed, chile pepper, or other strong seasonings) cut into ½-inch pieces (about 1½ cups)

Salt, to taste

Freshly ground black pepper, to taste

1 cup canned imported plum tomatoes, drained and chopped

1½ pounds dry pasta (Marcella uses a full recipe of pappardelle, though)

2 tablespoons good butter

⅔ cup grated Parmigiano-Reggiano cheese, plus more for serving

1. Cut the bell peppers into 4 sections; discard the seeds and cores. Peel the sections with a vegetable peeler. Cut into 1-inch pieces; set aside.
2. Put the oil and onion in a large skillet over medium-high heat. Cook, stirring, until the onion turns pale gold, about 5 minutes.

Add the sausages; cook for 2 to 3 minutes. Add the bell peppers; cook, turning occasionally, for 7 minutes. Season with salt and pepper; stir well. Add the tomatoes; reduce the heat to low. Cook for 20 minutes, until the oil floats free of the tomatoes. Meanwhile, cook the pasta. Finish by adding the butter to the sauce. Place the pasta and sauce in a serving bowl; toss. Add the cheese; toss. Serve with more cheese at the table.

•

We all sat down together for this meal in the dining room, which has robin's-egg-blue cabinetry hand-painted with alpine flowers, and is filled with majolica and antique china. It has a fireplace, too, which we lit to keep us warm long enough to eat, before moving our party back to the big fire in the living room for another storytelling session. As large and rambling as the house was, it seemed to be the homiest place in the world—its age, the unmodernized kitchen, the rustic sunrooms, a little area for watching football, children's chairs and board games, a guest book, family photos, a record of connected lives, a home for several families at once.

In the morning, we took a long walk across the Donald Ross golf course lined with log fences and through the neighborhood surrounding the Eseeola Lodge. Then everyone naturally fell into closing up Dot's house: cleaned out the refrigerator and washed the towels as if it were their own home, then packed their cars and said goodbye.

I didn't have to leave yet—I really had no place else to be—so I went to sit on the side porch made of stone. When Dot came out to find me, I asked if there was anything else I could do.

"No, I love that you are the most low-maintenance person I have ever known," she said.

"Nobody has ever told me that before," I replied incredulously. Maybe I was not who I thought I was.

I ended up staying for four more days, but at Dot's real house, right around the corner.

She had most of a bushel basket of organic red peppers left from the girls' weekend. "We're going to make that pepper dish for Greg," she said, while we were unpacking her car. Greg is Dot's boyfriend, a slender, goateed painter and sculptor with a North Carolina High Country accent. I liked him immediately because he peeled the peppers for me, which is a pain, while describing what his family ate when he was growing up in this area: pinto beans and corn bread, but also leather britches, which I'd never heard of—basically dried green beans, reconstituted.

Dot had been divorced for years, and her two kids, Cole and Locke, split their time between parents. Locke was with her father, but there was a photo of her in Dot's office from a wry series Dot had shot of women wearing their divorced mothers' wedding dresses. Locke has her chin in her hand, looking as if she can't believe she ever agreed to pose for the photo, but also looking gorgeous, like Dot, which made me wish I had a daughter, too.

●

I slept in Locke's bunk bed, in her pink and lavender room, and woke up at 8:30 to the syrupy-sweet, smoky scent of red bell peppers on the grill. "How wonderful," I said, standing over the charred vegetables. "And how bizarre."

"I love to cook in the morning," Dot said. She had filled the sink with salad greens for a wash and already put up some peppers in olive oil. It was a home-cooking no-brainer, and I decided I'd adopt early morning cooking, when I was fresh and rested, so that I'd never be too busy or tired to make a nice dinner for myself.

I was free to do things differently from the way I'd learned, or the way I'd been told was the only right one. I could operate in the kitchen any way I wanted, any way that made me happy.

In the afternoon Dot took me to an art gallery nestled on a nearby hill to show me some of her astounding, richly colored photographs of dead birds. It sounds morbid, but she'd shot them so close up—on one patch of feathers, an ebony beak, and the rest a blur—that these ordinary things were strange again. You had to recalculate what you were seeing. The images were like spirits, proud and soft, but gone.

"My brother told me to shoot these," she said.

"I don't know what you mean by that," I said. Her only sibling, her brother, David, had died when we were in college—a suicide brought on by his bipolar illness.

"I mean that I was asleep and dreaming, and David was there and he said, 'Photograph the birds.' It happened; I don't care what anybody thinks," she said.

So I told her about the cardinal thing, which I'd kept to myself until now. "I can't even miss Oliver the person," I said. "I have to have a bird. And I can't stop being so fucking mad." I may have been realizing that fact for the first time, right as I said it. I was so angry. And I was still amazed by the fact that I ever could have loved people (the Engineer, members of my own family) who seemed to see my grief as useless and annoying.

"You got out," she said. "Something was telling you to get out. Maybe Oliver was watching over you. I believe that is possible. I do." I thought about being back in Barcelona, when I fell. I'd seen Oliver's face for the last time then.

Late that night we took a walk with Dot's two dogs, a giant white Great Pyrenees named Shug and sweet Rosie, a geriatric border collie. It was so dark I truly could not see a single thing as we made our way through a stand of trees, even though the stars were bright; I kept tripping. Dot grabbed my arm and turned on her cell phone flashlight to light the path. That simple act, a friend lighting my way for me, stayed with me. Other people could keep me safe; they didn't have to be the source of pain.

When I went to bed that night, in Locke's lavender bed, I let myself remember Oliver without pushing him away, and I considered the idea of Oliver's watching over me. For the first time, it didn't hurt to think of him. And I went to sleep.

I didn't know it at the time, but after that weekend Dot would become the best friend I've had in my life, and I would visit her and Locke and Cole again and again. We would take trips together, confide in each other, light the way for each other no matter how dark it got.

As my relationship with Dot grew closer, Locke and her brother, Cole, began to feel like my family. Cole, who was fifteen, can make getting lost in the forest a culinary adventure. I discovered on one trip back to beautiful Linville, which sort of became my third home, that he goes frog gigging in the middle of the night, hunts with a bow and arrow, and knows what to do with a deer or a turkey or trout once he's killed it. (I have two of his recipes for venison sausage, which he demonstrated for me after I asked him why he kept loading more deer meat into the freezer.) He catches trout with his bare hands, which I watched him do during one visit, in the freezing cold, plunging into a stream and disappearing several times before coming up with a fish—three of them within ten minutes, actually. "You have to make your hands like water," he said, wiggling his fingers.

When Cole caught the trout, we brought it back to the house, and he and his friend Noah built a smoker in the backyard with an old bedsheet and some sticks. Obviously, most of us will have to use store-bought smokers for the stovetop or outdoors, which are available online. A few days later we had the delicious trout pâté that Dot's mother always requests for her birthday party.

Dot's Smoked Trout Pâté

Makes 2½ cups

If you own a smoker, smoke 2 to 3 medium trout in your backyard, picking the bones and skin from the trout. Otherwise, buy smoked trout at the grocer. For this recipe, I use two 5-ounce packages.

> 1 (8-ounce) package cream cheese, at room temperature
> 1 to 2 garlic cloves, depending on your preference
> Lemon juice, to taste (I use about 2 tablespoons)
> Salt, to taste
> White pepper, to taste
> A few drops of Tabasco sauce, to taste

Crumble the fish into the bowl of a Cuisinart. Add the cream cheese, garlic, lemon juice, salt, pepper, and Tabasco. Use the Cuisinart blade to combine all the ingredients into a smooth pâté. This is good on anything, but I like it on thin slices of chewy French bread. When I put it on a bagel, it reminds me of my regular Saturday lunch in New York City, when I got the smoked trout special at Zabar's down the street from my apartment, then took it to Riverside Park to eat in front of the community garden.

Note: I have on occasion also added a couple of teaspoons of pre-pared horseradish; delicious.

●

Not much later, I barged in on their beach vacation, during which Cole and his friend Noah fished in the ocean, pulled a bushel of clams out of the marsh, and steamed them in beer and garlic. When I hugged Dot goodbye, I said, "You know I'm trying to steal your family, don't you?"

"That's fine, they love you, you can be their aunt," she replied. "After all, I think of us as sisters."

●

But on this first trip to see Dot, when it was time to go, she led me out of town just the way Wyler and Portia had, arm waving out the window of her car before she headed back to her own life. I drove in my own direction. With nowhere else to go, I was heading back to Galax, back home to make a plan.

Thirteen

THE STUFFED PANTRY

When I arrived back at John and Mariah's, it was getting close to dinnertime. No one was there, so I opened the tall double-doored kitchen pantry to see what I might use to make a meal. The stacks overwhelmed me, so I looked in the refrigerator where I found a packet of sliced dried beef (for creamed chipped beef), which sent me reeling back to the pantry, then to the overstuffed upright freezer in the laundry room, which released an avalanche of frozen foods I could not identify. There was no way I was opening the second refrigerator in the basement storage room or the mini fridge in the bar.

Aunt Mariah's daughters, my sister Elaine, and I all agreed that Mariah's food-storage situation had reached critical mass many times over. And we'd said so, repeatedly. It was not really fair of us to criticize, since we were always welcome at John and Mariah's house, where they used the pantry and refrigerator to feed us. She would certainly never inspect our refrigerators, but even if she did, she'd never rudely comment on them, however shocking she found them.

But now I went back to the pantry and refused to look away. I simply wanted to process the immunity to disposal Aunt Mariah had given the old jars of relish and the sugarless candy no one eats, a vacuum-packed side of Scottish salmon that was six years old, seven different brands and grinds of grits, assorted boxes of pasta with only a few strands or shells or tubes rattling in the bottom—useless together, not enough for a meal alone. There was also grape jelly that no one in the family liked, boxes of saltines and Ritz crackers with most of the sleeves opened by the grandchildren, and assorted homemade canned goods from forgotten gift givers. Boxes of oatmeal, both instant and steel cut, one unopened jar of jumbo Spanish olives stuffed with almonds, three types of barley, Jordan almonds, a six-pack of Nabs, four open bottles of raspberry and other flavored vinegars, a high-to-low collection of olive, walnut, and hazelnut oils, a Hershey bar, and a small pile of two-cracker packets of restaurant Captain's Wafers.

Before I'd left for Portia's, Aunt Mariah had climbed the step stool to get a jar of apple butter, which had been on the highest shelf in the back, along with hoarded jars of Martha's pickles. It sat on the marble-topped island, brown and conspicuous, as I walked through the kitchen to load the car. Aunt Mariah said, "Here's some home-made apple butter; you can take that as a hostess gift."

"I'm not sure—"

"It's homemade," she interjected. This was the only way for her to get surplus food out of the house. She couldn't waste it. She had to ride it out attached to visitors. I took the apple butter to make Aunt Mariah happy.

It's much easier to cram new items on top of the old than it is to coldly cull them—even when some of them are turning into poison. As I stared into the dusty depths of Aunt Mariah's pantry, I realized this was the half-assed way I'd been living for the past year, obsessively examining the muddled contents of my brain, looking for something good and intending to toss out the bad, but just leaving a lot of rotting stuff in there instead.

As far as her refrigerator and pantry went, I imagine Aunt Mariah had her reasons.

For me, however, my inability to discard expired ideas and attitudes was beginning to seem dangerous.

I had to start a new story, rather than continue an old one. As a pretty neurotic kid, I'd believed I'd somehow grow up to be like Barbie, driving a lavender convertible with flower decals, wearing lots of cute outfits with matching purses and mod hats, and marrying a cute boyfriend with a crew cut. Or I'd tried to. In the back of my head, I think I knew that even if I became Barbie someday, I'd be Barbie the Divorcée, whose foldout house contained a table set for one, with plastic food that came in tiny single servings.

I wanted to put the lessons I'd learned to work, but the new affection I had for Galax outweighed my fear of being alone forever. I went to movies and had more dinners with wonderful Mary Margaret and her friends at one of the two good Mexican restaurants in Galax (mushroom quesadilla, every single time), but I didn't see her as much as I would have liked; I was shy about asking her to spend more time with me. I went with Becky to a giant arts and crafts fair out in the countryside, to scout possible artists for the gallery downtown, and later went to the gallery's holiday party on Main Street. When Aunt Mariah mentioned that she was going to the holiday concert at the Baptist church (even though she was a Methodist) and that I didn't have to come but I could if I wanted to, I went, and the preacher was a man who used to show up bareback on a horse in the summer when we were all teenagers and whose cute brothers wore Future Farmers of America jackets and played on all the sports teams. The choir included the woman who sang "Leaving on a Jet Plane" and "I'll Never Fall in Love Again" in the yearly talent show with Elaine, and a woman whose husband I kissed at a basement party long before they were married. The choir director was the daughter of the vice principal of my high school. They were all still here, continuing the lives they'd begun years ago, with their children and jobs and joyful choral expertise, and I was back with nothing to show for whatever it was I'd been doing since I'd left. What had I been doing, exactly? I seemed unable to recall a single worthwhile thing.

●

On November 6, my birthday, the first since Oliver had died, John and Mariah took me into Winston-Salem for a movie and dinner at their regular spot, the Village Inn. I kept thinking it was the first of all my remaining birthdays that I would no longer share with him. I remember I had vanilla ice cream for dessert.

When we got home, Aunt Mariah took me upstairs to the attic off the big bedroom to show me the decorative eggs she'd brought home from their trip to Russia. While we were sifting through stacks of photos and papers, memories she'd built with the family she'd created, I found a framed photo of Oliver with his child, then a baby, asleep on his chest, both of their eyes closed, at peace, which caught me off guard. I put it back quickly, closed the drawer.

"Oliver had happiness in his life," Aunt Mariah said.

She tended to say the perfectly right thing, allowing you to have your own thoughts instead of loading you down with her own. That there had been a time in my life when Aunt Mariah and I had not been close was unbelievable to me now, and I wanted all that time back.

We went back down to the breakfast room, I made us cups of decaf, and we waded into a conversation about my mother, who'd been one of Aunt Mariah's best friends for so many years. They'd raised us right across the street from each other, in houses too small by far, while their husbands, who were brothers, were on the road selling furniture for the family business. They were so poor that Aunt Mariah would pack sandwiches for John to eat in the car the first few days of the week. On Friday nights Mom would occasionally get a call that our St. Bernard, Butterfly, had gotten into the school gym and was running around during the high school basketball game; Aunt Mariah would have to stand in the street between our two houses, like a sentry watching eight cousins, all under the age of ten, until Mom had driven down to the gym and retrieved our enormous dog.

How could a friendship of such long standing fade? It all came down to two pivotal events when we were kids: my mother had stopped talking to their mutual close friend Millie and there had been my parents' divorce, which caused more disappearances. Our circle got smaller and smaller. "She divorced everybody," Aunt Mariah said, not knowing that I'd always felt my mother had divorced me, too, back when I was a kid. That sometimes it felt like she was surprised to see me—(oh, are you still here?).

"Millie was devastated, she never understood," Aunt Mariah said. "And she never stopped caring about your mother. Neither did I." I knew the feeling. I'd still do anything in the world to have an intact family.

When I was in college, my mother moved away from Galax with her new husband, her former costar Emile de Becque. There was not really much room in her life for any of us after that. When I visited their home, I felt like a guest who'd come at a bad time. I'd occasionally get boxes of my stuff in the mail, things that were taking up too much room in their home together but that I certainly didn't have room for: a box of my sports trophies or childhood books, my photo albums.

In college, and for a long time after, I often had no place to go, no place I felt comfortable during the holidays. Aunt Mariah and Uncle John must have thought I was with my own family, but there was no home left for us. And I always wished that I could have come to John and Mariah's at Thanksgiving and Christmas. But Millie and Al were there, and I felt as if I had been the one to hurt them. I was too shy, not fully formed enough, to push my way in and get the happiness and love I missed: to tell them I still wanted to be a part of the family group.

Later, my mother and her sister, Pat—her only sibling who lived just an hour away from Galax, with a husband and five kids of her own, and whom we saw a handful of times growing up—stopped speaking. Even though they never saw each other. They managed to be angry over the phone, I guess.

In the intervening years it had begun to wear on me, trying to figure out how to navigate the minefield of who was and was not speaking to whom, feeling guilty if I ended up on one side, getting rejected if it appeared I had chosen another.

After Oliver's funeral, I sent an email to everyone, asking if we might patch things up before someone else died. Nobody responded except my brother Michael, who wrote, cryptically and, it would turn out, noncommittally, "Family is all there is."

•

I'd have taken anything. I had an enduring fondness for my off-kilter childhood, its flashes of love and strange glamour, even if they were just for public consumption. It was mine, and I wanted it back.

But nobody seemed to care. Elaine and I—who had managed to remain devoted and unquestionably loyal despite her years of stand-offs with other women in my family—weren't talking, even though we'd never had a fight. Even though we hadn't been around each other enough to have anything to fight about. And even though I was almost never mad at her.

I was afraid that eventually I'd be completely alone, in a family of seven that was now six. And that because I didn't know how to be with normal people, I thought that I'd keep picking people who punished instead of loved.

It's not like I was exactly innocent. Not long after I'd started working at the *Chicago Tribune*, Elaine, Lisa, and then my mother had stopped talking to one another again, for reasons I never understood, even though Elaine talked to me frequently (almost obsessively) about how angry she was without ever talking to Mom or Lisa. I didn't see how that made sense. You're mad? Talk about it. I got caught in the middle and it made me miserable.

But it finally struck me that the act of stonewalling a loved one—simply freezing them out and never resolving anything—was a learned trait, maybe even an inherited one, which I'd begun to exhibit myself. I admitted to myself that I'd stopped speaking to a handful of friends, or allowed our relationships to wither away out of hurt or anger over some stupid thing. I wanted to unlearn it before it was too late.

I missed my friend Julie, one of the dearest friends I'd had in life, whom I had stopped talking to over something that had seemed monumental at the time but was in fact silly, not long before leaving New York for Chicago. So I gathered up my courage and apologized to her, tried to explain myself, my terrible family trait, making excuses for doing something that now embarrassed me. And, miraculously, Julie accepted me back into her life with so much grace and kindness. There were people who accepted apologies! So I apologized to the other friends I'd frozen out, really *hurt*. Two of them took me back happily. One wasn't interested, which was fair enough; I'd been a jerk. Another was simply unreachable. I still miss her.

"I'm afraid I might have put my faith in the wrong Nunns, Aunt Mariah," I said, full of decaf.

"You didn't have any choice, did you?" she asked.

But I often felt that *everything* that had gone wrong in the life of my family could have been prevented if only I'd tried harder, been more vigilant about the feelings of others. Including my relationship back in Chicago. Despite how unsustainable it had become, I was the one who had ruined it, by *drinking*. And now I had no right to happiness.

"But Emily, that's not all that happened. And he should have helped you with your wine," she replied matter-of-factly.

What? This seemed practically insurrectionary to me. I had never considered the idea that a kinder, more loving person might have been there for me, shown up at Friends and Family Day at Betty Ford, put his faith in me the way I had in him. Rather than worrying more about how it made him look that I needed help, someone who really loved me would simply have helped pull me up rather than pushing me further down. Including back when I told him I could not drink.

Maybe I'd had no choice about whether I was around loving, stable people when I was a little kid. But I had that choice now, and my family was beginning to strike me as more grotesque than tragic, like a *Jerry Springer* episode.

The family I got did not have to be my reference point for my place in the world, which was enormous and beautiful and full of great things that had absolutely nothing to do with them or with their silly fights. It was also a world where many people would sacrifice anything for parents and children, brothers and sisters. Where people stayed connected no matter what because that is what families do.

I had to let go or be dragged.

———

Fourteen

IF ONCE YOU HAVE SLEPT
ON AN ISLAND

Dot rang me up not long after my birthday, and it turned out that we were both at sixes and sevens over the upcoming holidays. I was not invited to be with my siblings Elaine and Michael in Santa Barbara; Dot's kids, Cole and Locke, were going to be with their father. I had plans to be at Pawleys Island at Thanksgiving with John and Mariah and Toni and her gang, but asking to then barge in on their Christmas seemed like pushing it, though they'd made it clear I was welcome always.

"We should take a trip," Dot said.

The words *Cumberland Island* came out of my mouth before I could think. I'd been wondering how I'd make it through cold gray winter; being outdoors had been the only way to stem my frequent bouts of fruitless overthinking. Cumberland, a magical place I'd visited ages ago with my first New York boyfriend and his family, was warm enough to stay outside all day long at Christmastime.

Dot made a reservation so fast I had no chance to back out. She invited her friend Elizabeth to meet us there. It was the best impetuous decision I'd made in years, even though it reduced my rapidly dwindling financial resources.

Geographically speaking, Cumberland Island is the largest (fifty-six square miles), most ecologically intact barrier island in North America, where an almost preposterous array of wildlife lives in its true natural environment—beach and dune, maritime forest, salt marsh, tidal creek, freshwater pond. It was designated by the National Park Service as a protected national seashore in order to stop development back in 1972. The only way to get there is by ferry from Fernandina Beach, Florida, off the southernmost tip of Georgia.

Philosophically speaking, if you can't put your life into proper perspective here, you may as well give up. The ferry ride over is lovely, with dolphins cresting all around. But once you head up the sand and shell path from the dock—past the marshy shoreline, through an archway carved in the thick wall of trees inhabited by tremendous white wood storks—you're in a strange and different world, where it becomes possible to see life in a beautiful new way.

On the short hike to the Greyfield Inn (the only place to stay, unless you camp), Dot and I immediately saw one of the posses of wild turkeys that zip around the island then come to a sudden halt en masse. Wild horses were roaming between long silver-gray tangles of Spanish moss draped over ancient live oaks—their lower branches stretching such great lengths horizontally that they touch the grass then rise back up and outward again. You can recline on these branches without leaving the ground. Armadillos (which we would see frequently) live in the forest with bobcats and wild boar (who remained invisible to us). Alligators and loggerhead turtles lay their eggs on the beach.

It was only about two in the afternoon on Christmas Eve when we reached the inn, a graceful, four-story, antebellum-style mansion, and yet the rugged island naturalist and photographer, Fred, was already prepping the giant stone grill for a Christmas Eve oyster roast before dinner.

The air was damp but not cold. I was going to eat oysters by a fire on an island. I was fortunate.

Since Elizabeth was taking the last ferry and was not meeting us until dinner at eight, Dot immediately headed off with her camera. I climbed the wide steps leading up to the grand veranda that stretches the length of the Greyfield. The rocking chairs, two giant porch swings at each end, and a chest of blankets for napping: it had changed very little in the years since my first visit, when I'd read *Anna Karenina* for the first time on one of the swings, under one of the blankets, on a chilly, mist-gray day.

At one point, the Carnegie family owned about 90 percent of the island; the Greyfield was built in 1900 as a residence for Lucy and Thomas Carnegie's daughter Margaret Ricketson, whose own daughter converted the imposing house into an inn in 1962. She left a massive, age-worn collection of art, furniture, books, and island artifacts intact inside, so staying here was like getting the chance to visit rich old grandparents (who feed you constantly but have no phones, no television, few cars, and room for twenty-seven guests at a time). In the open living room/game room, the dashing portrait I remembered of Lucy—dressed like a chic gypsy in an emerald-green sack dress with a long red headscarf tied pirate-style around her head, a knife on her belt, asserting her style under the burden of being a Carnegie—was still there, along with taxidermy animals atop cabinets, and alligator skulls and shells decorating the deep sills of the ceiling-high windows.

Dot and I ran into each other back on the porch and decided to take a bike ride around the island, which was originally occupied, thousands of years ago, by the Timucua tribe of American Indians, then later followed a familiar progression—Spaniards, war, Brits, plantation owners, more war, rich private citizens, encroaching development. Today, having been taken over by the National Park Service, the island is scattered with a number of giant empty houses along the shore, whose owners released their property to the government (for a price, of course). We didn't run into another human on our ride, but if we had, it probably would have been someone dressed in a forest-green National Park Service uniform.

We pedaled and pedaled for miles over the same wide sand paths used by the horse-drawn carriages that once carried the Carnegies back and forth to Gilded Age parties, through strange, dense forest where muscadine grapevines clung to the branches of pine, hickory, cedar, and live oaks, all twisted together in a canopy of van Gogh whorls. The lush floor was spiky with saw palmettos and resurrection ferns.

The dunes here were as high as fifty feet in spots, swathed in wind-sheared trees, sea oats, and clumps of fluffy muhly grass, the sand stirred into undulating acid-trip patterns by the wind.

We left our bikes behind and climbed up and over the dunes, and the breathtaking beach rose in front of us like a scene from a Bergman movie: a desolate blue, gray, yellow-brown vista of sky and sea, sand and wintry vegetation. Scruffy wild horses were standing like statues on these dunes, looking at the ocean, as if this view were completely new to them, too.

It spread out forever and when we walked along the lonesome beach for a very long time, we didn't feel the need to talk at all.

I picked up huge shells and some of them were full of life, literally occupied by conch and other animals. Other things were dead; I still have the tail of a horseshoe crab I brought back.

When it started to get dark, Dot was so engrossed in her photography work that I rode back alone, on Christmas Eve, through this surreal, almost prehistoric landscape back to the inn, where the lighted windows guided me home.

I arrived with plenty of time before dinner to claim the outdoor cedar shower, where the combination of cool ocean air and steamy heat felt purifying—it seemed to allow whatever faint bitterness was left inside of me to float away like vapor. It was more than worth the slight embarrassment of wearing a turban towel as I returned to my room by the only indoor route, through the inn's kitchen, where the cooks chatted me up and invited me to taste things as I passed through.

When I got back to our room, a sweet haven with William Morris floral wallpaper and two ornate mahogany beds dressed in white chenille spreads, a note ("Sweet Dreams from Greyfield Inn") had been placed on my pillow describing the next day's weather ("High: 70; Low: 42"), the time the sun would rise (7:22 a.m.) and set (5:32 p.m.), and the exact moments when the tide would be at its highest (10:30 a.m.) and lowest (4:29 p.m.) then highest again (10:18 p.m.).

Promises from nature that couldn't be broken.

I would rely more on nature, which is always there to comfort you, even if it is mad at you. Watching the sea through my window, past the marshy woods, I felt as if I was breathing easily for the first time in years and years and years. Just as my mind tried to find troubling thoughts, to relocate worries about repairing my life, I instead sank into the bed and fell asleep in my turban, not dreaming, until the sound of footsteps crunching across the tabby drive underneath my window woke me.

Sleeping on an island really works. I felt hungry for what lay ahead, not just here on this strange, ethereal island, cut off from the rest of the civilized world. I was hungry for the very *next moment* of my life.

Which just happened to be dinner.

The straightforward food they make in the Greyfield kitchen is perfectly delicious but also suited to an atmosphere that has little to do with perfection, everything to do with comfort. There's fresh local fish and the vegetables they serve come from the inn's own organic kitchen garden, where giant turnips, roses, herbs, carrots, tomatoes, and orange and lemon trees were still growing when I went exploring later, even in late December.

By the time Dot got back from the beach, her friend Elizabeth, whom I'd never met before but loved immediately, had arrived. The Christmas Eve oyster roast had been underway for half an hour; I'd gobbled down at least a dozen. Fred cooked bushel after bushel of them, using a wide shovel to scrape them from a grate over the fire and pile them at the end of a long wooden table once they'd begun to open from the heat. Twenty or so of us, dressed for dinner (a couple of men were in dinner jackets), stood on the grass in the dark, awaiting each batch with our giant napkins and oyster knives, until the rocky shells were barely cool enough to pick up and pry open, then with tiny forks we speared them—barely cooked, warm and briny— and dipped them into little pots of good horseradish, cocktail sauce, and sherry butter warming over a chafing candle. After slipping them into our mouths, we tossed the shells into the hole in the middle of the table built expressly for the oyster-roast ritual.

When it was all done, I felt slightly spellbound, as if I'd eaten the sea.

Up in the house, people were making themselves cocktails in the tiny honor bar off the library and digging into a spread of hot canapés, artisanal cheeses, and some sort of fabulous dip with crudités over in the living room, before gathering near the gigantic, roaring fire while a chilly ocean breeze floated in through the front door screens. Elizabeth, Dot, and I sank into one of the old velvet sofas to socialize.

I felt like I was in a Victorian novel. We talked to the four daughters of a local harbormaster, one of whom had also married a harbormaster, and they'd all come over together for Christmas dinner. A mysterious man who had sailed around Cape Horn and all around the world sat down next to me and told me that the thing he missed most at sea was bread, so he had learned to bake.

Baking bread even though you're at sea.

Suppertime at Greyfield is communal, a concept that I had always dreaded as enforced socializing. But that was before the three of us—single women on Christmas Eve—sat down at a long table with nine people we didn't know and ended up making new friends.

The food at the Greyfield must have had something to do with everyone's gregariousness. It is old-fashioned in a way that I love: Why would you stop making something as marvelous as beef Wellington just because someone more fashionable or younger had purchased a sous vide machine? Dinner was fresh red snapper, vichyssoise, fat broiled scallops, lovely organic salads, including a southern version of stacked caprese with red and green tomatoes—simple and gratifying at the end of a long day spent outdoors. The kitchen also turns out an abundance of old-fashioned sweets: crème brûlée, mini apple cobblers with whipped cream, and dense *pots de chocolat*. That first night, we had real Christmas Eve dessert—gingerbread with a tiny scoop of vanilla ice cream sprinkled with cinnamon that made me go straight into the kitchen after dinner to ask for the recipe. It was more like an English pudding than any gingerbread I'd had, and it came to the table buttery and warm, with the ice cream barely beginning to melt.

I make this gingerbread a lot now, but the first few times I tried it, it seemed like ginger brick. Fixing my mistake was a simple matter of using an electric mixer rather than stirring it by hand, as suggested by the chef in her recipe. Thank goodness I recalled that chefs have stronger arms than most other people and will do most everything by hand to avoid dirtying a piece of equipment. The mixer was exactly the help I needed to lighten the batter up.

It's important to persevere when undertaking a recipe you love.

Greyfield Inn's Gingerbread

(from Chef Georgia Kelly)

Serves 8

2 cups all-purpose flour

¼ teaspoon baking soda

2 teaspoons baking powder

½ teaspoon ground cloves

1 tablespoon ground ginger

1 teaspoon ground cinnamon

½ teaspoon salt

4 ounces (1 stick) unsalted butter, plus more for the pan

1 cup boiling water

2 large eggs, beaten

1½ cups dark molasses (this is basically an entire jar; I've had better results using the cheap grocery store stuff over organic boutique brands)

1. Preheat the oven to 350°F. Grease a 9-inch square ceramic baking dish.
2. Sift together the flour, baking soda, baking powder, cloves, ginger, cinnamon, and salt in a large bowl.
3. Melt the butter in the water. Using a hand mixer, incorporate this wet mixture slowly into the flour mixture.

4. Add the eggs and molasses, continuing to mix until well blended (be careful there are no lumps of dry ingredients).

5. Pour into the pan and bake until a toothpick inserted into the center comes out clean, 50 minutes to an hour. Let it cool for 10 minutes. Serve very warm with a scoop of vanilla ice cream sprinkled with cinnamon, whipped cream, or warmed orange marmalade. Or all three.

●

The next day, in addition to a revelatory gingerbread recipe, I also had new friends from our dinner conversations, Malcolm and Judy, whom I later visited with in Charleston—a town that holds the oyster roast in special esteem, in large part as a way of connecting to others.

I felt my life opening up like a beautiful magnolia blossom on this island. That may sound like the corniest thing you've ever heard, but it's the truth.

For lunch the chefs made each of the guests a picnic basket covered with a checked cloth, labeled with our names, and we went right into the kitchen to pick it up whenever we felt like eating. That was my idea of genuine hospitality: welcome to my kitchen. Coffee was always somewhere in the house, depending on the time of day, which was luxurious and nerve-racking, because I really love coffee and will drink all of it. If you stayed around the house to eat your lunch rather than taking it on an outing, soup was set up. We did this only once. The New England clam chowder that Dot, Elizabeth, and I ate under a live oak one afternoon, with a horse grazing nearby, was sublime and perfectly authentic, despite our considerable distance from the Northeast. Mediocre clam chowder is one of those things that can be fine when it is the only thing you know. I probably could have even eaten it from a *can* all my life and been perfectly content. But having this soup, in this spectacular place, reminded me I could make it myself, with fresh fat clams when I could find them, just enough potato and sweet cream, and a pale slick of salted butter on top.

New England Clam Chowder

(adapted from Greyfield Inn's Chef Alberto Gonzales)

Serves 4 to 6

4 strips thick-cut bacon, diced (this is easier to do when the
bacon is very cold from the fridge)

4 tablespoons (½ stick) salted butter

1 small onion, diced (about 1 cup)

3 celery stalks, chopped (about 1 cup; I like to include some
of the pale tender center stalk and some of the delicious
leaves)

½ cup all-purpose unbleached flour

2 cups chopped clams, or 4 (6½-ounce) cans chopped clams with
their juice (see Note)

3 cups milk

2 cups heavy cream

6 medium red-skinned potatoes, diced

Salt, to taste

Freshly ground black pepper, to taste

Tabasco sauce, to taste

Render the bacon on medium heat until it begins to darken and crisp. Add the butter, onion, and celery. Sauté until the onion becomes translucent. Add the flour gradually, stirring as you go, to soak up all excess fat. Now add the clams with their juice, milk, and heavy cream. Stir and add the potatoes. Raise the heat and bring to a boil, turn the heat down to low, and continue to cook until the potatoes are tender. Season with salt and pepper as well as a splash of Tabasco. Serve with oyster crackers and hot sauce on the side, if desired.

Note: If you have access to fresh clams, you are very lucky. Buy them frozen if they are available. I added an extra can of clams once by accident and it was really good; you may, too, if you'd like.

•

One day I joined a group of guests in the back of one of the few trucks on the island for the afternoon tour with Fred the naturalist, which involved sitting on benches in the back and being slapped across the face by palm fronds hanging from trees that lined the sand roads.

We zipped past the rusted shells of cars from the 1920s and '30s that were half-buried in the sand, as if someone had pulled over during a long-ago car rally and decided to walk away from the past. Fred taught us about the island's various ecosystems, the complex science of the dunes. We visited small graveyards (Henry "Light-horse Harry" Lee was buried here but was later exhumed and moved to Virginia to be reburied with family, alongside his son, Robert E.), and two miles south, Dungeness, the mysterious ruins of the original Carnegie estate, an expansive self-sustaining compound that at one time included not just the pristine, intact version of the enormous crumbling 1880 Queen Anne house destroyed by fire, but gardens, pergolas, and more than two hundred outbuildings that contained a gymnasium, pool, and squash court as well as long-gone housing for the farmers of cash-crop cotton, dairy, and poultry, a house for the estate manager, and a boat captain's house. It was dazzling, a ghostly empire still clinging to the marshy shore (and also disturbing, with its whiff of Reconstruction-era tenant-farmer servitude).

Fred stepped on the gas once we hit the open beach, speeding along until we arrived at one of the island's distant two-and-a-half-mile jetties built from majestic gray stones, some much larger than we were. The ecosystem the jetty created through the years had become home to multihued sea creatures—some spiky, others undulating—including one that looked like a cobalt-blue party balloon growing out of the sand. Animals I never would have encountered had I not joined this group of people in the back of a truck.

Another afternoon on a bike ride, Dot and I wandered into the yard of one of the grand old houses whose owners clearly were among the many former residents who had agreed to give up their homes once the National Park Service took over. A glimpse through the windows—the pale-yellow walls of a sunroom were hand-painted with faded green marsh scenes, egrets in flight—hinted at the kind of charmed life the family must have once lived here, and how sad it must have been to give it up and simply leave it behind and empty. We ate oranges dropped on the ground by an overachieving tree (the island once held enormous orange groves) that was still doing its job even though it had been abandoned. Dot shot photos; I swung on a rope that sent me floating into the marsh-lined woods, with a million birds watching from above, the way the children who'd once summered here must have done, and would probably always remember.

●

Fred took Dot out with her camera to look at birds. More than three hundred species live on or migrate to Cumberland Island, including the Wilson's plover, American oystercatcher, black osprey, least tern, clapper rail, egret, painted bunting, pileated woodpecker, hooded merganser, and assorted owls, egrets and herons, gulls and terns, warblers and thrushes, and a cuckoo. There are even snipe, which I'd previously believed to be an imaginary bird. I found Dot and Fred down on the dock over the marsh with a tragically beautiful dead pelican they'd found under a tree; the three of us stood together overlooking the marsh at dusk as Dot photographed it in the remaining sunlight, still radiant with life.

Things were being born here, too, even in winter. In the past few decades the coast of Cumberland Island has become a calving ground for the North Atlantic right whale. One of the most endangered marine mammals in the world found its way back here in late December in order to survive.

I felt a spiritual attachment to those whales and to the earth in this unspoiled, otherworldly place, where the changes the natural world inflicted upon itself—the wind shear, the wearing away of the dunes—were often naturally reversed, self-healed. Coming here moved me forward, just a bit, by leading me back to things I had forgotten to value. Life is advances and reversals, wave and particle. And you absolutely can't avoid the inherent duality of the world—love and loss, peace and upheaval, life and death—no matter what tricks you try, including giving up. Life finds you.

Two days didn't seem like nearly enough time to spend on Cumberland Island. At the same time, it had the power of years on me. Maybe I would go to culinary school and think about nothing but food for the rest of my life. Maybe I would fall in love again. Maybe the man would break my heart, as if he were following instructions he found pinned to my shirt. Maybe he wouldn't. Maybe I would be alone for a long time and be sad too often. Maybe the happy life I'd always envisioned for myself would finally find me, and I would spend the rest of it rejoicing. Maybe I would find a group of friends in a new community who would welcome me and cherish me forever, and vice versa. Maybe I would stop thinking of life and the people in it as something that needed escaping. Maybe I would stop feeling like the kind of person everyone eventually leaves behind. Maybe I would stop acting like I was waiting to be left. Maybe I would stop being so frightened of losing a home that I resisted making one. Maybe I would fully realize that if I continued to live a life dictated by the expectations of others—especially people who cared less about who I really was than who they needed me to be—I would never have a life of my own. Whatever happened, I knew that if I fell again, and of course I would, I could get up again, reverse things. Because that's the way the world works.

We decided to stay an extra day, despite the misting rain that had begun. It felt like some grand message to me: *staying is what you do when something makes you feel good.* Elizabeth went kayaking alone in the windy rain that had begun late on our last afternoon and worried me and Dot sick when she didn't come back until after dark, when the rain and clouds had disappeared and the stars and moon were so bright and clear, so close, that the entire island seemed silver-plated from the light. But she came back.

And when I got back to Galax, in spite of the fact that it had turned into a place that made me feel better, I found I was finally ready to leave.

Fifteen

BRING OUT YOUR DEAD

Back in late November, I had tried replanting one of Aunt Mariah's hanging ferns down near the woods. A few pink roses and purple irises were still blooming somehow, but the ground was too hard for me to dig a hole: *time to move it along.*

I could have lived forever in Galax, but then I'd have spent all my time down in John and Mariah's basement going through the stacks of photo albums, trying to piece together *exactly* what had happened to my family: *we all looked so happy on that trip to Colonial Williamsburg!* That was a zero-sum game.

Also: I'd had a dream up in the pink bed in which Oliver scowled at me in his usual way and yelled, "Get over it!" He could have been referring to any number of things I'd screwed up or was avoiding or could not, for the life of me, make sense of, but my takeaway was that Oliver had been gone for months and he was doing much better than I was.

But getting over it was not going to help me one bit if I wasn't also building a new way to live. So I decided to move to Charleston, South Carolina, a place I'd fantasized about since college, when my friend Mary (a mutual friend of Portia's) had brought me home with her one spring weekend. Her father had taken us out in his rickety motorboat with a bottle of whiskey and a bottle of Perrier to wrench live oysters from the gorgeous marsh, standing in waist-high water. I tasted she-crab soup (basically a thick mesh of crab with butter, cream, and sherry) the first time that weekend. It had seemed like heaven to me. My plan was to pursue freelance writing while searching for a real job: anything related to my abandoned career as a food writer and features reporter.

Portia and Mary met me in Charleston and helped me find an old loft to live in.

That January I slept on an air mattress at night while waiting for my things to be shipped from my Chicago storage space. During the day I rode my bike all over the peninsula, stopping to read the landmark plaques on gorgeously preserved eighteenth- and nineteenth-century houses and churches and municipal buildings, lasting and living vestiges of early American history, spread out in disarming, rainbow-hued rows along palm tree–lined cobblestone streets and alleyways. I coasted past hidden courtyards and significant formal gardens, and somehow always ended up down on the Battery, where Charleston Harbor's beautiful waters sparkled in the sunlight but also reflected a fog of humiliation at the edges, since this was where the Civil War began with unwarranted high hopes.

Long before the rush of tourism and outside money transformed the peninsula into a refined Disneyland, people who'd lived here for generations had hung on to their family houses, their customs, their dignity—and their actual families—through notoriously shabby decades brought on by wars and hurricanes, not to mention horrendous errors in judgment, as well as forces beyond their control.

For me, Charleston's good qualities added up to a magpie form of self-respect.

The rest of my belongings had been in storage for so long I barely recognized myself in relation to them by the time the movers arrived. *Exactly what kind of person had dropped eggs and flour into the spinning bowl of this red KitchenAid mixer back in Chicago? What in the world had she been making? What had been her purpose in life?*

I didn't quite know.

But I thought I wanted to be more like Charleston. I wanted a modicum of indelible grace in the face of my disgraceful failures, to continue with some dignity whether I deserved it or not, not to mention a family that would never let me go despite my foibles.

It's good to have goals, even outlandish ones.

It wasn't lost on me that the local cuisine was partly responsible for the city's unique and enduring spirit. While the rest of the country had only recently begun to think it adorable to dine on grits and okra, Charleston's home cooks had never stopped being loyal to ingredients near at hand, which harkened back to early European, African, French, and West Indian antecedents and continued through the iffy late era of Junior League gelatin salads. Low Country cuisine—the corn, rice, and grits dishes made with the region's plentiful seafood, with such vegetables as tomatoes, squash, Jerusalem artichokes, eggplant, and butter beans, and fruits like native figs, peaches, and melons—had never gone away. You can ride your bike past one of the many persimmon trees, with the fat orange-red fruit hanging down like Chinese lanterns, and that night have persimmon pudding at someone's house. And when you ask a local who makes the best chicken bog, it's never one of the newfangled restaurants that have sprung up since the nineties, it's their grandmother or a neighbor or somebody who used to work for them; it's people from their family, extended or otherwise.

●

Preserves, relishes like chow-chow, pickles, and chutneys have always been an important element in Charleston cuisine, and the locals make their own rather than buy them at the store—because that's just what people do here, including my friend Mary's family. She grew up on the Battery, married her childhood sweetheart, Winn, and raised her own children in Charleston, like her family before her.

Long after the deaths of their parents, Mary and her brother, Harrington, have maintained the beautiful Charleston tradition of making artichoke pickle—which is really a relish or chow-chow—together with their own families. "Artichoke pickle runs deep in the blood of folks in Charleston and they hide recipes and believe theirs is the best—like chili in Texas. It's crazy!" she wrote when she sent me the recipe belonging to her late grandmother Eulalie on her father's side, handwritten on grandmotherly stationery. "She would be very upset at me for sharing it if she were still alive." Mary had driven me to the Limehouse Produce one afternoon to pick up fresh artichokes; I was surprised to see they were Jerusalem artichokes and that she was buying about a million of them, in a bag as big as a pillowcase. "We make a lot," she said. "But we also eat a lot of them." When I tasted the pickles for the first time at another cookout at Mary's, it reminded me of the way we treat Martha's Virginia Sweet Chunk Pickles in Galax and Courtland, which is to revere them. They're delicious and they *mean* something—they're a part of who you are. Why would you ever, ever let them go?

"We didn't learn how to make them until we noticed they'd almost disappeared from our cupboards. We taught ourselves out of necessity," Mary said. The first time out, she and Harrington were up until four in the morning ("we were drinking bourbon," she pointed out), and it stunk up her kitchen for a month. "We had no idea what we were doing," she said. She eventually took a lesson from her eighty-year-old uncle Tommy, who has his methods down to a quick science (and who cuts his artichokes into thick coins). Now Mary and Harrington make a big batch each October, so they're ready for the holidays.

And as long as their kids decide to make them, too, and on and on, they'll be around forever, connecting their family in a way that goes beyond blood.

Mary's Grandmother Eulalie's Mustard Artichoke Pickles

Makes about 1 dozen 16-ounce jars

3 quarts artichokes, knobs removed, thoroughly washed, and
    soaked in cold water overnight

2 quarts cider vinegar

4 cups light brown sugar

2 teaspoons celery seed

2 teaspoons mustard seed

½ teaspoon red pepper flakes

Scant ½ cup salt

1 cup all-purpose flour

1 teaspoon turmeric

4 teaspoons dry mustard

4 cups chopped onion, cut into 1-inch pieces

4 cups chopped cabbage, cut into 1-inch pieces

2 cups chopped celery, cut into 1-inch pieces

2 cups chopped green bell pepper, cut into 1-inch pieces

1. After the artichokes have been soaked overnight, chop them into uniform 1-inch pieces to match the rest of the vegetables. (Mary and her brother use a Cuisinart food chopper to do this.)

2. To make the sauce, in a very large pot, mix together the vinegar, brown sugar, celery seed, mustard seed, red pepper flakes, and salt and bring to a boil, then turn down the heat and simmer for 10 minutes.

3. In a small bowl, mix together the flour, turmeric, and dry mustard. Remove about a cup of the liquid to a small bowl and slowly whisk into the flour mixture. Slowly stir this mixture back into the pot.

4. Add all the vegetables and the artichokes to the pot, return to a boil, and cook for 20 minutes more over medium-high heat. Turn off the heat, and start sealing in prepared jars while hot.

●

Months later, as I attempted my first small batch, I tried to conjure a picture of my remaining siblings and me making pickles together—carrying on any southern family tradition besides being completely, predictably dysfunctional. It would be like cooking with a bunch of Elizabethan mimes, the whole undertaking somehow ending in a bloodbath that nobody would ever discuss, because, you know, they weren't speaking to anybody else. And yet I longed for all of us to be together anyway, making anything at all. And for that reason, I cherish Mary's recipe; to me, it's a naïve receipt for hope.

So I settled in, in my own way, looking for a job and for examples of how to make some kind of new home in Charleston even though I had the feeling that if home is where the heart is, I was going to be lost for a while.

I found an old side-street coffeehouse full of newspapers and locals, a great place to cut my hair, and a greenmarket I liked attached to an actual farm out near the ocean.

And I started attending a few remarkable AA meetings, one of which was held in a historic church a few blocks away from my apartment, on Meeting Street, which had the distinction of making no effort whatsoever to be remotely anonymous; no one bothered pretending they didn't know last names or what you did for a living. We were going to figure it out anyway, in a place as insular as Charleston. And I really liked that. No one seemed particularly ashamed.

One of the rakish alcoholics in a poplin suit and bow tie suggested I join the Charleston Library Society, so I did. Opened in 1748, it is currently housed in a Beaux Arts confection not far from my apartment. It quickly became my favorite place to be. I walked to their evening concerts and noonday lectures, held among the historic busts and framed documents that only hint at the depth of the archives of the country's third-oldest library, in a city where so much significant history happened. When your book is overdue, you receive a polite handwritten postcard reminder that looks like it was mailed from the eighteenth century.

One night I went there alone to hear a local music collective perform selections from *44 Harmonies from Apartment House 1776* by John Cage, music that struck me as a reflection of the nature of life: beautiful noises followed by almost unbearable silence, with snatches of remembered music recast for the present. And for the first time since I'd been going to the Library Society, I could have sworn I saw a ghost in the stacks.

This was normal in Charleston. It felt oddly comfortable. My friend Holly, whom I'd found by seeking out the food groupies and writers I knew from social media, joined me on early morning walks. We were on a particularly gorgeous cobblestone street near the Battery when I stopped to admire a robin's-egg-blue home with polychromatic flowers pouring out of its window boxes.

"That one is really lovely," said Holly, a cookbook author. "It's haunted."

"Yeah, yeah, yeah," I replied.

"At the upper-left window, at the right time of day, you'll see him looking out," she said matter-of-factly. It was a fact that the city gloried in.

Sometimes it felt like I was living in the afterlife. From the horse-carriage tours that clip-clopped underneath my window several times a day, I culled an interesting if not cohesive oral history of the city, including the fact that the pink hotel next door had not only been slept in by George Washington, but that it, too, was haunted. "A fire swept through here and destroyed pretty much everything!" I heard a young man yell cheerfully to his horse-drawn audience. And, "People here ate too much, drank too much, and spent recklessly, which is why they died very young." Every significant piece of architecture had a guilty, tortured spirit still pleading its case, moving the sheet music from the piano to the sunporch, snuffing the gaslights. Many nights when I pulled into my parking space off Queen Street, tourists were gathered around my spot, listening to one of the hipster tour guides. "In that building there," one of them said, as I got out of my car and stepped into the crowd, "two spinster sisters died but their ghosts remained." He was pointing to the back of my own building. Great.

Charleston was where unresolved sadness came to live. So in a way it was perfect for me and also a kind of beautiful trap. My undigested grief could go on forever here, virtually unnoticed and normal. And yet despite all the ghosts, there seemed to be no better place than Charleston to learn to reconnect with living human beings. They're so curious and social it's almost impossible not to connect. Tell a local you're a writer, they give you the name or email of five writers you should know. You're a *food* writer? You must get in touch with Nathalie Dupree and the Lee brothers. And on and on.

So I reached out, I definitely got around: parties, food functions, the Spoleto Festival USA. I met people for dinner, including my internet foodie friends Cathy and Brandon, who were in town for the

Charleston Wine and Food Festival, which we wandered together the next day. I even had a handful of dates; the one I was drawn to in particular, however, was a recent widower, a kind of cowboy in mourning. We both knew it wouldn't work. For the most part, though, I was allowing only people from the past into my apartment. Toni and Richard and the girls came to town to sightsee; their giant white poodle slept in my giant otherwise empty bed while the humans stayed at the haunted pink hotel next door. Dot and her daughter, Locke, arrived for Locke's spring break; they slept in the giant bed while I took the couch. But I wasn't ready to let new people into my home, into my life, just yet. It wasn't good enough, I wasn't ready, I had nothing left to offer! I had this idea that things had to be perfect before anyone new could enter my house.

I decided to take a class on how to make that happen at the Charleston Academy of Domestic Pursuits, the brainchild of two very funny and elegant Charlestonians I'd met, Suzanne Pollak and Lee Manigault. The academy's motto was "Live at Home." Its aim: to teach a generation of people used to going out for supper how to plan a dinner party, throw an oyster roast, set a table, make jams and pickles, and even catch a fish, among other skills once necessary in slower, more traditional times. It offered etiquette classes, lessons on how to get invited back to someone's house, and how to avoid feuds at your dinner party. I took a dinner-party class, held at Lee's home, which also happens to be one of the country's finest examples of Georgian architecture, the Miles Brewton House. The house is like a museum, but Lee's family actually lives in it like normal contemporary people. While I admired Pollak and Manigault and their ethos ("Learn to Build a Beautiful Life"), they attained a more advanced form of socializing than I was yet capable of.

Soon Elaine came to visit. "I brought you a present," she said when she arrived, handing me a little package that contained a pale-blue decorative dish with script that read:

> *"Sisters make the best friends in the world."*
> *—Marilyn Monroe*

We'd patched things up before I'd relocated, in our usual way: by adhering to the unspoken pact that we would simply ignore whatever crime had led to the rift. I was so happy she wasn't still angry with me; I never worried about the fact that it kept happening, more regularly, with no real explanation. The way it had happened with her and my mother, and with my other sister, who were no longer in my life as a result.

She was what was left of my idea of home, and I adored her. We rode bikes together like twelve-year-olds, stopping at every single house that struck us as gorgeous, peering through the windows and curlicued iron gates in a way that verged on invasive. One man who caught us sidling up to his piazza as he brought in groceries turned out to be the friend of an old friend of mine from the *New Yorker* and invited us inside for a tour. Elaine, a Santa Barbara socialite, knew a prominent Charleston family, and when we visited their graceful mansion, she told them that she loved the city so much she and her husband were planning on buying a house and retiring here, which was news to me. But it made sense: Charleston seemed so perfect. (In fact, so perfect that people were lulled into forgetting its dark past.) We went for oysters at Amen Street at suppertime, had lunch at Husk, and browsed all the antiques shops on King Street during the day. In addition Elaine rearranged all my living room furniture and bought me a plant stand at an antiques store for the giant fern in my bathroom. She mentioned that it looked like I'd lost some weight and that my hair could be an inch shorter at my age, with my cheekbones. I tried to disengage whenever the subject of my appearance arose, several times; I just drifted off. "Robert E. Lee was standing on that balcony . . . ," I heard a tour guide say below my window, as I floated in my private ether, like one of the ghosts, there but not there.

Late one afternoon I drove Elaine across the dazzling Arthur Ravenel Jr. Bridge, while the sun was beginning to go orange and pink and the Cooper River and the harbor were bright silver with pastel stains. The city looked like an ancient topographic map. It made me unspeakably happy. "Look! Isn't it beautiful?" I said.

"Did you know you have a really long hair growing out of your left arm?" she replied.

After Elaine returned to Santa Barbara a set of bar stools arrived, since I had no bar stools at my kitchen counter (because I don't really care for bar stools), along with the bright yellow ballet flats she'd bought for herself on King Street but decided she didn't really like. She had offered to buy me a pair of my own, but I had declined. More gifts, more money spent on me, even though she had complained to our family and my friends about all the money she and Kevin had spent on similar things before Camp Betty not long ago. "You should probably put your winter clothes in storage; they look messy," she said.

Rather than make me the least bit mad or even annoy me, all of this broke my heart in a way that felt familiar. And for the first time, it worried me a little.

If I refused to accept her gifts and money and "advice," it would irritate her and bring on a stretch of silence; if I *did* accept, I ran the inevitable risk later, when she was displeased about some unrelated thing, of her anger over the money she'd spent on me.

Either way, I was aware that I could become devalued, like clutter that needed to be discarded forever.

She couldn't help herself. And I suppose I'd always seemed to her like unfinished business, regardless of how wonderful my life had been at any given point, how much money I was making, how gorgeous I looked, how prestigious my job was, what kind of man I'd snagged, or how much her ideas about what kind of person I should strive to be did or did not match the kind of person I actually was. Or how much those ideas and suggestions might have hurt my feelings. I, in turn, had always been glad to have what I interpreted as support. It was all I knew. I'd always loved her with every bit of my heart.

After she left Charleston, I missed her the way I always have, with a wistful, familiar emptiness. But this time it almost felt like pity, and I wasn't sure if it was for her or for me. She was so critical of herself that it gushed over into my life in a way that my rational brain told me was completely inappropriate and sad. But in my heart I think I actually wondered, *How was I supposed to know how awful I was when she was gone?*

A few weeks later I was invited to a very small dinner party that was smaller and far more casual than any gathering I'd attended since arriving. And it was there that I finally realized the great case for the other side of the coin where socializing or connecting in any way at all is concerned: the side where waiting until everything was magazine-pages perfect or even very well organized at all before you entertained could make you very lonely.

It was at Chef Robert Stehling's. His restaurant, Hominy Grill, had been my favorite place to eat in Charleston since I'd written about the burgeoning restaurant scene for the *Tribune* years ago. I made it a point to become better acquainted with Stehling and his wife, Nunnaly, as soon as I moved to town.

Chef Stehling served a simple pasta with fried chicken liver sauce, which we ate sitting around their kitchen table, with the breeze blowing through the screens. The food was incredibly delicious. But it threw me off. When I got home I wondered, *Why hadn't Stehling made something that I (and food critics everywhere) knew and loved him for?* Dishes that reflected his deft interpretations of Charleston home cooking without smothering it in "innovation"—country captain, shrimp and grits, catfish creole, luscious tomato pudding, perfect shrimp and okra beignets, with buttermilk pie and hummingbird cake for dessert.

I managed to feel a bit . . . disappointed.

After giving it way too much thought, it dawned on me that perhaps Stehling was simply *being himself,* cooking what he liked to cook when he was away from the demanding kitchen at Hominy. I'd been allowed into his and his wife's home like a friend taking an evening walk past their house at dusk: *Come on in and have some supper.*

And isn't the whole point of letting others into your life supposed to be that you get to be who you really are rather than who everyone else expects or even wishes or demands you be?

And shouldn't bringing together people you care about *relieve you* of rather than burden you with the insane goal of perfection—not just because it will wear you out and cut you off from a world full of flawed and wonderful people, but also because it simply is not possible? *The pursuit of perfection is a fool's errand.*

I wanted to be able to throw a dinner party with unspectacular—or even pretty bad—food and know that my friends and family would still be happy that I invited them. And would show up at my next dinner party.

You can learn a lot thinking about dinner way too hard. And after I'd done that I knew that if I really wanted shrimp and grits—a dish Hominy is most well known for—I had to rely on myself. I recalled that I had already created a version of the archetypal dish that represents who I am rather than what the world expects from classic shrimp and grits. I happen to prefer it.

Emily's Shrimp and Grits–Style Risotto

Serves 4

16 large shrimp (about ¾ pound), peeled and deveined

2 lemons, juiced, several slices of peel reserved

3 sprigs fresh thyme

6 tablespoons olive oil

½ teaspoon crushed red pepper flakes

4 strips thick-cut bacon, chopped

2 garlic cloves, finely chopped

1 cup chopped fresh flat-leaf parsley leaves

1½ cups chopped plum tomatoes (about 3 medium)

1 cup dry white wine

2 cups fish stock

2 to 3 tablespoons unsalted butter

1 small onion, finely chopped

1½ cups sliced mushrooms

1 cup long grain Arborio superfino rice

A few dashes of Tabasco sauce, plus more for serving

½ cup half-and-half, warmed

4 scallions, sliced with some green tops

1. Place the shrimp in a bowl with the lemon juice, a few strips of lemon peel, the thyme, 3 tablespoons of the oil, and the red pepper flakes, and toss to coat. Let marinate for at least 30 minutes.

2. In a medium skillet, cook the bacon over medium-low heat to render the fat; remove with a slotted spoon once the bacon has cooked to golden but not crisped and drain on a paper towel–lined plate.

3. Add the remaining 3 tablespoons oil to the bacon fat in the pan; cook the garlic and parsley together until very fragrant. Add the tomatoes to the pan and cook for 2 to 3 minutes over medium heat. Add the shrimp (with its marinade) and cook for 1 minute per side. Add the wine; bring to a simmer, removing the shrimp after 1 minute. Set aside in a covered bowl. Add the fish stock to the remaining liquid and keep at a low simmer.

4. In a Dutch oven, heat the butter over medium-high heat and sauté the onion until golden. Add the mushrooms, and cook until golden. Stir in the rice and cook until translucent.

5. Over a period of 20 minutes, add the stock mixture ½ cup or so at a time, stirring until all the liquid is absorbed with each addition. When all but about ½ cup of liquid remains to be added and the rice is al dente, stir in the bacon and shrimp and a few dashes of Tabasco. Finish the dish with the warm half-and-half and a squeeze of lemon. Put the lid on the Dutch oven and let the risotto rest for 5 minutes before serving topped with the scallions and more Tabasco at the table, if desired.

●

I created this fairly amazing dish and made it exactly the way I wanted it to be. It's delicious.

But another insight that followed my dinner at the Stehlings' was this: I was chicken liver pasta to Elaine (and to the Engineer, too, probably), but she kept hoping for shrimp and grits.

And somehow it had never occurred to her that that chicken liver pasta, while not what she'd ordered, might be exactly what I wanted to be. What I was *meant* to be. I'm not sure that it had ever occurred to me, either.

•

Months passed. I was *moving forward,* I told myself. I was living in the *present.*

But I wasn't really living in my own apartment, nor was anyone invited in. As hard as I'd been trying to create a home—baking bread, buying flowers, the things I used to do—I began staying away from my loft as often as possible. *It's not like anyone is keeping my dinner warm,* I told myself. So I took off. I spent a week at an insanely wonderful pheasant hunting lodge in Thomaston, Georgia, at Portia and Buddy's invitation. I went to Atlanta to see Toni and the girls, to Galax several times, to the beach, and to Washington, DC. I went to New York a few times, where I rekindled an old friendship with Julie, whom I'd foolishly stopped speaking to many years before. I took so many trips that I noticed I was becoming more comfortable with two suitcases than at home with a whole houseful of beautiful stuff, all of which meant less and less to me as time went on. I slept in so many beds that I started taking pictures of them, so I'd remember where I'd been.

I traveled through the green and corn-gold farmland on roads lined with sweet peas and purple clover to Arcadia, Indiana, to visit my friend Tom, a former photojournalist and professional chef who farms and raises about half of his own food and cooks it for his wife and two young daughters; he documented all of this on his blog, *Bonafide Farm.* Tom showed me how to make meaty duck burgers with French butter and a great burned okra dish with potatoes and basil.

I stopped by Aunt Mariah and Uncle John's on my way to Washington, DC, where I visited my friend Cathy Barrow, who was just starting to work on her fantastic book *Mrs. Wheelbarrow's Practical Pantry.*

I attended the pie-making class she was teaching in her home the weekend I arrived and learned how to make not just several kinds of pies and tarts but a terrific and easy method for great crusts. She also fed me according to the premise of her book, which teaches you how to make things at home that you wouldn't normally dream of attempting, how to preserve practically everything, and gives recipes for putting it all together in a way that is the definition of sustainability. Down in her basement pantry, the shelves were chockablock with vivid jars of prettily conserved vegetables (including slender asparagus and green beans lined up like soldiers), soups, fish (tuna in oil, chunks of pink salmon), meats, chutneys, mincemeat, vinegars (fig, tarragon), sour cherries, peaches with ginger, pears, Meyer lemons, Cara Cara oranges, and other fruit, as well as sundry pie fillings (cardamom peach, apple, blueberry), Cathy's triple sec and Limoncello, lemon curd, meat, poultry and fish stocks for soup, and soups, too. It was like a fallout shelter where the worst event could only result in beautiful meals. When I left it was with a dozen jars containing vegetable soup, chutneys, pickles, and jams as a present.

But the gift I valued most was a recipe for Cathy's favorite comfort food, the sour cherry pie created by her mother, who'd taught Cathy all about cooking and preserving. "We'd watch Julia Child together when I was a kid," she said. Now that her mother is gone, Cathy makes this pie for her stepfather. It is the perfect combination of sweetness and tartness—an aspirational pie that also reminds me of the power of food to preserve memories of people we love.

Sour Cherry Pie

Makes one 9-inch pie

2 (1-quart) containers tart cherries
Scant 1 cup granulated sugar
3 tablespoons cornstarch or tapioca flour
Juice of 1 lemon
½ teaspoon almond extract
2 pie crusts
1 tablespoon unsalted butter
2 tablespoons heavy cream

1. Stem and pit the cherries over a bowl to catch all the juices. Put the cherries in a large bowl and add the sugar, cornstarch, lemon juice, and almond extract.

2. Roll out one crust and fit in into the bottom and up the sides of a deep-dish pie pan. Pour in the filling and dot the top with the butter. Roll out the remaining crust. Either form a lattice top or stamp out stars or hearts with a cookie cutter and lay them across the pie filling. Crimp or flute the edges decoratively. Brush the top crust, not the edges, with the heavy cream. Freeze the pie for 1 hour.

3. Preheat the oven to 425°F. Bake the pie for 20 minutes then reduce the heat to 350°F and bake for an additional 45 minutes, or until the filling is bubbling. If the crust browns too quickly, cover it loosely with foil. Cool on a rack for at least 1 hour before serving.

Cathy Barrow's Best Pie Crust
(adapted from Cathy's mother, Jan, and grandmother, Bea)
Makes 1 crust

4 ounces (1 stick) unsalted butter, ice-cold and cut into cubes
1⅓ cups all-purpose flour
¼ cup ice water

1. In a food processor, pulse the butter and flour until it's sandy and in pea-sized lumps. Add the water and pulse until the crust comes together in a ball. Form it into a disk and chill for 4 hours, or overnight (better).

2. If you don't own a food processor, blend the butter and flour with your fingertips. (If your hands are naturally warm, cool them under the faucet before you start.) When the butter and flour are sandy and in pea-sized lumps, add the water and blend with your fingers until the dough comes together. Turn it out on a countertop and press the ball out with the heel of your hand, pushing away from you. Gather the dough, push away again, and gather. Form the dough into a disk, even if you think it's not very homogenous. Chill for 4 hours, or overnight.

•

And one of the several times I visited New York, my friend Dot and I had dinner with Amanda Hesser, the cofounder of Food52, a website that had changed my life when I was back in Chicago, when she still ran the enterprise out of her own kitchen. (It has since become so successful she and her partner, Merrill Stubbs, have had to move operations twice to larger quarters.) After the staff had left her house, she made a delicious dinner for me and Dot and her husband and twins, including a simple celery salad with sherry vinaigrette and shaved Parmesan that both Dot and I began to make regularly. But the thing that I recalled most distinctly about our visit with Amanda was that just minutes after she'd cleaned up the kitchen at the end of her long day, she suddenly started getting out flour and sugar again.

"What are you doing?" I asked.

"I forgot to make a thank-you cake!" she replied. It was 9:00 p.m., and she started baking a cake for someone who'd done something nice for her. A habit I have since begun to emulate.

After I got back to Charleston from these trips, I found that I never wanted to be at home—I didn't want to work on my job search and freelance writing at my beautiful desk. The weather was so perfect I could carry my computer down cobblestoned Chalmers Street, pass through the curlicue wrought-iron gates surrounding Washington Park, which had opened in 1818, and work outdoors undisturbed almost all day, until a chamber music group began practicing outside one of the adjacent buildings, behind a high brick wall. Past all the blossoming trees, I could see the steeple of St. Michael's Episcopal Church and hear the bells on the hour, and later in the afternoon the tinkling murmuring sounds of other people's after-work cocktail parties, which was good enough for me, really. Hovering at the margins.

It was in this park one afternoon that I'd noticed a stupid cardinal fluttering way too boldly at the corner of my vision, over near the monument to General Beauregard. While I no longer believed that every cardinal that got too close to me or hung around just a bit too long was my brother Oliver, this bird reminded me, in a sudden breathtaking jolt, that I was alive and Oliver was dead.

I never spoke about Oliver to anyone anymore—it inevitably got me in trouble. But I now thought about him every single day, convinced that I alone carried an obligation to keep him alive, not hide him away. And since I could not talk about it, this duty was like a heavy garment that I could not take off, no matter how beautiful and warm the day, or how many cherry blossoms were in bloom. I wore it everywhere. And I was pretty sure I would forever.

But in this park, surrounded by birds and cherry blossoms and tourists and one guy I suspected was a drug dealer and so many other living things, it occurred to me that I was confusing how I felt about Oliver with how I felt about myself. He was gone, had escaped the pain he was in. I was still here, imprisoned by my own guilt. I had not fully abandoned the world, nor had I found a way to live in it.

I was the ghost, trapped in the foyers and libraries of people and places who'd long forgotten me, and who might have never loved me at all.

So what were my options? I'd equated having a home with losing a home for such a long time—for most of my life, actually—that it almost felt more comfortable floating around. But didn't I have an obligation to settle down, live the way the rest of the world did, even if it meant faking it?

A few months earlier, at the end of a visit to New York City with Dot, I had told her I was sad about going back home, that I always was when I had to return from a trip. It reminded me of staying outside until dusk as a kid in order to avoid going inside to possible chaos, and, later, dreading returning to my own apartment in Chicago whenever the Engineer and I were not talking. "Home is highly overrated," she replied, laughing, and I knew it was because she loved to travel, was comfortable everywhere, comfortable with herself.

So I gave myself permission to give up on the idea of a true home for a while, until I could be more like Dot.

It was time to travel again, with even bigger purpose, back into the land of the living. It was time to wake up from my beautiful, restful Charleston dream.

Sixteen

CITY OF MIXED EMOTIONS

It was easy to decide where I had to go next: Chicago, City of Mixed Emotions. If I'd learned anything at all since I'd blown up my life in order to escape it, it was this: if you can never stand to face what you should be grieving—a home, a family, a job, a way of life, how a person died, how much cruelty you'd been willing to accept in exchange for ostensible love, how much everything that has happened in your life, both good and bad, is your own damned fault—you'll always be lost. Things you bury prematurely come back to you, eventually. They always do. I had not left my burned-down past behind simply by moving to Charleston. I had to face Chicago down.

This, of course, was my own brand of dime-store self-analysis. I would obviously need the help of a professional to get me through this trip. But the professional I chose was a chef rather than a therapist. After all, food had been leading me the right way. I'd begun understanding its limits, trusting its virtues. I almost never felt bad about food. So before I'd even left Charleston, I made an appointment to drop in on a man I'd admired in the most comprehensive way, from my earliest days in Chicago, Chef Bruce Sherman of North Pond restaurant. His ninety-year-old Arts and Crafts bungalow was always my birthday spot, not to mention the only place I trusted enough to submit to the otherwise loathsome idea of brunch. Even though I admired him, in all the time I covered food and restaurants in Chicago, I had never had a conversation with Sherman that wasn't for work. So I was surprised that when I asked him to make me his ideal comfort dish, he complied.

When I got to the city, I felt perfectly fine. *Why, it was nothing more than a bunch of tall buildings and a beautiful lake!* I'd been invited to sleep on a foldout bed in the living room of one of my oldest Chicago friends, Anita, while I was in town. Dropping my suitcase in the hallway of her high-rise apartment, I realized I'd never spent much time in her home. We'd always met somewhere else, at the movies or a restaurant but never in our own apartments. In retrospect, it seemed odd to me. "What the hell had I been doing in Chicago that was so important that I couldn't pop in on my friends?" I asked her, as we were watching a little TV, getting ready for bed one night. "I always thought you were so busy," she said. Ha. Busy avoiding true friendship? I knew I'd escaped something, but it seemed like I'd also left behind a home here, too. I had not kept in close touch with my Chicago friends since I'd moved away, even though I thought about them all the time. And that was my own fault and terrible loss.

By the time I'd left Chicago, I had lost my faith in myself, questioned my strength, lost my place in a community, and sometimes lately it even seemed I'd lost my place in the universe—like an astronaut trying to reenter the earth's atmosphere at the wrong speed and at the wrong angle, my ship had bounced off the surface and hurtled away into limbo.

But that was then, this was now. I made sure I got to see my friend Jessica, who had picked me up at the hospital. She was engaged now, to a man who clearly adored her, so we all went together to my post-breakdown comfort spot Great Lake for Nick and Lydia's perfect pies and farmers' market salad. I felt like I'd seen her just the day before, the food was as good as I remembered it, and everything seemed so easy. Why had I ever felt otherwise about friendships—that it required courage and trust I could not spare?

•

I left Anita's house a little earlier than I needed to, remembering that North Pond is always a little hard to find, located down a leafy path through Chicago's Lincoln Park, right before you fall into the pond. It was easy to overlook it. Plenty of people in Chicago did, for years.

Sherman was overlooked, too, a quiet national treasure, in my opinion, not willing to change his style just so he could outshout a city full of louder chefs. When he finally won his first James Beard Award in 2012 after five nominations, it had been more than a decade since he'd hung a sign on the bungalow identifying his food as "Seasonal Cuisine." (North Pond has since earned a Michelin star, too.)

People said, "Oh, that's nice. What season will you be open?" He was that far ahead of the curve and was one of the first chefs, along with Frontera Grill's Chef Rick Bayless, who cultivated close, working relationships with sustainable and artisanal farmers and ranchers and dairies who often were struggling. Now the practice of naming your farms on your menu has been standard for some time.

While his staff was getting ready for lunch, we talked about how North Pond came to be.

"It wasn't deliberate, as far as I know," Sherman, a Chicago native, said. He had cooked in high school and had always been fascinated with food, but as the son of an affluent banker, he followed the expected path (Ivy League degree in economics, followed by the London School of Economics), before he figured out that "as an adult, I could decide what I did." By the time he was twenty-six, he owned a successful catering company, which he was perfectly happy to sell after he met his wife, Joan (who worked for CARE), with whom he moved to Haiti.

"It wasn't until I was thirty-five, living in India, that I realized I wanted to be a chef," he said. So when his wife finished her posting in Delhi, they moved with their first child, Emma, to Paris, where he studied cooking at a government vocational school recommended to him by the venerable cookbook author and teacher Patricia Wells.

Then it was back to Chicago with his young family (including another daughter, Kate), a few apprenticeships under local chefs, among them Prairie Grass Cafe's great Sarah Stegner, who was at the Ritz-Carlton back then, and the opportunity just two years later to take over North Pond, which had been more of a casual nuts-and-berries café, with a corrugated aluminum overhang where the spectacular sunroom now is.

The French influence surprised me. As pristine and elegant as his food is—the menu conjures jewellike images (Beet, Watercress Salad: Roasted Red, Chioggia, and Gold Beets, Watercress, Cured Sardines, Parmesan, Orange, Pistachio)—I had always thought of it as very creative American, the kind of beautifully constructed, multicolored dishes you'd eat if Georgia O'Keeffe were your grandmother and loved to cook. As sophisticated as it is, it doesn't seem to brag about its time abroad, happy instead to elevate the stature of rustic seasonal ingredients to edible art.

But the food made sense, given Sherman's life's trajectory. The influences of Southeast Asia, London, Paris, and even the home cooking of Haiti were all present, and I loved finding out that he'd taken such a circuitous path—presumably without too much drudgery and angst along the way?

"Well, I wouldn't say that," he responded.

In addition to renovating and restoring North Pond to its Arts and Crafts glory, there came a time when he was up against so many disasters all at once that he woke up one morning and told his wife that he just didn't want to go to work.

"Within weeks, staff I'd inherited walked out," he told me. "They were drinking tequila in the bathroom right before diners arrived, threatening me. I had to file a police report. Pipes and other essential things broke, the power was going out, and there were so many other setbacks."

His beautiful restaurant, which looks like a prairie church, seemed possessed.

"It was one of the most difficult years I've ever had, just head-scratching, 'is this really doable' difficult. And you're not supposed to feel that way about a restaurant you've just started," he added.

Finally, Sherman took a mystical turn, determined to do anything to get North Pond headed toward the restaurant he knew it could be.

"We called in a Native American shaman to rid this place of evil spirits," he said, looking at me like he was joking. "He did incantations. . . . I was thinking the place was built on Indian burial grounds."

Obviously, he didn't give up. "You just have to put your head down, hunker down, and make it work."

Sherman also admitted that the repeat misses for a James Beard Award had a real effect on him. "Oh, it mattered. It was frustrating. And I was bitter every time. But this is what I do and this is who I am. I can't be any other way. I just do what I do."

Which made so much sense to me. He was the king of circuitous paths, stubbornly true to himself, compared with so many successful chefs known for bandwagon approaches to food trends.

Besides, he pointed out that none of the bad times or the disappointments matter, in the end.

"It's just that much sweeter when you meet the challenge. You could say that about the Beard thing, it's much sweeter after six years. And about life, I guess. It sounds trite, but people who don't have to try hard don't have the same treasure at the end of the rainbow. You could give up, of course, and there are certain times when you might have to. But often you do have the tools to overcome enormous problems. You just have to have the wherewithal."

I told him I had doubts about how in the world I'd find my own way.

"That's always going to be a part of us. If we're not doubting ourselves and our ability, we're not going to be on our game," he said.

"Look, there's still stuff that stresses me, but I remember: What am I worried about? There's nothing else that I aspire to, except to be this, what I am."

At that point I didn't need to hear another word.

But then he said: "Should we cook?"

My favorite words. We'd talked about the possibility of a great, sloppy burger, but when he mentioned an egg dish that he made for his family—"cheesy eggs finished with Dijon mustard, a little cream, and chives"—I decided that was a path I'd like to go down.

"You know what? I know it would be fun to do this in the kitchen, but they're trying to work in there," he said. He disappeared, returned with an industrial burner, and then sped off once again, returning with a giant *boule* (an almost-black, dome-shaped bread) and the rest of his ingredients. We set up a makeshift kitchen at the hostess stand, which was also our dining table. After he'd sliced the bread for toast and started the eggs, he had to run back into the kitchen. "Here," he said, handing the spoon off to me, and I finished the long-stirring process over low heat that makes soft scrambled eggs so beautifully delicate and creamy.

When he returned he toasted the bread and spread it with apricot jam while I tossed a little arugula salad he'd splashed with a little olive oil and lemon juice. He spooned the perfect eggs over the jam. After he'd piled a bit of the dressed arugula on top, he took out a giant knife and sliced the egg and jam toast crosswise into six pieces for us to share. It was wonderful: creamy perfect eggs together with crunchy and chewy textures, sweet and bitter flavors. If you think this dish sounds like a bad idea, you should know I thought so, too. Jam and eggs? But you just have to trust Bruce Sherman. In the end, his way of doing things tends to turn out just right, despite what you or anybody else may think.

Chef Bruce Sherman's Cheesy Eggs on Toast

Serves 2

2 tablespoons unsalted butter

4 large eggs

2 tablespoons whole milk

Fine sea salt, to taste

White pepper, to taste

5 to 6 ounces Uplands Pleasant Ridge Reserve (or good Gruyère)
    cheese, finely grated

2 teaspoons crème fraîche or heavy cream (optional)

1 tablespoon Dijon mustard

2 teaspoons finely chopped parsley

2 teaspoons finely chopped chives

1 to 2 thick slices per person (depending on loaf size) of *miche,*
    boule, or other rustic loaf

Apricot jam

For top salad: a good handful of baby arugula, extra-virgin olive
    oil, lemon juice, salt, and white pepper

1. Preheat a small sloped-sided pot over *very* low heat. Add the butter.
2. Whip the eggs and milk in a bowl and lightly season with salt and pepper. Add to the pot.
3. Over very low heat, stir continuously with a wooden spoon or rubber spatula. If the eggs begin to firm up and coagulate, turn down the heat. Stir constantly for 10 to 15 minutes—switching to a small whisk when the eggs begin to curdle—until the eggs eventually become creamy and custardlike.
4. Take the pot off the heat and stir in the cheese, crème fraîche (if using), mustard, parsley, and chives. Season with salt and pepper.
5. Toast the bread and generously spread with apricot jam.
6. Place the warm eggs on top of the jam layer. Before serving, dress and season the arugula to taste and arrange on top.

———————

Seventeen

HOT WHEELS AND PINTO BEANS

Toward the end of my journey back from madness, I was met on the dark road, in the tangled forest, by a terrible and powerful dragon who took me to his cave. Or, to put it in more quotidian terms, I drove to Knoxville, Tennessee, to visit my father, after years of taking the longest, loneliest, most damaging, numbed-out circuitous path to make sure I didn't run into him by accident. And I also ate at Ruby Tuesday. Twice.

Of course, in past years it's possible that I would have been too drunk to care if I'd run into Daddy, as we've called him all our lives, in spite of the fact that we never saw much of him after he and my mother divorced and he slowly drifted out of our lives.

But now, alcohol and I were quits, and I'd have to face the monster with all my senses dialed to "acute." That had me worried.

"Just hurry up and get here," Elaine commanded by phone from Galax, where she'd flown from Santa Barbara for a visit with John, Mariah, Toni, and the girls, but also to drive to Knoxville to check on my father—about whom, it had become glaringly clear, it was time to "do something."

Elaine already had a plan in place for our trip together.

"We'll leave at 6:00 a.m., spend the day going through his things, take him to dinner, and leave the next morning," she said.

So bossy. I'd always obeyed her, and would do so now, even at my age, as if I were still a child and she the only human in the world standing between me and full-blown chaos, still grateful that she had made sure I joined clubs, played sports, read the right books, ran for class president, applied to college, and thought about what my plans were.

The truth is that as a child I'd always recognized in the back of my head that there was something missing: that mysterious superglue that held families together even if they were a little weird or had devastating losses and tragedies, or affairs, or alcoholism, or a child who wasn't perfect, the way everyone always claimed we were. Strangers would walk up to my parents after church at the Midtowner restaurant when we were still little, to say, *You have the most beautiful family, so well behaved,* and we smiled up at them in our Sunday school clothes. (This always thrilled me: maybe my mother would see it, too! We were wonderful!)

My brother Michael noticed it, too. "Why can't we just buy the Galyens' old house?" he'd asked, when my parents started building our giant glass and stone house up on a hill, which my mother had begun to throw all her hysterical energy into planning, collecting pages from house magazines and stopping in at decorating shops in Winston-Salem to glean ideas each Wednesday, the day she went for her psychiatric appointment. She went way overboard to make sure this place we were going to live in was "unusual": a working soda fountain in the bar, a basketball court that could be turned into an ice rink, a fire pit for all the neighborhood parties we'd never have, a vine-shaped brass fountain that tinkled beneath the open staircase in the indoor stone garden, zebra wallpaper in her bathroom, a bidet, handmade quilts that matched our wallpaper exactly, a Murphy bed in Michael's bedroom, and a white piano in the jungle-themed living room, where a large ceramic monkey in a turban held a glass tabletop above his head.

"Why can't we just be normal?" Michael frequently said.

But no kid, however controlling, could keep my parents from divorcing, fix our broken hearts, teach us the value of a family or how to have and keep one, avert our loneliness or sadness or general casting about for our purpose, or give us the plan for life that had never been handed down to us by our parents, because they didn't have one either. Except in Mom's fantasies, which included her turning us into a singing group like the von Trapp family. That lasted one week and ended with some tambourines and guitars being thrown on the floor, and her silent, wounded disgust with our lack of enthusiasm and talent.

We were all simply set decor in an anxiety-filled movie, punctuated by Mother's drama and bouts of depression that left me always afraid that she would eventually kill herself and leave us behind with no one.

After my mother asked him for a divorce, Daddy never came to get his books, which he cared about more than anything else, so there was not much hope that he'd be coming back for us, either. No one was coming to rescue us.

We saw him in Galax less and less after that, until it was clear that he had now based himself in Knoxville, selling furniture, carrying his fabric samples in the saddle-leather case that was always in the trunk of his car, and spending weeknights in hotels along the way. Sometimes, I still saw him at my grandmother's pink, daisy-wallpapered house, where the stone walls were studded with the pretty fairy stones (shaped like crosses) that Toni, Susan, Lisa, and I had helped her find on a trip to Fairy Stone State Park.

I'd ride my bike over to visit, in the months after the divorce announcement, and Grandmother and Daddy would be in separate rooms, reading. And the less he came back to Galax, the easier it became not to think of him at all. Daddy who? He had been a voice on the phone a couple of times a week ("Tell your mother I'll be at the Days Inn in Kingsport until Wednesday")—there but not there. And on the weekends, regardless of how thrilling his arrival was to me (the hard, brief hug that made me gasp like a bellows, the smell of his Old Spice, his crisp white shirt and gorgeous tie), after the divorce he kept his distance, like a banished prince.

I was able to avoid the topic of Daddy for many years after. My mother and Emile moved out of town to places I never felt comfortable visiting, my parents didn't pay for college, they didn't pick me up for holidays, show up at parents' weekends, comment on my awful grades, or ask whom I was dating. They weren't interested, which seemed normal.

But wherever Daddy was and wherever I happened to be, I always knew he was reading a book, smoking a cigarette (until he had a heart attack), and drinking coffee silently. He was out there.

After Elaine and I had discussed our plans to take charge of Daddy's welfare at last, and I had hung up the phone with Elaine, these sorts of memories made my stomach hurt. They brought back a lifetime of wondering, however subconsciously, what the hell I'd done, or hadn't done, that would cause a father not to stick around to see a daughter doing all the things she did, or didn't do, growing up. Incidentally, what I'd done was score thirty-four points against Blacksburg High School on my incredibly awful basketball team; I was president of my class junior year and planned the whole prom (but didn't have a date when the prom itself rolled around; my friend Lyn had to get her brother to come home from UVA, put on a beige tux, and kiss me at the door); was picked to attend the statewide leadership camp at Virginia Girls State; won first place at fourteen for forensics (with my dramatic reading of a piece by Erma Bombeck, about the trials of motherhood—my mother's idea, of course); won a Voice of Democracy speech award; was on homecoming court; was an editor on the yearbook; won trophies for Sportsmanship, Best Female Athlete, Best Tennis Player, Best Basketball Player, among other trophies that clogged my bedroom; was in practically every community theater play my mother directed. I was like one of those subway buskers, playing all the instruments at once: banjo, knee cymbals, pedal drum, and a pennywhistle in my mouth. *Hey, look at me.*

What I didn't do was date very much even though I was reasonably attractive. I still recall too vividly the case of one cute basketball player who would come to stand at my locker, during which time I pretended he wasn't there, that I wasn't available to have my heart broken by anyone. Undeterred, he showed up at our house on Saturday mornings, ostensibly to play basketball with my brothers but really to wait in the playroom between all of our bedrooms for me to come strolling out of my bedroom. I was surprised to see him there, and so happy, but I walked right past him, a foot away, and didn't say hello. Ever. He finally went away and started dating one of my friends.

There was just something that kept me from allowing myself to be loved. I made sure it never happened, regardless of how valiantly men have tried.

My crimes started early, the summer before first grade, when I suggested a game called Catch and Kiss, just so I could catch Ted Winship, who had red hair, pale eyelashes, freckles, thick glasses, and was probably hyperactive. He claimed he took "peppy pills," which he stored in the Winships' mailbox. He would open the box, pantomime taking a pill, and run away like Jerry Lewis. He was absolutely irresistible to me; he could ride his bike backward, sitting on the handlebars.

"Let's play Catch and Kiss!" I yelled. I snagged Ted by his shirt and threw him on the ground in a stand of pink azaleas in the mayor's front yard, where my entire neighborhood played Kick the Can until the sun went down each summer. I pushed the copper-marigold hair up on the back of his sweaty, freckly neck and kissed him there. I can recall this now with exquisite clarity, the slightly sour but lovely scent, the slippery feeling of my lips on his skin. Thrilling!

I looked up and a group of the preteen kids who grew up with us on Sunset Drive were staring at me, silent. Obviously, no one else had joined in on my game.

"I'm telling!" screamed Oliver, who was Ted's best friend at the time. And he went straight home and told on me. I was six; Oliver was seven.

When I finished my long, slow perp walk back to the house, I lifted my unaffectionate heavy Scottish terrier, Sukoshi, onto my lap as my mother sat me down and looked at me seriously, sadly, and said, "We don't give our kisses away for free." I was Hester Prynne, and the village had condemned me.

I learned permanently that if I, in particular, liked a boy and he liked me back, there would be trouble with a capital *T*. As far back as my memory stretches I knew that male attention would get me busted. In first grade, I made the dreadful mistake of telling my mother that I "liked" Will Goad. I trusted her with this information despite the Ted Winship incident because I was madly in love with her, wanted her to share my love for someone else; also, nothing was real until she herself had owned it. In retrospect I think she identified with me, confused the two of us, which made her particularly hard on me in a misdirected way.

Will Goad had perfect posture, which I really admired, straight glossy bangs like Mr. Spock, and large delicate nostrils. His skin was the exact color of the "flesh" crayon in the Crayola box.

I told my mother some of this, and she promptly told everyone in the family, "Emily has a crush." As if I was not human. They, in turn, made fun of me in a *Lord of the Flies* way. Which I never understood: all four of my siblings had naturally moved into the stage of life in which you attach yourself, however confusingly, to another small human being outside of your family.

Naturally, when Will Goad was chosen to be the Groom of Springtime in my first grade play, I told the music teacher that I'd be unable to accept the proffered role of Bride of Springtime.

She frowned. "Why ever not?" she asked, genuinely confused.

What little girl would turn down this role? I was going to be the *Bride of Fucking Springtime,* which was the equivalent to being a Disney princess today. The thought of standing on the old wooden stage in the wooden firetrap auditorium at my elementary school, while my mother—the only real actress in the family, who'd been deprived of fame only because she'd extruded the five of us—was in the audience, watching me get married to the Groom of Springtime, seemed dangerously wrong. Holding his hand, wearing a wedding dress and a crown of flowers, and being serenaded with songs of springtime innocence by this boy with great posture? I had a feeling things would turn out badly for me.

Rather than pointing out that I'd already portrayed Springtime in our kindergarten drama, I insisted that I had stage fright, a condition I'd heard about from my mother; her favorite singer, Barbra Streisand, had this disorder and she got onstage and sang her heart out anyway. My teacher picked another tall blond girl to play the bride, and I ended up in the back row, as one of the nondescript supporting flowers, singing a song called "Flowers, Flowers, Everywhere," whose lyrics were exactly those words, repeated, with swaying. But it was a relief, nonetheless, not to be the star.

Never be the star! Even as a first grader, I got that somehow. And the bride thing probably got lodged in my brain, too: never be the bride.

Just to be accurate about how much was going on in my simple mind at the time: I remember on the actual night of the play, which was thrilling in its own right, I got to wear mascara with my flower costume, and lipstick, which my mother applied then blotted with a tissue, her face close to mine, before we headed to the auditorium. It was dreamy. There was wedding cake—a sheet cake, really—for everyone after the play was over, moist and white, with vanilla frosting, each square piece decorated with a pink or yellow flower.

Through the years, all around me, everywhere, my friends—and both of my sisters—would develop these dangerously forbidden crushes, flirt with boys, fall in love, and receive whatever kind of love that was returned at that age, while I ended up yearning but never getting any of this. I have no memory of a boy holding my hand at the movies, a first kiss that meant something (I got kissed the first time, inappropriately, by a twenty-one-year-old guy who was the lead in one of my mother's plays, after the curtain call), or a boy who called me at night even if it was just to hang up on me the minute I answered, just to hear my voice.

I didn't care if it was stupid, gross love. I was left out, and it felt like I had a sturdy bubble enclosing me, hung with a sign that said: GO AWAY. *Why did this happen to me in particular?* I often wondered vaguely, the way kids are doomed to wonder things without the capacity to try to find answers. *Why did I get the bubble? How do you take this thing off?*

I never realized I was protecting myself.

For a long time, into my early teens, I thought no one noticed the bubble or the sign. I thought I was just not anyone's cup of tea. Until one Saturday night, when I was fifteen, my brother Michael installed himself outside my bedroom door, plastered, having drunk beer in the woods with his friends, who were seniors. Our bedroom windows were sliding glass doors, and Michael's opened onto the garage, for easy escape and reentry.

I had been in bed for a while, after riding around with my friends Lyn and Amy (who had her driver's license) *American Graffiti*–style, up and down Main Street in Galax from the edge of town then up the highway to the Pizza Hut and back. As we got older, boys arrived at Ann's basement rec room, and people started pairing off while I played pinball or made prank phone calls.

"Guys like you, Emily," Michael said, drunkenly. He almost never talked to me directly; maybe this was a prank? "But they think you won't go out with them."

"Well, I would," I said, from my canopy bed, in my girly room, with the ice-blue shag carpet and the wallpaper decorated with bunches of violets tied in blue ribbons. I was amazed he'd noticed my problem. "Who likes me?" I asked.

"Guys," he said. "But you have to go out with Barry Bannon first."

"No, I do not," I said. Barry Bannon was perfectly nice, but he was no Ted Winship. He had a voice like a duck's, slicked-down yellow hair, and he said stupid things. Which made me feel sorry for him.

"Why Barry Bannon?" I asked. But I knew: if I'd go out with Barry, certainly I'd go out with anybody who asked.

"Michael?" I said, waiting for an answer. He had gone back to his room. I later heard him snoring.

So I eventually accepted a date with Barry Bannon to the Baptist Church Sweetheart Banquet, on Valentine's Day, which fell on the Monday after my first college weekend visit to Elaine in Chapel Hill.

This college trip was like a dream. We went to parties, a basketball game (her tall boyfriend, Woody, was on the team) against NC State, her Shakespeare class taught by a Jesuit priest who made my heart leap up when he read aloud. We ate at her sorority house where the girls were pretty and smart and seemingly not weighed down by the latter fact. And the guys flirted openly with me at the Shack, gave me sweet cocktails, danced me into a corner so that Elaine couldn't see us, and tried to neck with me. One guy in particular wanted me to stay on Sunday to go to a sorority dance with him. It was as if they hadn't heard about me and my bubble, here in 3-D Chapel Hill. Also: I think the cocktails might have helped.

The guys at my high school wore jeans, work boots, Converse high-tops, and T-shirts emblazoned with the logos of hard-rock bands or auto-parts dealers. Some of them wore overalls. In Chapel Hill they wore starched pastel shirts, smelled like soap, cut their hair short, and wore loafers with no socks and ridiculously short khaki pants. They reminded me of Daddy when he would come home on weekends, dapperly dressed, yet manly—but they paid attention to me, they saw me!

I had to go back to stupid sepia-toned Galax to go on my date with Barry Bannon, instead of to the dance with a man I still think about today. He's married, living in Charlotte, with children who are in college now, like everyone else in the universe.

The Sweetheart Banquet was an excruciating farce: me, wearing a dress for someone I didn't like. However, Barry won the raffle prize, a giant red-satin heart-shaped box decorated with plastic roses and full of Pangburn's Millionaires, which are sort of like turtles—a chocolate-covered patty of caramel and nuts.

I accepted them from him at the end of the evening, at the front door of our house, while he grinned at me like an insane person, as if we were going to kiss, which we did not. Before I went to bed that night, I crammed two or three of the Millionaires into my mouth and slid the rest, nestled in the red heart, under my bed so no one would ask about them and I wouldn't have to share. I was fifteen. Daddy had been gone awhile. I ate a couple each night until they were gone.

•

I felt okay when Elaine and I started out on our trip to Knoxville, on our Daddy errand. As we drove through the velvety rolling mountains that lay between Virginia and Tennessee, we had the radio tuned to a station that was playing the kind of soul/beach music Elaine loved in college.

"Get up, get down, get funky, get loose!" Teddy Pendergrass sang, on the radio, in the early morning light. "Write that one down," Elaine said. "I want to keep a list of songs like that."

Elaine's plan was that we'd check into our hotel near the airport first thing, and then go over to Daddy's apartment to assess his living situation in preparation for his eventual move to live with my brother Michael in California. Then we'd take him to dinner, spend the night at the airport hotel, and be out of there in one day. Bam!

It was a good, optimistic plan, but not at all what happened.

•

The last time I'd been to Knoxville was when we drove there to pick up Daddy for the long drive to Elaine's first wedding, in Greenwich, Connecticut, on the lawn of a beautiful inn. (She wore a delicate ring of tiny flowers in her straight blond hair, like a crown. A string quartet played. My mother was distractingly flighty and nervous, as if she was the focus of the event, but my grandmother, who was dressed in a blue floral dress and looked like an Easter egg, was calm and beaming the whole time.)

I mentioned this to Elaine. "Good to know," she said, not unkindly. She was all business. *This was not going to be crying time,* she seemed to be saying. *This was going to be working time.* That's how she has always gotten through things. And I really wanted to emulate her.

During that first visit, for the wedding, Daddy's apartment had been neat as a pin, almost sterile. His books were arranged on shelves in the middle of one room like library stacks, and in his kitchen there was a Crock-Pot full of chili that he needed to put away before we left for Greenwich.

It was a cute little bachelor pad that seemed staged, as if he wasn't staying long, as if it was a hotel room. In fact, in his bathroom, there was a giant glass bowl full of the same little hotel soaps he'd collect on his weeklong work trips and hand over to us every Friday night when he got home. These little soaps were gifts, in my opinion, and I loved them. He was giving me something! I can recall every gift he gave me. A cassette player and some cassettes of the Mamas and the Papas, an obscure band called Tartaglia (who did a great version of "Good Morning Starshine"), Roger Miller, Sonny and Cher; a hand loom with skeins of yarn; a Dunlop Maxply Fort tennis racket, which he took me to purchase in Winston-Salem and once grabbed from me as I was hitting balls against the garage wall, used it to slap a few shots, then went inside. Also, a book of Cole Porter lyrics. If he went on real trips, to Chicago or New York, we got even better gifts: the boys, hatchets in leather cases, and I got round hippie sunglasses that came in an accordion case with four sets of interchangeable colored lenses: yellow, purple, gray, and blue. So groovy. He knew I was groovy!

Later, he started collecting first editions. I was living in New York writing about theater and food for the *New Yorker*, and boxes of books of plays and books about food would arrive, culled from entire estate collections he bought, looking for something valuable. And that was nice; he seemed to know what my interests were.

Rather than check into the hotel once we arrived in Knoxville that June day, we went straight to Daddy's place, since it was only 11:00 a.m. He greeted us at his door barefoot, in khakis and a polo shirt, his face both happy and worried. I don't think I ever noticed how pale his eyes were becoming, like a light flickering on and off. He used to be so tall.

"Well, come on in," he said, finally. He'd remembered we were coming. When Elaine had called him to tell him we'd be making the trip, he'd asked, "Why?"

There was a pair of brand-new penny loafers on the living room floor. But otherwise, the apartment looked exactly like what I think Elaine and I had both feared: the home of someone who was no longer taking care of himself, who couldn't see the dust on the floor or the dead plants, who ate the wrong food, didn't care about visitors, and probably had not had one in some time.

I felt breathless and dizzy as we stood around in his tiny living room, waiting to get down to business—and getting past how ridiculous and almost surreal it was that we were even standing here, in this mysterious place, after all this time.

What was he still doing here? With neighbors who seemed to be exactly the kind of people who should be living in this complex—the kind of people who had nothing and no one, who matched the neighborhood's deterioration over the last twenty-five years or so, as time had rushed by, after my father had moved in. How had this happened?

I got down to work, trying to be like Elaine.

Okay! Three things, to start:

1. Daddy's right foot looked swollen, and we were confused about the oxygen situation; there was a tank in a closet off his bedroom, but where had it come from, and was he using it?
2. He couldn't remember how to use his computer and had been without the internet for months, convinced that his computer was broken. This was just one of the things he couldn't remember.
3. His finances were a complete mystery, although we knew they were not good. And one entire investment account was missing.

After establishing our main goals, we made an appointment to see his doctor at 3:00 p.m., and then we'd eat an early dinner.

"Are you hungry?" Elaine asked.

"Yeah, I guess I am," he said.

"Where would you like to go?" she said. "We can go anywhere you'd like."

He seemed confused. "I wish there was someplace just to get a bowl of pinto beans and some corn bread," he said.

"Is there?" I asked, because that sounded perfect to me, too. In fact, this combination was one of the leading comfort food meals in the poll I had taken before starting my comfort food travels.

But there was no place to get pinto beans.

"Ruby Tuesday is nice," he said. I had to close my eyes. I tried to think of someplace else. Ruby Tuesday was up on the treacherous strip of suburban-spread highway between his place and our hotel near the airport. But old people love Ruby Tuesday.

So we had until two thirty to get things in order, before finding the doctor's office.

I started taking pictures of the contents of his place, to give us an idea of what had to be gotten rid of and what we'd be moving to California where he'd be living. It was easier to look at his place with my camera than with my eyes, which I had to keep closing, hard, as if things would be happier when I opened them.

Daddy followed me around a little, curious, as I did this. It was his stuff, although I couldn't imagine what he'd want with the nondescript travel posters and ratty old couch that had been in my grandmother's den, the crummy coffee table stacked with folders and some children's toys (a football, a small tennis racket).

He kept his eye on his most precious things, the two Le Corbusier chairs that had been in our house when I was a kid, the ancient Victrola that had been his father's, which he'd kept in his office, a room decorated with red and navy flocked houndstooth wallpaper, which was situated off the ridiculous pink laundry room, with the pink washer and dryer and freezer where my mother kept extra cuts of meat and chicken for our big family and chocolate cordial cups for parties (which I unwrapped from their gold foil and consumed when no one was around). There was my grandmother's crystal lamp sitting on a piecrust table, the single ornate gilt mirror left over from the heyday of the family mirror plant, and shelves and shelves of books.

"I'm going to have room for my books, aren't I?" he asked.

"Daddy, you can take all your books, don't worry," I said. And he relaxed.

"I'm so glad you girls are here," he said several times. "Two gorgeous girls, here just for me."

In Daddy's office, Elaine had started going through his financial files, which looked neat as a pin, but she found them undecipherable.

"Emily," she whispered. "We have to figure out where the missing money is, what he lives on each month, what has been coming in and going out."

Which was more than I'd ever done for myself, frankly, but I didn't mention that. Elaine, back in PR-executive mode, was the quick and efficient leader to my stunned workhorse.

She soon had our father's banker on the phone, who told her, "Your dad is quite a spender," among other things, including the fact that Daddy would need to come by in person the next day to sign some things. She tracked down and had a long discussion with his best friend, David, who, it turned out was much younger, and one of his few remaining living friends. David drove him to their Kiwanis meetings each week. "Your dad is one of my favorite people," he told Elaine.

Meanwhile, I spent time on his confusing PC, trying not just to get him back on the internet but figure out where the hell his hard drive, applications, and documents had gone. It was indecipherable, so I located a Geek Squad guy in the phone book who tried to help me log on over the phone, but we couldn't make it work.

"I told you. I've lost all my files," Daddy said. "That daggum store forgot to put my stuff on my new computer, and I've lost all my files. All my records of my books were on there," he said. He had, however, somehow retained photos of Catherine Zeta-Jones and some other comely stars in fetching pinup positions, I discovered.

We made an appointment for the computer guy to come over early the next morning, once Elaine and I realized we'd be there another day.

Meanwhile, Daddy got tired and went to his bedroom, which is what I imagined his army barracks in Korea had been like: a bare utilitarian bed—no quilt or bedspread, just a blanket, and old flat pillows, nothing that hinted at the least desire for comfort or luxury, except for a second small television and a gigantic collection of old movies on DVD. He turned on *The Bridge on the River Kwai* and began watching it on his own while we buzzed around in other rooms.

"No, I don't have cable," he said, when I stuck my head in to ask. "Why would I want that?" And I suddenly recalled that this was just the way he had been since the divorce. He'd never really wanted anything once he'd lost his family.

After my grandmother died, and we were divvying up her house full of Bombay chests, and dressers, china, silverware, jewelry, art, and other heirlooms left over from her own mother, he found and held on to exactly three things: a broken crystal glass that had been his grandfather's shaving cup, a couple of books on Picasso, and a volume of Audubon prints, which he sat and read while the rest of the family went through the entire contents of her house, from attic to basement.

During this first afternoon in his apartment, Daddy went all lost on us a couple of times.

"What is this?" he asked me.

"A pen," I said, twirling it around like a baton.

"What's this?" he asked, pointing at Elaine's bracelet; she presented her wrist for him to examine it.

At one point, I opened up a fresh page in the notebook where I'd been writing everything down and making lists, and on it Daddy had written, "Close your eyes." Beneath this, he'd drawn a wavy octagon, beneath which he had written, "I fell."

I recognized his tiny scrawl, which was like reading hieroglyphics. He kept notebooks listing all the books he'd read.

We took a break, leaving Daddy so we could take a nap, and drove to the hotel across that nondescript stretch of highway that seemed to go nowhere (although in the distance you could see the unbelievably beautiful smoky-blue Tennessee mountains).

We rested on our separate beds, but it didn't feel like rest: my head hurt as if my scalp was being stretched back by an extremely taut ponytail; my chest felt constricted, wrapped tight in a way that was keeping something from escaping. We freshened up, checked our email, put on lipstick, and talked about the next day's plan, while CNN played in the background. When two thirty arrived, time for the doctor, I felt better. Maybe help was on the way.

I'd located the medical center on my phone's GPS, but after we'd been driving for ten minutes, Daddy remembered exactly where his doctor's office was and started giving us bossy directions. When we pulled into the parking lot, he jumped out like a kid going for ice cream and made a proud beeline across the scalding hot parking lot and into the freezing-cold reception atrium.

A nurse came almost immediately to take him for blood work and to have X-rays on his foot. And when he was returned to us, to wait for his actual appointment with his doctor, he was in a mood to chat. Something had cheered him up.

Unbidden, he brought up his own father, Poage Nunn, who, as it happened, had left him, his brother, John, and younger sister, Judy, when my father was a much younger kid than I had been when he left us—rarely to be heard from again. Poage's former father-in-law, my great-grandfather, fired Poage from his position in the furniture factories after Poage and Bea's divorce. Poage went back to Pulaski, Virginia, where he'd grown up, before becoming a railway conductor and meeting my grandmother Beatrice when she was a schoolteacher in Austinville, near Galax.

"How come Poage never came to see you?" I asked.

"He couldn't drive," Daddy said. "He loved to ride horses, though. He was a big horseman, but he couldn't ride all the way from Pulaski to Galax." I wondered if he couldn't drive because he was a drinker, but I didn't ask.

Poage's father, Riley, he pointed out, "was a mean old sonovabitch. He'd be sitting on the porch when Mama would take us to visit, with a shawl on his lap, reading a book. When we pulled up, he stood up and went inside and never said hello."

I'd seen pictures of Poage from the days when they were all still young, but I never met him. He was a great dresser and looked a lot like F. Scott Fitzgerald, with that Jazz Age wavy hair. I'd seen a few shots of him on horseback, too.

"I liked him," he said, which seemed like the saddest understatement I'd ever heard. "He was a good guy." He added, "I used to visit him once a month. We'd shoot the breeze."

I barely knew Poage existed until the day he died, when I was in fifth grade. I was awake early one weekend morning, preparing for a Girl Scout event, and was in the kitchen putting emergency food in my pack.

Suddenly, a scary sound filled the small house: Daddy weeping loudly, in what seemed to be a tortured kind of pain, a grown man crying with no throttle on.

I followed the sound through the dining room, down the hallway to our rooms, and into my parents' bedroom, where he was sitting on the edge of the bed, leaning over with his head in his hands, weeping. I stared at him, stunned, until my mother made me leave and closed the door behind me.

Daddy continued, "I was at the hospital, visiting him, when he died. He was there having some tests. He was a good old man. When a nurse came back in to take him to a test, I went down to get a cup of coffee. When I came back, he had died."

According to Daddy, the nurse told him that Poage was upset that Daddy had left the room. "She told me that he said, 'I wonder why Roy didn't stay around?'"

Which struck me as fabricated and poignantly deluded: I knew Daddy had been at home with us when Poage died.

In his imagination, Daddy had been both the good and loved son—whom Poage had been happy to see—but also the bad son who abandoned Poage on his deathbed. Daddy had shown up, but at the crucial moment that everyone always remembers, he had let his father down. For a cup of coffee, he had given up the last chance to let his father give a damn about him, the last chance to tell Poage whatever it was that my father could have found to say to him.

He was there, but not there, as always. Guilty even though Poage had never bothered to be anything like a father to him, and had never even met his own grandchildren.

That's the way it is with guilt, even if you made the whole mess up—you never win. It's a closed maze with no way out into normal feelings.

Elaine and I went into the examination room with Daddy. The nurse came in and he flirted with her, and she sweetly flirted back. She bent down and lightly held his two extremely unattractive feet dangling from the edge of the paper-topped table, taking a closer look. I had to look away.

"Okay, Mr. Nunn," she said. "Do you know who the president of the United States is?" He rolled his eyes, shook his head, and gave the correct answer to her question. And he gave the correct answer to a whole series of questions clearly designed to detect the onset of Alzheimer's or dementia. He might have hesitated on a couple. But he was proud of his performance and followed each answer with a Jack Benny–like, rim-shot remark.

While the nurse and Elaine were talking to Daddy, the doctor came in and began reviewing Daddy's files on a computer. He was handsome, his dark Indian face so solid, with beautiful eyes. After we'd gotten through the basics—Daddy was indeed supposed to be on the oxygen, at night only, for chronic obstructive pulmonary disease (COPD); his heart was doing well; the doctor would fill us in on the tests next week, etc.—I told the doctor the story of what our family had been through over the last year or so, leaning in close so Daddy couldn't hear.

The doctor listened so raptly that I found myself falling in love, wanting to kiss him, and not just a peck on the cheek. I told him, half-whispering, about things Daddy had stopped doing that he absolutely loved, like tutoring children in reading at a nearby school after doing it many years because, as he put it: "I don't remember why. They took a break for summer, and forgot to tell me to come back. Or I forgot . . , I guess I don't know." And also that I thought this activity had been keeping him alive.

I told him that Daddy's best friend, David, had said Daddy was so convinced his money had been stolen that he cried, and that he'd once rented a car while his jeep was in the shop and had forgotten to take it back.

"Why are you still driving that rental, Roy?" David had asked.

"What rental?" Daddy had answered.

I told him that Daddy claimed to walk thirty minutes every day and see friends on a regular basis, but we didn't think that was true. He said he drove to Target every week, to walk around the store several times for exercise, but we suspected it was his effort to have human contact, and that he ended up buying things he didn't need (there was a child's guitar in the back of his car, and that children's sports equipment in his living room), spending quite a bit of money each month there, according to bank records Elaine found. And I told him about our long on-and-off estrangement, Oliver's death, my own breakup, breakdown, and hospitalization.

He stopped the conversation there and explained that Daddy was depressed.

"Often, when older people are isolated, a traumatic event like losing a child can send them into a deep depression. This can look like dementia." And then he prescribed Daddy's regular drugs but included the antidepressant Celexa, which is what I'd taken for the last year or so.

"Make sure he takes it," the doctor said. "We should see an improvement."

That my father was depressed hadn't occurred to me. Two months after Oliver's funeral, Daddy had sent us an email that ended by saying, "I have not yet come to accept Oliver's death. Maybe later." Which I had just ignored. Maybe I blamed him in my torrent of self-pity and had lost my compassion.

We left the doctor to have an early dinner at Daddy's restaurant choice, Ruby Tuesday. Daddy flirted with the young waitress, of course, and also had a cocktail. I took his picture, and that seemed to make him happy.

"You girls kill me," he said for the second or third time that day, beaming, while Elaine and I had coffee. "I may have said this, but I don't know how I'm ever going to thank you. You're just the two greatest ladies in the world. And I'm the luckiest father in the world."

And then he asked the question he had asked on the rare occasions I'd seen him, in the few years before Oliver died, the same question Oliver himself had asked me once, in a moment of rare intimacy. "How come your mother and sister don't talk to anyone in the family?"

"Who knows," I replied. I didn't really understand it myself, he was an old man, and all that was over. "I think it's hereditary."

We dropped off Daddy at his house, got him settled, and made plans to see him the next morning at around eleven, after he got back from his bank and when the Geek Squad guy would arrive.

"I wish you didn't have to leave," Daddy said. "This has been the best day of my life."

Elaine and I drove straight to the hotel and slept like two dead people, but not before eating a lot of crap from the hotel vending machines. Well, I did. She actually just had one square of homemade fudge from the gift shop.

The next day, after several hours of work, the guy from the Geek Squad said that the computer was perfectly fine. It needed a new modem, which he would come back and install as soon as it arrived, show Daddy how to log on, and print out large-type instructions for him to pin on his bulletin board in case he forgot; he agreed to be on call to help Daddy, on retainer from Elaine.

I walked around the office absorbing what I saw on his bookshelves and walls, which were covered with familiar photos of us kids (when I was three, still dressed for church, in a formal grouping my grandmother had taken during her studio-photographer years, with our St. Bernard, Butterfly, at the center). Some pictures I'd never seen before, others were recent—my author photo for Food52, blown up to an 8 x 10. Where had he gotten this? There was a photo of Oliver shaking Ronald Reagan's hand, from his days working for the California Republican Party after college; Michael and Oliver in Santa Monica, the former in jeans, flip-flops, and a windbreaker, the latter in a charcoal-striped business suit. And quite a few photos of my mother.

Portraits, their wedding photos, with Mom leaning her head shyly against Daddy's shoulder, her hair cut short like Audrey Hepburn; Mom posing with Daddy's best friend, Budgie; Mom's sister, Pat, who was maid of honor (her giant toothy smile lined in red lipstick) in a photo of the bridesmaids dressed in silver-blue organza gowns, which looked as if they would rustle pleasantly when the bridesmaids danced.

No other pictures of women hung on this wall, aside from a pretty younger woman Daddy might have dated after his divorce from his second wife, Brassy Lou (long story, short marriage), of whom there were no photos at all. To me, it was like a museum dedicated to a family that had never happened, and I wondered what kind of happy story someone might make up about them a hundred years from now. But to him, I realized, it was the story of his life, despite its lack of continuity.

As a hedge against the pity I felt creeping into my locked-down heart, I reminded myself that Daddy chose to be remote, unavailable; he had chosen this life. And I held on to that as Elaine and I opened a drawer in which Daddy had been keeping a manila folder on every single one of my siblings, adults now, virtual strangers that he usually saw less than once a year.

Elaine and I went through each of them. Hers was full of professional photographs from her year as a model in Japan, wedding photos, pictures of her and her husband, Kevin, and school photos. Mine contained many of my old school pictures, too, with my blond braid or my crooked bangs, an assortment of articles I'd written for various magazines and the *Chicago Tribune,* and an old newspaper clipping of me in the Girl Scout fashion show, probably in third grade, dressed in a gray flannel shift dress with a white collar, reading a newspaper, wearing the round hippie sunglasses he'd given me and a beret.

Michael's included pictures of his graduation from the police academy, so handsome and happy, and photos of him with his son, Charlie, who has turned out to be a wonderful person. There was a folder labeled "Oliver," but it was empty. Where had he put the contents of Oliver's file?

And this: an old file titled "Moi." No one else was around to do it, so Daddy had been keeping a record of himself.

My heart thumped. I could feel it in my chest, as we investigated these drawers he had whittled his life down to: a folder labeled "Awards and Notices," which included a yellowed newspaper clipping with him in uniform, as Soldier of the Month, in training before Korea, along with copies of his commissions and discharge. His MBA was in there, with Kiwanis notations, and copies of a newspaper article, from over five years ago, focusing on Daddy's many years as a reading tutor at local grade schools. A dozen or so copies of the glossy photo used for the piece were there, in which Daddy sat, smiling and rumpled, in corduroy pants and a V-neck sweater, before a circle of smiling schoolchildren positioned on the floor all around him.

He had saved his own letters, birthday cards, and a Mother's Day card he had sent to my grandmother, which he must have taken back after she died. In one boyish, eager-to-please letter, written on Camp Chimney Rock stationery, he remarked, "The fellows enjoyed the cookies you sent," and "We visited the girls camp, and that is as far as my story will go"; it was punctuated with language that, as Elaine pointed out, sounded like it came out of a 1940s movie. In reference to some of the camp's rules: "I personally thought it was a lot of rot!"

I wondered if Grandmother had actually baked the cookies. She tended not to pay as much attention to the boys as she had her daughter, Judy, who stayed home and attended the local high school, while the boys were shipped off to Staunton Military Academy, now defunct. In fact, at lunch the day before, he retold the story about how one year, Grandmother had completely forgotten to pick up him and his brother, John, during Christmas break. "The whole campus had emptied out, it had gotten dark, and even the janitors were gone," he said, laughing, but she finally sent a driver.

"She made a lot of hams," he said, when I asked what she made for them to eat besides the cakes and cookies, "but she didn't cook. We had a lady who made all of our food; she used to kill a chicken every Sunday, right in front of us, and it would run around the yard without its head." But most of his childhood meals were at Staunton.

In the mix were black-and-white photos that had nothing to do with us: of him at Michael's, a local pub where most of his social life had taken place when he was in his fifties and sixties, maybe seventies, before it closed and that crowd broke up. He had talked about this place a lot when I saw him in Galax or called him on the phone. There were color shots, including one with a tired-looking woman in the bar, and vacation pictures of him stretched out on a chaise next to a pretty younger woman at a beach hotel and posing as he shook the hand of a uniformed captain on a cruise ship, wearing a three-day beard and dressed for dinner. So he had had love after us, hadn't he?

Elaine pointed out a black-and-white photo I hadn't noticed hanging on the wall, a *Mad Men* assortment of couples at a dinner club, in which my father sat next to a woman who was not my mother, a pretty blond woman who looked like someone I would have liked. It used to hang on the wall going down to our basement, which I remembered because she had a Band-Aid on her leg. Daddy must have liked her very much.

"That picture used to make Mom crazy," Elaine said. "She wanted Daddy to take it down." But I had been too young to remember that sort of thing, the more adult interactions that Elaine had been audience to. I didn't even remember the two of them having a conversation about it.

The folder gave me a sense of urgency, as if it might disappear. There was a thick stack of photographs and reading plans from his years of tutoring, group pictures of each elementary school class, and individual photos of so many boys and girls, cute in the way that all preadolescent children are, with their names on the back in Daddy's handwriting. There were hundreds of children whom he saw each week, during those years—and who came to adore him. One hand-drawn card on yellow construction paper—to which a little blond girl's photo was pasted—read: "Dear Mister Nunn, I love you, Love Emily."

I stole that one, just put it in my notebook and crammed it into the giant bag I'd been carrying everywhere like a hobo since I'd left Chicago. But there were at least fifty other handmade notes with drawings, including one in which the stick-figure student and a weightier Daddy were holding hands and reading. Toward the back of the folder, apparently after he'd started forgetting to show up, many of them told Mr. Nunn that they hoped he'd feel better soon.

We spent most of the last hours going through banking files that Elaine needed to take back for further examination, making lists of the rest of the family's phone numbers and emails, reminding Daddy that he had money, and that if he was scared, he just had to call one of us. And that he didn't have to buy hundreds of dollars' worth of stuff every time he went to Target.

Toward the end of the day, he sat down beside me on a stool next to his desk chair, where I was sitting in his office/museum/library. Elaine was in the living room on the phone.

"What happened with Oliver?" he asked. He seemed so small, I was afraid he was going to fall off the stool. I tried to get him to switch seats with me.

"What do you mean?" I asked.

"What happened?"

It was a question that hung over us all, but that no one had ever talked to him about.

"Well, Oliver was gay, Daddy."

"I know that."

"And I think he struggled with that. He wasn't built to live that life, especially in the South. He loved his wife and child. He told me that the last time I talked to him. But I think fighting his feelings got the best of him finally. He had a monster, all his life. At least he thought of it as a monster. But it was really the fact that he felt he had to keep it a secret that was the monster. He couldn't accept it."

I reminded him of the story Oliver once told me. When we were little kids and Mom came into our rooms at night to say good night and tell us she loved us, he thought to himself, *Not if you knew.*

How could a person go a lifetime living that way? I'd always wondered.

I told him that in the last three or four years of his life, Oliver had been drinking pretty much all the time, after years of sobriety. I told him about our phone conversations before he died, that Oliver knew we all loved him and wanted to help him. I hope he knew; I wasn't really sure.

"I don't think he really had a chance after a certain point," I said.

Daddy's eyes were wet and sad, but he had no other expression on his face.

"I'm an alcoholic, too, Daddy," I said, finally. "It had me by the throat, but I'm okay now. I go to AA, but I was in the hospital after Oliver died, after my breakup. And then I was at Betty Ford. None of us drinks anymore. But I think it's going to be something I always struggle with like a lot of our ancestors did. I'm not up against as much as Oliver was. And I'm going to be fine."

We just sat there for a few minutes. I think this was the most I'd ever said to my father in one sitting.

"I'm sorry all that happened to you," he said, at last, looking into my eyes, and my heart broke into a million pieces, all over again.

And then I started laughing. Over Daddy's shoulder, hanging on the wall, I saw a portrait of our entire grown family, probably the last ever taken, at my younger sister's wedding (where I got drunk, made out with one of the groomsmen whom I ended up dating even though he lived in San Francisco and turned out to be a pothead and a Deadhead). Daddy had placed a small square of double-sided foam tape over the face of my mother.

But it made me sad, too, of course. He'd been mad at her almost all his adult life, I realized, and he just withdrew. We were alike: we couldn't get over someone discarding us when we loved them so much. He had loved a narcissist, and I had loved her, too, and had found others so much like her, people who knew how to break my heart correctly, the way it should be broken.

"Well, it happened to you, too, Daddy," I said. "It was hard for you, too, and everybody knows that. You lost a son."

"Thank you," he said, and he held my hand for a minute, the same way he had during Oliver's funeral.

"I still sometimes think I'm going to get a phone call from Oliver," I told Daddy. "To tell me a joke. Remember? He'd call, tell you a joke, and just hang up. Or leave the joke on your answering machine, with about three minutes of his laugh?"

"Did he do that?" Daddy asked, smiling, but not remembering.

"Sure he did, all the time. You hear what happened when the Pope went to Mount Olive?" I asked.

"No, what?" he said.

"Popeye beat the shit out of him."

That made him laugh.

•

We all decided that we'd have another early dinner at Ruby Tuesday. All three of us ordered a steak, with salad bar, and it was absolutely delicious, the exact right thing to do, and it came with biscuits.

"Daddy, this is close enough for you to come here by yourself, for an early dinner," I told him, while we ate. "The waitresses will remember you."

"But it won't be as much fun without you two girls here," he said.

"This has been the best time I've had in years. I don't know how to thank you."

We hung around for a while, back at Daddy's apartment, where I noticed that among other toys he'd clearly bought for his schoolkids, he had four big plastic bags full of Hot Wheels. I started fishing through them.

"You want to take some cars?" he asked. "There are some trucks, too."

"I love Hot Wheels," I said. But did I need them?

"Well, take as many as you want," he said, smiling.

So I leaned over, dug my hands into the metal, and came up with seven cars I really wanted. That seemed like too many, so I put back two. He was offering me something, and for once I took as much as I could allow myself to take.

The plan was we'd spend the night at the hotel and get an early start the next morning for Galax. So we wouldn't see him in the morning.

Elaine and I hugged him goodbye and assured him that we'd be in touch—that we'd be back for him.

As we pulled away in the car, he stood in the Tennessee heat, in the doorway of his small apartment where he'd lived forever, the sun in his eyes, his face crumpling in real pain. He did not want us to go. I couldn't bear to look at him any longer, so I took his picture. Elaine blew the horn, and he waved but didn't go inside. The next morning we drove past Ruby Tuesday, then past Daddy's turnoff, and it made me so sad to know he was there that my eyes filled with tears.

Heading back to Galax, after an hour or so on the horrible interstate, the landscape turned into gentle hills that looked like they'd been upholstered in green velvet. We passed the exits for Hungry Mother State Park and Claytor Lake State Park, where we swam as children. The hills looked so soft and peaceful I wanted to go to sleep on them.

"When you were growing up, did you ever want to lie down in a field?" Elaine asked me as she drove. Her voice had changed from PR executive back to sister. "I used to do that. I would just go lie down," she said.

But we didn't stop to do it. Neither of us was hungry, so we just kept driving away from my father. I wished that I had made him a pan of corn bread and a pot of pinto beans before we'd left.

Magnificent Sour Cream Corn Muffins

(adapted from Marion Cunningham)

Makes 6 large or 12 medium muffins

1 large egg plus 1 egg yolk, at room temperature

4 ounces (1 stick) unsalted butter, melted, plus more for the tins

1 tablespoon vegetable oil

¼ cup milk, warmed

1 scant cup all-purpose flour

⅔ cup white cornmeal

1 tablespoon baking powder

2 tablespoons granulated sugar

½ teaspoon salt

1 cup sour cream or plain yogurt

1. Preheat the oven to 400°F. Grease the muffin tins.
2. In a medium mixing bowl, whisk the egg, egg yolk, butter, oil, and milk until well blended.
3. Combine the flour, cornmeal, baking powder, sugar, and salt in another bowl and stir with a fork until well mixed.
4. Add the dry ingredients to the egg mixture and stir until blended. Finally, stir in the sour cream.
5. Spoon the batter into the muffin tins so each cup is three-quarters full.
6. Bake for 15 to 20 minutes, or until the edges of the muffins are slightly golden and a toothpick inserted into the center comes out clean. Remove from the tins and serve hot. But they're also delicious at room temperature or toasted the next day for breakfast.

Pot of Pinto Beans

Serves 10 to 12

2 pounds dried pinto beans, picked over and rinsed

2 slices (about the size of a Hot Wheels car) country ham, side
 meat about the same size, or small ham hock (if you use
 country ham, the beans won't be greasy, however)

Salt, to taste

Freshly ground black pepper, to taste (optional)

1. Soak the beans overnight in a big pot with water to cover by 2 to
   3 inches.
2. Rinse the beans a few times then put them back in the pot with the
   ham. Add water to cover, bring to a boil; reduce the heat, simmering uncovered until done, about 3 hours. If the water gets too low,
   add some more. Salt to taste only after the beans have become
   tender. They should be slightly soupy, not thick like baked beans.
   Add pepper, if using, but no need to go nuts.

●

Elaine and Kevin remodeled my divorced brother Michael's second
bathroom so he could share it with his son, Charlie, who also lived
there; bought new furniture for an extra bedroom; and turned the
dining room Michael never used into a library with big comfortable
chairs and lots of shelves. Afterward, Elaine went alone to oversee
moving Daddy's things out to California; she didn't ask me to go
along. She sent us siblings an email with a video attachment of
Daddy's last Kiwanis Club meeting, as he accepted an award of appre-
ciation for all his years of dedicated service. In another email, she sent
a photo of him reading the *New York Times* in the Knoxville airport
lounge, looking frail but content, as if it were a happy surprise to be
flying to California, after a lifetime in the South, returning to a family
he thought he'd lost decades ago.

Eighteen

IN SEARCH OF NEW RECIPES

I missed my own family, too, and despite all rational evidence to the contrary, I kept thinking I could get it back, the way it used to be. Even though my idea of "the way it used to be" dated back to the year I was fourteen and was mostly a product of my imagination. My cooking trips had made me hopeful.

So a month later I took one more trip, on Amtrak's Southwest Chief, to see Elaine in California, cutting across the top of Missouri (which made me think of square pizza) then straight through corny Kansas, dropping south through the eastern corner of Colorado, along a remarkably crooked path through the Land of Enchantment (New Mexico), onward through Arizona, stopping very close to the Grand Canyon, and ending up in Los Angeles, where I would visit a chef before driving up to Santa Barbara, a place I later began to think of as the City of Utter Confusion.

I had been thrilled when Elaine invited me out there. "You can watch Maggie while Kevin and I are at Wimbledon," she said. I would interview some chefs, explore the Farmers Market, do some writing. And then when they got back home after a month of traveling, we'd hang out the way we used to! Before Oliver had died. *We would start to become a real family again.*

I rode part of the way with many troops of Boy Scouts, a traditional sight on the Southwest Chief every summer, as thousands of boys travel back and forth from a rugged 130,000-acre scout ranch near Cimarron, New Mexico, for their annual jamboree. A group of them tumbled and wrestled into the booth directly across from me to play cards, even though the car I'd settled into with my book was mostly unoccupied.

They were shy, freckled, chubby, smart, bespectacled, skinny, goofy, pushy ding-a-lings who reminded me of circus chimps, but they turned into gentlemen when I interrupted their game to ask them about Boy Scout eating habits. One of the tallest, their alpha male, answered for them as if he were on CNN. "We eat *trail food*," he said, enunciating perfectly. "We *do* cook over campfires. Pop-Tarts and dehydrated spaghetti. On a normal campout we'll cook over a real fire. Things like stews, chicken Alfredo, beef jerky." I loved these Boy Scouts.

"We make the beef jerky," added the freckled one, who had buzz-cut hair the color of a peeled papaya. "It's easy to do if you have a dehydrator."

By dinnertime we had just passed the Mississippi along the border of Missouri. At six the next morning, we awoke to the smell of coffee and the sight of Kansas's dusty brown terrain, which we'd exited by breakfast time (delicious thick French toast with real maple syrup). Colorado's dry oxbow lakes were behind us by lunchtime, and we headed briefly into sage-green high country before the train took a turn due south and we entered a dark tunnel, which deposited us in New Mexico. At first it was nothing but mile after mile of rocky red landscape, but as we whizzed onward it changed from flat expanses and faraway mesas into giant, hulking mesas that were thrillingly strange and suddenly close enough to hit with a tennis ball from the train window, if the windows had opened. We had lunch (veggie burgers, green apple salad, and iced tea) south of the Santa Fe National Forest and by dinner, I'd spent most of the afternoon mesmerized by the wide open blue sky, sudden flashes of deep orange flowers I'd never seen before, unfamiliar birds gathering near a rare stand of deep green trees, and tiny cars rolling slowly along in the distance. Where in the world were these cars going? At one point a freight train appeared, and it stretched on for such a long time it became comical. It made me feel very small, in a good way. How little of this giant world we'll ever get to know, how short our lives in it are. *So get on with it.*

●

Somewhere along the way, a man in his twenties boarded the train. It was during dinner hour. He started yelling indecipherable things— about animals' rights and their human souls?—and slowly began to remove his clothing, peeling off his shirt and dropping it in the aisle, shoving his backpack into a booth in order to unbuckle his belt while toeing off a boot. "Sir, please don't take off your clothes," someone said, loudly but calmly—a passenger or a porter, I was not sure. But he kept going. He was stripping, as if that would make his garbled message clearer. He was finally subdued in the next car, by several men. At our next stop, a large Gothic structure fronted by a chain-link fence, we all looked out the window where awaiting the naked guy were men in plainclothes with a German shepherd, who tried to pounce on his backpack as he was handcuffed. We were carried away from him and his messy, deteriorating life in our metal tube. I felt both protected from him and deeply sorry for him. The thread that separates us all; I wondered what his grief was, exactly, and remembered a line from *The Year of Magical Thinking,* Joan Didion's book about the death of her husband, and how it made her understand, among other things, the "shallowness of sanity."

If I'd never left Chicago that terrible winter, begun to move out into the larger world, I never would have understood that you are never really absolutely safe in it, no matter how much you enjoy the idea of being carried along, protected by a structure you've built or that has been built for you. No matter how much you wish to look away or pretend you are completely removed from life's messiness, it jumps on. And, to paraphrase the Boy Scouts, it's best to be prepared.

●

Aside from the dazzling, lonesome views, it seemed to me that just about everything interesting happened in the dining car. At dinner I took an open seat with a couple of men who seemed to be traveling together and with another who was clearly traveling alone. I'd read on Twitter that Amtrak fare was surprisingly good, so I went ahead and ordered the ribs. "These are actually pretty good," I said after I'd tasted them. The couple, who had ordered them, too, agreed, and we admired the nicely cooked carrots but laughed about the stiff round ball of mashed potatoes. "High school cafeteria style," said one of them, smiling. The lone man remained mysteriously quiet. "These containers of dressing are a big waste, though, for such small salads," said the other of the two men who were traveling together.

"But it's all about American comfort food," the quiet man finally said, rather passionately, as if we'd hurt his feelings. After lovely coconut cake, a waitress placed a bill in front of the quiet man. Nobody else got a bill, of course (it was part of the ride), so he was forced to reveal that he was Daniel Malzhan, the executive chef for all of Amtrak's dining cars, traveling on his company pass. He paid for his meal and disappeared.

The next afternoon, somewhere around Wagon Mound, New Mexico, I found him in the observatory lounge and mentioned that comfort food was also an interest of mine. He seemed unimpressed, but I sat down anyway to ask him how he came up with the menus.

"When you're on a long trip, meals are the highlight," he said. "But people are nervous because it forces them to socialize. The food has to be a magnet, because the train is kind of a captive community."

I was reminded of how *excited* we'd get at mealtimes, back when I was in the hospital; how the ritual of eating helped us open up to other people in distress. In this Amtrak brand of captivity, as voluntary as it was for us, food was also one of the things we had to look forward to. We wanted a reason to be together, even though we were all strangers.

In that sense it was no different from real life.

"Food has turned into a national pastime," Malzhan continued. "We're all experts. But in this job, I have to figure out what we all have in common, and narrow it down to five or six meals." Here was a man who had learned what we all have in common. And it was *ribs*.

Malzhan was saying one thing about the comfort of food, but I was hearing this: if you remain captive to a certain way of life, you will end up eating the same six meals, over and over.

A terrible fate. I asked him if he'd consider giving me a recipe for one of his favorite dishes.

I gave him my email, never really expecting to hear from him. A few weeks later, he sent me this beautiful summer recipe, which was beyond comforting—another gift from the trip.

Chef Daniel Malzhan's Grilled White Nectarines with Sweet Basil, Homemade Crème Fraîche, and Wildflower Honey

Serves 4

"Summer always brings a plethora of wonderful stone fruits, which makes for memorable eating. Herb-scented nectarines fresh off the grill make a wonderful, not too sweet and very flavorful dessert when paired with basil crème fraîche and drizzled with honey. While this recipe calls for white nectarines, peaches and plums are also great should a substitute be required."

> 1 cup heavy cream (for the crème fraîche)
>
> 2 tablespoons buttermilk (for the crème fraîche)
>
> 4 white nectarines, firm but not hard
>
> 1 small bunch fresh basil
>
> 2 tablespoons extra-virgin olive oil
>
> 4 tablespoons wildflower honey

For the crème fraîche

Combine the heavy cream and buttermilk, mix well, and transfer to a glass container. Cover and let stand at room temperature for 24 hours. Stir the thickened cream well and refrigerate covered. This will keep for 10 days. (While you will use most of the crème fraîche in the recipe, not all of it is required. And, as you are going through the 24-hour process to make the crème fraîche, I always advocate doubling the recipe so that you'll have additional left over to use in other ways.)

1. Wash the nectarines and cut them in half, removing and discarding the pits.
2. Select and set aside 4 basil sprigs as a garnish for the final dish. Roll together 8 large basil leaves, cut them into fine strips, and then cut them crosswise into a smaller mince.
3. Combine half the minced basil leaves with the oil and then add the nectarines to the basil oil, coating them on all sides.
4. Mix the remaining minced basil with the crème fraîche and refrigerate.
5. Prepare a hardwood or mesquite fired grill to cook the nectarines, or preheat a George Foreman–style panini grill if that method is more appealing. When the heat source is very hot, grill the fruit on both the cut and rounded sides for about 90 seconds per side.
6. Plate 2 nectarine halves per person with 1 half rounded side up, the other half cut side up. Using a teaspoon, make two quenelle-shaped dollops of basil crème fraîche for each serving placed next to the peaches. Then drizzle the honey across the fruit and the crème fraîche.
7. Garnish each dessert with a basil sprig and serve.

●

Today, when I make this, my memories of my last trip out West become bittersweet. Which is better than bitter.

As we began making our way through Arizona, I met an extremely old man who seemed to be trying to tell me something, too. I later wondered if I'd imagined him.

"You going to the Big Gulch?" he asked me at the coffee station. I was surprised he was able to maintain his balance, rocking back and forth as we were. I cocked my head.

"The *Grand Canyon*," he clarified.

"Oh no, I'm not stopping this time around. I'm staying on this train to LA, then heading to Santa Barbara," I told him. As if I was in some kind of rush.

He shook his head sadly. "Oh, that's too bad for you."

Later, I would wish with all my heart that I'd gotten off, witnessed something I never had, something so close, rather than rushing back to ground I'd covered too many times.

We create our own prisons, never noticing that we are free to leave them; even when the door is wide open, we return to old ways of life, old structures because they seem comfortable.

During this visit it took almost no time before Elaine and I were not talking. And my plane didn't leave for two weeks.

But I couldn't bear another person in the family not speaking to me, so I apologized even though I wasn't sure what I was apologizing for. (Elaine used to tell me that I should have a name tag that read: HI, MY NAME IS EMILY. I'M SORRY!)

We made up, precariously but rather insanely, without really resolving the strange, vague matters at hand.

I went home. And after that, Elaine drifted further and further away, not returning calls, sending brief responses to my emails, or cute pictures of animals in lieu of conversation.

When I got back to Charleston, staying in dark places, which my downtown Charleston apartment had come to represent in several ways, began to seem like a plan that wouldn't work. But staying on my path, moving along, *had* worked, even when it had been lonely.

I found a garden house cheap enough for my laughable budget (which now included withdrawing the remainder of my depleted IRA), close to Folly Beach, with a screened porch in back, a patio garden off the main bedroom, and a yard barely big enough to mow. It seemed so perfect, filled with sunlight, a kitchen more than big enough to cook in, that I nabbed it on the spot.

My friend Mary was just a bike ride away. One day there was a strawberry festival going on down the street, at a nearby farm, with pig races. I had skylight windows in the pitched living-room ceiling, where I saw the cat from next door above me, cleaning his paws, then he'd suddenly disappear. I planted clematis, sweet peas, and jasmine next to the roses and rhododendron that were already there, along with some exotic native South Carolina trees and flowers I didn't recognize. The house even came with a dog, a skinny mutt who showed up in my yard every few days, insisting that I throw his ball. It was fantastic.

The only major downside I could see from the start was on the outside: a hulking tree in the backyard that was gray and gnarled, a dead ugly thing that I knew was going to have to be chopped down and sawed into pieces to cart out to the curb. I could worry about that later.

When late November rolled around I wasn't invited to Santa Barbara to have Thanksgiving with Elaine and Michael and my father.

At Christmas, when I dumbly asked what we were all doing, Elaine said that she and Kevin were leaving the country.

But later, I saw pictures on Facebook of my brother Michael and a pretty girlfriend, smiling for the camera, celebrating at Elaine's house, a tastefully decorated Christmas tree in the background.

In January I got her on the phone and worked up the nerve to mention the Facebook picture. She was cool—something about having to stay in town last minute because Daddy had seemed upset and confused and they didn't want to leave him alone.

"I'm afraid there's something wrong with our relationship. It makes me sad," I said, somewhat dumbly.

"You're creating drama where there isn't any—once again," she responded. Did she think everything that had happened back in Chicago—the death of our brother, my awful breakup, the loss of a home and a child and dog, the trip to the hospital, my guilt and shame and sadness—was just my imagination?

The family and the home that I was always on the verge of losing had become my model, and I was desperately loyal to it—would do anything to keep it, at my own peril.

Even my cute house seemed to be hinting at me, *Your idea of home barely exists, and what's left is pretty dismal and probably needs rethinking.*

As it got warmer I noticed that this house's air conditioner was not working. The landlord's husband "fixed" it and also broke my grandmother's antique mirror and glued it back together without telling me. I opened the windows for ventilation, but the screens had giant holes, so mosquitoes, enormous flying palmetto bugs (basically giant roaches), and several apple-green lizards moved in. I was covered in bug bites. It was as if I was on safari without a tent. "Screens? You don't need screens," said my landlord. "It gets broiling here. Turn on the air conditioner." Meaning the air conditioner her husband had not fixed.

One day my stove made a burning electric odor, sizzled loudly, and turned itself off permanently. The deliveryman who dropped off the used replacement stove pointed out that my kitchen was like "Armageddon."

"Excuse me?"

"You see that wire right there?" He pointed to one dangling where the stove had once been, below which sat a growing puddle caused by the broken ice maker in the fridge.

"You step in that water? That's gonna blow you to kingdom come."

And yet I stayed.

Soon a giant rainstorm turned my yard into a pond, made my patio disappear, and then filled my living room and kitchen with two inches of water. How could I not have noticed the cracks in the foundation, the mismatched paint, the missing hardware, the gaps in the windows, the fact that my sweet little house was uninhabitable?

●

By March, Elaine and I were completely estranged. As usual, I didn't really understand how or why. This time I felt especially desperate in my conviction that Elaine had completely cut me out of her life and would never let me back in, even when I begged.

Which I did. I was pathetic. Like Liv Ullmann in *Scenes from a Marriage,* when she lies down on the floor and wraps her arms around her mean husband's legs, trying to keep him from leaving. That was me.

I shouldn't have been surprised, though. This, at the end of the day, was the way my family worked, or didn't. Unlike a lot of messy families I knew, who managed to be in the same room despite their eccentricities and differences, we stormed apart and then eased back toward one another again and again—an unhappy push-pull that got us nowhere. Lately, the cycle always seemed to get stuck in the push, at least for Elaine. She wasn't speaking to my younger sister, or to my mother, or, now, to me.

And it had begun to occur to me that there was no way back to break the cycle between me and Elaine unless I could be the exact sister she wanted, unless I could meet what seemed to me impossible and often secret standards.

I recalled years earlier, when I was living in New York City, Elaine was in town from Santa Barbara and had set me up on a blind date with a friend of Kevin's. ("If I weren't married to Kevin . . . ," she'd said.) We were going to meet them at La Grenouille. I arrived at her hotel after work at the *New Yorker* in a navy silk suit, which she disapproved of, even though she'd given it to me. "Here, wear this," she said, holding up a pale gray Donna Karan suit on a hanger, along with a cream blouse. When I emerged from the bathroom, she tucked a kerchief in the breast pocket.

"You look *great*," she said, standing beside me in front of the mirror. I started laughing. She was wearing almost exactly the same outfit, down to the pocket square. We could have been twins, except my blond hair was curly and hers was straight.

"What?" she said.

"We look like a nice lesbian couple from West Hollywood, in town for a film festival," I said, snorting at how funny I was. She didn't laugh. I wore the suit. The blind date reminded me of Rodney Dangerfield. ("I hear they have a Women's Studies Department now at Amherst," he said. "I studied plenty of women while I was there, and I didn't get any credits for it." *Ba-da-boom.*)

She could *not believe* I wasn't crazy about him. But then again, she'd always confused the two of us this way. Rather than someone separate, I was an extension of her whom she seemed to love but wasn't sure she liked. That I didn't loathe myself had always seemed to be a curiosity to her. Or maybe she was loathing herself through me, by proxy.

Either way: it was all over now.

For a while, my alienation was lonely and quite terrifying. It seemed as if my family history had been erased, the good with the terrible, and that I had no right to happy memories at all. Looking at photo albums made it worse: my connections, all gone. How had I gotten here? To this new level of alone? I often woke up in the night or in the morning with a clenched stomach, as if freshly punched, remembering. Had Oliver felt this way at the end of his road?

And then it was just stupid and absurd: I had no intention of moving to Sicily like my youngest sister, and I sure as hell wasn't going to kill myself. That seemed so much like slapping myself in the mouth at the dinner table back when we were kids: punishing myself so no one else would have to get their hands dirty. Although I'd be lying if I did not admit I had to go through hell again before I realized this, that I found myself circling a very dark and dangerous hole. I'd been apologizing to my family, worrying about them, and forgiving them—apparently without being forgiven myself—all my life. Back then I could not be angry at them so I became angry at myself instead.

But at this moment, miraculously, I felt relieved in a way I never had before. And I would come back to it for comfort, again and again.

Because I finally realized that trying to understand my family's bizarre patterns of devaluing and discarding people closest to them was so much less important than realizing that the patterns were just that—a systemic dysfunction—and that I could escape the system.

•

I knew I was one of two things, and had to decide, once and for all, which it was:

1. The worst, most unlovable person on the face of the earth.
2. A person with one of the most exquisitely screwed-up families on the face of the earth, whose tangle of misdirected anger, sadness, and bitterness led them to pull apart rather than together.

Luckily, thanks to the friends and family still in my life, I had built up just enough of a strong core to pick door number two. And that, I am certain, has made all the difference.

I knew my truth, and trying to change what other people needed to think would only wear me out. I realized my lifetime of unrelenting guilt was, miraculously, baseless. And that maybe, instead of losing my mind, I had simply been going through the pain of finding it.

So it was okay to leave my pretty, deteriorating house and my broken idea of home behind.

I put all of my things back in storage with the help of my friends Mary and Winn, who made chicken on the grill the night before I left, the same way that they had back when I'd arrived in Charleston. We had their artichoke pickle with it. I packed two suitcases and my favorite cookbooks and drove up to the mountains, to Linville, North Carolina, to visit Dot, Locke, and Cole.

I wasn't sure exactly where I was going or why, but as the air began to smell like pine and moist earth and the road became winding and narrow, this is what I told myself: *You have not been rejected, you have been released.* I told myself, *Stop trying to return to places and people who are prisons. Run, while you still have the chance.*

I ended up staying in Linville much longer than I had expected, and certainly longer than Dot imagined when I showed up. But I couldn't help it. They had always made me feel so much like a part of their family.

I rented Dot's beautiful guesthouse (which has a great kitchen with a gas stove) for six months, during which time she became that particularly wonderful kind of friend whose kitchen you know as well as your own, although I never could find the olive oil. I don't think there's a better kind of friend. Dot and I cooked together a lot, often with Cole and Locke and Dot's great boyfriend, Greg. We hiked in the mountains with visiting friends. Took the dogs for long walks practically every day. Through that winter, even during the bitterest cold, I would walk across her backyard with a dish I'd made, to add to all the other dishes we'd all eat together. Her cats and her giant white Great Pyrenees, Shug, would come back for snacks and sometimes sleep on my bed.

Dot and I played in the Scrabble tournament down the winding road in Celo, a community full of artists and Quakers, some of whom lived off the grid, where the owner of the Celo Inn served all the competitors homemade grape soda and an apple cake flavored with rosemary, which was out of this world. We went to movies in Boone, and civic meetings to stop the town of Sugar Mountain from horning in on Avery County's water supply. We visited the Penland School of Crafts, an hour or two away, near Spruce Pine, a city that reminded me of Galax, except for the fact that it had the Knife and Fork, an amazing restaurant where Dot sometimes had dinner parties. I made summer rolls with mango and shrimp, which I steamed over the mango peels, and sometimes, if it had been a good day, I'd allow myself to think about my own family.

I'd set aside the huge hand-printed cookbook that my aunt Judy had made years ago—*Cooking: Recipes From the Files of Judith Lucinda Nunn Alley*—to mail back to Aunt Mariah, but during the cold winter, when the snow piled up against the door of the cottage, I couldn't bear to part with it yet. I took it out like a photo album, along with my folder of recipes Elaine had given to me, and my food notebook, to remember all the good things about my family.

Sometimes it was hard to accept the fact that rather than going down in a plane crash that I had no power to stop, they'd all, one by one, chosen to leave me out of their lives. How does a person say goodbye to her entire family? The only person I'd known who'd done it successfully was Oliver.

What my father regained—a family of sorts—I would have to lose, as though the remains of my tattered tribe could contain only a certain amount of love and forgiveness, as if one of us had to be displaced to make room in a closed system that could only become smaller.

But I still had this: I had forgiven Daddy. Somehow, after my trip to Knoxville, a dark place inside me had faded and softened. I could see past my remaining hurt, fury, and selfishness, and realize how alone he'd been, without a family to call his own. I understood now how that must have felt. He'd shown up at the funeral, frail and embarrassed, and held my hand, tears rolling down his face, when other members of my family hadn't come at all. He had never tried to hurt me.

We were a lot alike, retreating when we desperately wanted to connect, feeling too hurt to ask for love, and waiting around alone, half-hoping love would show up. He never did a truly unkind thing. And I don't think he ever blamed me for not recognizing how alone he was, for not coming to get him sooner. Which is all I think he'd wanted forever: his family back. For people he'd loved to understand him, accept his limitations, and love him back.

•

As much as I wanted to run away from the world I had to remember—to remind myself often—to stop being like my father. I didn't want people I loved to continue to think for a lifetime that I did not. At any given time, people do the best they can with what they have on hand: they improvise. Some of us are better at it than others.

Realizing this made it easier to be sad rather than angry. And for that I feel like the luckiest person in the world. Sadness can't devour you the way anger can.

•

After forgiving my father, I discovered that I was finally capable of beginning to grieve for Oliver, at least a little bit, and remember him not as a saint but as the complicated, extremely difficult, angry, funny, brilliant, melancholy middle child he was. I stopped making lists of terrible people throughout history who should have died instead of him, even though I think it would have made him laugh. But I did not stop thinking about him so intensely that it brought me to tears every time I saw a stupid cardinal. He hurt a lot of people, some of whom have forgiven him, some who never will. And I've hurt people, too. But I'm alive to apologize to those people, and I have. For some people, I will never be able to make it right—and I have to accept that. I know that every life has value, that everyone deserves forgiveness and support, especially from their own families. But those things sometimes never come. That's the way it is.

I got stronger. Sometimes I felt peaceful.

In the spring, before all the people from Charlotte had opened up their summer houses and after the lavender and fuchsia rhododendron began to bloom, I got a job in the kitchen of the Eseeola Lodge, where the French chef hired me as a prep cook, in spite of my limited professional experience.

"Ee-ma-lee," he said, glancing at my résumé. "You could be working at the *New York Times*! I don't know what you are *doing* here. You are unusual, so I am going to hire you." It seemed like faulty logic. But I didn't tell him that I'd once interviewed at the *Times* a year after I'd started working at the *Chicago Tribune* because I was so homesick for New York, and that they'd hired someone else. I didn't tell him my confidence in my abilities—journalistic and otherwise—was a little damaged. I just said thank you. I let him think what he wanted to, because maybe it was true. Maybe the person I'd been was still in there, somewhere.

But that was all on me now.

I started over, truly. In my own life and in the rigid hierarchy of a professional kitchen. Almost every morning, from May to November, I showed up ten minutes early in my chef pants, cheap white T-shirt, black baseball cap, and grotesque nonskid shoes that looked like bumper cars, over which I donned a heavy white chef jacket, a long white apron, and two clean towels, tucked into my apron—so many clothes.

I was near the bottom of the ladder, the person who comes in during breakfast service, chops things until there is nothing else to chop, then does whatever else needs to be done according to the whims of the chef. But I began to rely on the order in the kitchen, which was permanent no matter how frantic the day became. The busier it got, the more efficiently the system in place seemed to function: it was built on teamwork, so it was full of safety nets.

The giant kitchen was always hot as hell—and then someone would turn up an eye on the industrial gas stove behind me, and say, "Don't let that burn." My glasses were fogged with steam, smeared in butter or chicken fat. I bandaged self-inflicted cuts from my new knives and had burns and bruises of unknown provenance, not to mention sore arms from carrying giant pots full of food. When I bled, frequently people didn't say, "Are you okay?" They ran over to make sure there was no blood on the food. And that was fine. It was six-day-a-week labor that paid next to nothing and sometimes lasted twelve hours at a time. I never saw Dot, Locke, or Cole. I didn't socialize. The minute I got home, I would fall asleep—sometimes on my couch, sometimes in the bed—until it was time to go back to the kitchen. The only new people I met were cooks and dishwashers and culinary students, mostly men. I worked so hard, for so many hours, I barely noticed the changing seasons of North Carolina: pink spring, green summer, orange fall. I never wore a dress, and no lipstick. It seemed okay.

This grueling job made me happy even as it wore me out. I was eager to roll sushi for hours, make hundreds of tiny tomato hors d'oeuvres (tomato, mayo, and provolone on rustic white bread, cut with the smallest biscuit cutter, decorated with minced chives), mix vats of really good chicken and tuna salad for lunch service and the snack bar on the golf course, carve five-gallon bowls of pineapple and honeydew and cantaloupe to mix with blueberries and the strawberries I'd washed and sliced, mold hundreds of tiny domed cheese puffs to be baked later for the cocktail parties of summer people, fillet eighty pounds of raw chicken breasts then cook them, with the massive amount of mirepoix I'd prepared, in a pot as big as a bathtub that I then had to clean (more foggy glasses). I loved scraping the gills from the portobellos, hated picking over the crabmeat for the elaborate seafood banquet, and was relieved to be asked to make fruit and vegetable arrangements to decorate a table.

Still, sometimes, my work was so meditative that it led me to wistful places where my feelings about the last year or so of my life welled up. But I kept slicing and stirring until I came out on the other side. I chopped chicken into tiny cubes for five hours without stopping, and when I got finished I no longer thought I was such a bad person.

It helped that all around me, every day, the distractions were beautiful: sizzling, clanking, splashing sounds and the lush, overwhelming scents of cooking. Suddenly horseradish filled the air, and lamb stock, the sweet strange smell of meringue being blowtorched by the pastry chefs into caramelized curls and peaks, underneath which was the most delicious coconut cake I'd had in years. The butcher was making sausage three feet away from me, filling the cases with pink, fatty meat, someone else was juicing a crateful of lemons, and a half dozen large butternut squash puddings were coming out of the giant oven behind me, to cool on rolling racks.

I got stronger physically—my muscles surprised me after just two months—and emotionally. So when the inevitable day came that the old Hungarian saucier named Attila focused all his red-faced fury about spilled onions in his walk-in refrigerator on me, I stood up for myself, however meekly. "My job description does not include onions," I told him, with virtually no sass, half-hoping he hadn't heard. He stared across the kitchen at me with furious eyes while everyone laughed at my lame defense, waiting to see how the encounter was going to turn out for the rookie. Attila moved on to something else. It was over.

In order for the kitchen to work, conflict could not last, didn't seem to want to last, and was rarely given a second thought: move forward or you're lost. After that day, Attila began to leave a cup of soup for me at my station at midmorning (heavenly cream of mushroom; lentil made with rich and murky lamb stock; tomato bisque; roasted red pepper with a spoonful of sour cream). It was the very thing to get me through to lunch: so restorative. When I carved fruit, I gave him pineapple cores to snack on.

The kitchen, I realized, is an especially good place to be if you've grown up in a system where loyalty was expected but taking love and support was rewarded with anger and guilt, as if you'd stolen something. Or where, if you couldn't be perfect, it always seemed that people would leave, or die, or ask you to leave. Where you might turn into the kind of person who would spend your entire life savings to prove that you loved someone, that you weren't a needy person just trying to *get* something. When in fact you'd lived a life of stalwart, almost isolating independence.

Until I trusted myself to create some rules of my own, this kitchen was my home. I began to live by the rules of the kitchen, where you could expect to get what you give.

One of the important things I learned—although it took me a

while—was this: if you're smart, you will become protective of your garbage can, where you have deposited pineapple peels and lobster shells and other very heavy stuff. Because at the end of each day, you alone will be responsible for cleaning up your station, scrubbing it down with steel wool and bleach, sweeping and mopping, and toting your own industrial bag of restaurant waste out to the Dumpster.

So: if you let other people put their garbage in your can, it's going to be way too heavy to carry. Just make sure the people you allow to do this are the same people who offer to help you hoist that bag at the end of the day.

I began working on banquets late in the summer. We dressed in starched white jackets and high toques for sunset parties at the lodge's mountain camp. Our food was perfect, artfully arranged, decorated with flowers, and served on silver trays. It was delicious, and we made sure that it never ran out and never looked like it ever could.

Occasionally, seeing other people's perfect weddings, with their groups of friends and family gathered all around them, beautifully dressed and thrilled to be a part of celebrating love, I became way too self-reflective: *me, me, me.* So I'd just go back into the kitchen and stand in the cold walk-in freezer for a few minutes. I liked the kitchen better for now, being in the background, in my chef's jacket covered in stains, stirring a sauce for someone else. It was enough for me back then—which is not to say I felt like it was nothing at all. I loved it the same way I had once loved the idea that life was a banquet, the dramatic Auntie Mame idea that we are here to take what is perfect while we can and reject the rest, to grab on to the best of everything before it disappears.

But now I knew what I wanted was love, people I could depend on. A family. I don't know exactly why none of my brothers and sisters had turned into that, for one another or for anyone else, really. They'd all been married, some remarried; none of the women had kids. I'd never been married at all. And now my remaining ties to my family were gone, against my will. I was rootless in a family of seven, now six. It was surreal.

Luckily, I had figured out that life was not a banquet at all but a potluck. A party celebrating nothing but the desire to be together, where everyone brings what they have, what they are able to at any given time, and it is accepted with equal love and equanimity. You can arrive with hot dogs because you are just too tired or too poor to bring anything else, or you can bring the fanciest, most elaborate dish in the world, and plenty of it, to share with people who brought the three-bean salad they clearly got at the grocery store.

People do the best they can, at any given time. That's the thing to remember.

I asked my boss at Eseeola, Chef Terry Dale (who spends his winters traveling around the country trying whatever the food world is raving about) for something that would be easy to make if you were tired, but that was still very sumptuous—something for a potluck—and he recommended a rich and soothing spaghetti squash casserole.

Eseeola Lodge Spaghetti Squash Parmesan

Serves 12

2 medium ripe spaghetti squash, split and seeded

½ cup canola oil

Salt, to taste

1 quart heavy cream

1 cup shredded Asiago cheese

1 cup grated Parmigiano-Reggiano cheese

White pepper, to taste (see Note)

½ cup panko bread crumbs (ask your grocer where these are; everyone has them now)

1. Preheat the oven to 350°F. Rub the squash with oil and salt and roast cut side down in a pan for 30 to 40 minutes, until easily pierced with a fork. Turn the oven to 300°F.

2. When the squash is cool enough to handle, scrape the strands into

a large bowl and add the heavy cream, most of both cheeses (save a total of about ½ cup for the top), and season with salt and pepper. Mix well.

3. Spread the mixture in a 3-quart casserole dish and top with the remaining cheese and the bread crumbs. Bake until golden and bubbly, about 25 minutes. Let sit for 10 minutes before serving.

Note: One of the things I learned at Eseeola is that chefs tend to use white pepper in dishes that are pale; I like the taste of both and use both, but try white pepper first if you have it.

●

A few months later, just days before the season would end and the restaurant would close for five months, I was setting up my *mise* again. Chef Terry stopped by my stainless-steel station, which I'd both bled upon and scrubbed down a million times with steel wool. I loved my shiny little corner, near pastry.

"You know what, Nunn?" he asked, half-yelling.

"No," I said, slightly afraid. (He always sounded like he was about to fire me, but it was way too late for that.)

"We had a bet when you started here that you'd last ten days. Chef Patrick said you'd leave like all the other weak ones." Over a dozen people had quit, just walked out on the job when it got too tough. "But you surprised the hell out of us," he said.

"Me, too," I said.

"Now you're a fucking rock star," he added, and went into his office, with no fanfare.

I was prouder than I'd ever been, because I had decided early on that I would not give up. In return, the kitchen had saved me. It had given me a place to cook when I had no one left to cook for.

I was in the cutlery room on my last day, looking for a ceramic platter to arrange fruit for a banquet. One of the upper-tier chefs was coming in as I was trying to go out, and when we bumped into each other the cumbersome plate slipped out of my arms and broke into large shards, like the pieces of a puzzle.

The chef, who didn't know me at all, raised his eyebrows, grinned, and said, "Way to go, dumb ass." I started laughing, but when I bent over to pick up the pieces I started crying; actually I was laugh-crying. Because it conjured something my friend Portia had said to me when I was visiting her house one weekend, the second time Elaine and I had stopped speaking after Oliver died. "I'm afraid it's permanent this time," I told her. (It wasn't, not yet.)

"But Emily, that's okay," Portia said. "You're feeling the pain of becoming the real you! The broken parts of you are coming together. And you don't need anybody telling you who to be. You are now free to be the real Emily. That's a blessing. Besides, we're your family now."

I knew it wasn't going to be easy. I still felt so alone. But I also knew this: I'd learned how to get back up again when I fell. I had begun to learn to trust people again, or I was trying. I took a lot of comfort in that, even as I wondered, *How was I supposed to know which pieces I wanted to keep, which I should discard?*

My answer almost always came back to food, which had rarely failed me.

Over the course of my journey, in the most random ways, food has reminded me of who I used to be—and therefore of the person I still am and can be. A brave woman not hiding out from the world but *living in it.* Someone who once baked bread every week, just so there'd be good toast, and who loved to make sabayon with fresh berries for dessert for a houseful of friends. Remembering this person, in turn, brings back people I miss but who are no longer available to me for various reasons—like ingredients my grocer no longer stocks.

Simply because I ate roasted chestnuts for the first time from a cart in Italy, when Christmas arrives I have acute memories of standing on a crowded street at dusk in Florence, with my first New York boyfriend, the sweetest man I've ever known. My capacity to love comes rushing back to me, reminds me that I've been dearly loved and will be again. I know that I'm capable of having the affection of a sweet and kind man because of him, but I also know that love is not guaranteed to anyone.

In his New York apartment, the Best Boyfriend would hand me the dinner we'd made together out the window of his kitchen so we could eat on the terrace. And, since he was the first person I went to Cumberland Island with, today when I think of him my thoughts then tumble toward oyster roasts, and the sight of oysters on a bed of ice, no matter where, can recall Charleston and my friend Mary and her wonderful father.

Which sends me back again to the Christmas Eve oyster roast they throw at Cumberland Island; the time Dot, Elizabeth, and I spent Christmas there, and Elizabeth went away in the kayak, and we thought she'd never come back. But she did. The people who love you come back, if they are able.

I've read that people recall the bad moments in life more vividly than the good. So I'm lucky that many of my memories tend to be attached to food, which tips the balance away from traumatic to curative; mournful to hopeful.

Because of food, I recall humor in bad dining situations: the cookout at which an unfaithful boyfriend suggested that we might need to get dental records in order to identify the chicken I burned. I remember my first peanut soup (luxurious and strange, at the King's Arms Tavern) and Lobster Newburg (so rich, at the fancy Williamsburg Inn) thanks to a disastrous family vacation my family took to Colonial Williamsburg with Millie and Al and Jayne and Tracey, the family I loved so much but lost early, because of my family's stonewalling curse.

Food has become my touchstone for understanding what real love is.

The best thing? Food makes it easier to give love, untangled. Since it keeps us alive, the smallest, simplest gesture can seem miraculous: *I brought you this soup.*

As much as I love the idea of Proust's madeleine, that tired little cake floating in tea, I don't really need to take a bite for food to work for me. The words alone make me feel hopeful: *piperade, confit, fricassee.* I can make any dish I want, and I try to remind myself that making food with other people is often an even richer experience than eating it.

Sometimes you have to work really hard for food to change your life. And sometimes it just shows up.

Take that gnarled tree back at my decaying house near the beach in Charleston. I thought it was dead and paid very little attention to it. But this misshapen thing produced tiny green buds, which turned into giant mitten-shaped leaves that began to grow so lushly I knew it was a fig tree. I wasn't sure it would actually produce figs, which are not actually a fruit but a mass of tiny flowers turned inward, but I was hoping so and began planning on making them into an elegant tart meant for pears, using a recipe by a Chicago chef, Shawn McClain, whom I wrote about for *Food & Wine*.

Once the figs came, though—enormous purple ones dripping with nectar—they filled the branches so quickly I could barely keep up with them. This tree just kept giving me more figs. I gave a lot of them away to my neighbors, and I didn't have time to make a fig tart more than once. Instead, I stood under the tree barefoot, in the damp grass, early in the morning or at dusk with a colander, and had fresh figs for breakfast and dinner.

I will make this fig tart again someday, for a dinner party or, better yet, a potluck.

Even when you have no faith in it, food can save the day, surprise you, change you, strengthen you. Share the food you love with an open heart and you'll find that people can do all those things, too. I did, and I was comforted.

Fig Tarte Tatin with Red-Wine Caramel

Serves 6 to 8

2 cups dry red wine

2 cinnamon sticks

½ cup granulated sugar

¼ cup water

2 tablespoons unsalted butter

2 pints large purple figs, hard part of stem removed, halved

1 (14-ounce) sheet all-butter puff pastry, chilled

Crème fraîche or whipped cream, for serving

1. In a small saucepan, boil the wine with the cinnamon sticks over moderately high heat until reduced to ¼ cup, about 15 minutes. Discard the cinnamon sticks.

2. In a 12-inch ovenproof skillet (I use cast iron), combine the sugar and water. Cook over moderately high heat, swirling the pan occasionally, until a light-amber caramel forms, about 5 minutes. Remove from the heat. Add the red-wine syrup along with the butter, return to the heat, and cook to dissolve the hardened caramel, about 1 minute. Add the fig halves to the skillet and gently move them around in the skillet with a rubber spatula to coat them, being careful not to damage the beauty of the fruit. Arrange the figs cut side down in the skillet in a pretty pattern with the stem ends pointing toward the center. Let cool for 30 minutes.

3. Preheat the oven to 375°F.

4. On a lightly floured work surface, roll out the pastry in a 13-inch square. Using the skillet lid as a template, cut out a 12-inch circle. Cut four 2-inch-long steam vents in the pastry and lay it over the figs, tucking the edge into the skillet. Bake for about 1 hour 10 minutes, until the pastry is deeply golden and risen. Let the tart cool in the skillet for 15 minutes, then very carefully invert the tart onto a large plate. Cut into wedges and serve with crème fraîche.

Acknowledgments

Special thanks to my extremely talented agent Nicole Tourtelot, who never let me go, and to agent David Kuhn, who pulled me out of a slush pile (both literally and figuratively) and turned my proposal into something palatable, with the help of Grant Ginder and Kate Mack. I adore all of them. At Simon & Schuster, thanks to my insightful and understanding editor Peter Borland and his wonderful associates Daniella Wexler, Daniel Loedel, and Sean Delone as well as to Elisa Rivlin, whose perfectionism and patience are epic.

My friends taught me that relationships can last, through thick and thin, and even if you rarely see them and even if you have been a jerk. I had long-lost ones who became steadfast again when I came knocking on their doors (Dot Griffith and her kids Cole and Locke Curtis, Wyler Hecht, Portia and Buddy Hendrick, Mary and Winn Tutterow). I had many virtual friends who became more than real along the way, and who shored me up again and again (they know who they are, and they mean the world to me); several of them invited me into their very real kitchens just because I asked them to (including Tom Hirschfeld and Cathy Barrow). In that realm, I also appreciate Merrill Stubbs and Amanda Hesser, whose creation of Food52.com gave me and a lot of other home cooks a groundbreaking virtual community and kitchen in which to gather; Amanda also allowed me into her home, served me a lovely meal, and taught me the power of the Thank You Cake. I have many old friends who could never possibly know the degree to which their love and support softened the sting of my various trials (Julie Welch, Jessica Reaves, Sara Olkon, Anita Russum, Mary Margaret Beamer Rector, Becky Webb Guynn, Mark Bittman, Mary Norris, Lucinda Hahn, Susan Thomsen, Andrew Boynton, Eileen Ryan Ogletree, Libby Hill Carson, Kevin Conley, Andrew Essex, Tripp Somerville, John Donohue). For their kitchen lessons, which are often life lessons as well, I am indebted to Chef Bruce Sherman of North Pond in Chicago; Chefs Terry Dale and Patrick Maisonhaute of the Eseeola Lodge, in Linville, NC; Daniel Malzahn of Amtrak; Doug and Vera Brown, of the sadly defunct Brown's Family Restaurant in Sparta, NC; Nick Lessins and Lydia Esparza of the late, great Great Lake, in Chicago; Chef Robert Stehling and his wife, Nunnaly Kersh, of Charleston's Hominy Grill; Suzanne Pollak and Lee Manigault of the Charleston Academy of Domestic Pursuits; and the staff, kitchen, and otherwise, at the Greyfield Inn, on Cumberland Island.

And most of all, thanks to my extended family, who gave me back the idea of home when I no longer had one: Aunt Mariah and Uncle John, cousins Toni Nunn and Susan Olson, and my aunt Judy Nunn Alley, as well as the Kello family—Martha Kello, James and Betsey Kello, Jim and Bob Parker, and the late Glynn Kello Parker, who passed away before this book was completed. And to my siblings and parents, whom I love madly, still, in spite of everything and whether they like it or not.

Finally, thanks to my Chicago therapist, Nina Uziel-Miller, who deserves a medal of some sort, and the Betty Ford Center, most specifically Ann Gallagher of the outpatient program, without whom I would, to paraphrase my late brother, "be lying in a ditch with a leaf stuck to my face."

Recipes